CW00670949

Leadership

Leadership

It's In Your DNA

Rhea Duttagupta

BLOOMSBURY
LONDON • NEW DELHI • NEW YORK • SYDNEY

First published in the United Kingdom in 2012 by

Bloomsbury Publishing Plc
50 Bedford Square
London
WC1B 3DP
www.bloomsbury.com

A CIP record for this book is available from the British Library.

ISBN: 9-781-4081-6834-9

This book is produced using paper that is made from wood grown in managed, sustainable forests. It is natural, renewable and recyclable. The logging and manufacturing processes conform to the environmental regulations of the country of origin.

Design by Fiona Pike, Pike Design, Winchester
Typeset by Saxon Graphics, Derby
Printed in the United Kingdom by CPI Group (UK) Ltd, Croydon, CR0 4YY

CONTENTS

THE COVER STORY

What the Cover means to me.

The cover is red – warm, rich and deep. It is bold. It is also the colour of blood, of what flows within us, which compliments the DNA metaphor. Imagine two people, like you and I, looking from the outside into this golden key of intrigue, a symbol of *the inner code* for our leadership DNA.

The cover, people have been kind enough to say, is creative but let me confess it came about by accident. I had tried four designers and was fed up with drafts I didn't like. Then against a looming deadline, I had one weekend left to resolve the final version. I became obsessed with doodling possible ideas. I sketched the key. I sketched the DNA strand. But it wasn't coming together somehow. Phil nailed the design for me in placing the DNA strand inside the key and letting it hang off an open key ring. As I did that my phone rang. I clumsily hit the mouse. When I came back to my desk the key had moved further up to the title. That gave me the idea of the key hanging from the ends of the DNA. I left the key chain open, not closed. That may seem strange but it is deliberate. Developing our leadership DNA is an evolving, life long journey – like an open circle of infinity. It is also like an open door where we are humble enough to invite other DNA keys belonging to our teams, mentors, coaches, family and friends. It is slightly crude but I like that. It is real. I wanted to give you a peek into how the 'inside story' played out. Terry from Bloomsbury gave it the final finish.

Thanks to Phil, Malcolm, Brian, Subrat, Daniel, Sanchita, Ma, Noeleen, Abhishek, Sundar, Paul, Sandy, Angela and Jenny who kept voting for the different versions over the last weekend of June 2012. At 23:50 we sealed the design. It was fun.

Simplicity is the ultimate sophistication. Leonardo Da Vinci

Terms in this book

Now if we are to develop a whole new approach to leadership, it is only fair we define some new terms for this "Leadership: It's in your DNA".

Leadership Leadership is first an attitude and belief, followed by the ability of one person to stand up and take ownership in walking taller and stronger on a new path or an improved current path.

DNA DNA is like a unique personal microchip we all have inside us. It is the nucleus of the cell, made of two strands, intertwined, that contains all the genetic information we are born with. But the intriguing fact about DNA is, other than being unique, it is capable of replication, thereby producing new cells to repair and replace old ones, and generate more fresh ones. On the note of originality and with my own fascination of DNA studies, this book's central urge is to take your existing DNA and to replicate a stronger leadership version of it, without losing the original.

Ingredients There are ten innate ingredients in our DNA which we all have from the President, to you and I and the 'guy on the street'. These ten ingredients, which form the ten chapters, are the code for our Leadership DNA already within us. These help us realise our leadership potential.

Key A symbol for discovery, opening, accessing, unlocking and enabling. This book is the key to the whole of you. You are its keyhole.

Blend It is a blend of ten ingredients because a blend caters to the individual requirements unique to each reader, who can blend the mix and match of the ten ingredients to suit his or her specific needs

Release Release means to set free, to unleash, to let out what is already within. The ten ingredients exist, they just need refining and releasing. Why not? Its your powerful leadership DNA after all.

MY *FOREHAND* RATHER THAN MY FOREWORD

I have taken the liberty to forgo a traditional book foreword and build on the imagery of a *forehand* from my favourite sports – tennis. I particularly want to invite your imagination to join me on Centre Court with my favourite tennis stars and their coaches. Leaders who I believe, from this perspective, show us the power of my ten ingredients, which will, in turn, illustrate my ethos – *Leadership: It's in your DNA*.

I can think of no better way to *set out my game* using my forehand, as I relish the parallels between sports and business. They say forehand is considered the easiest shot to master, perhaps because it is the most natural stroke. Just like my natural approach on leadership. I open with that because *inspiration is everything in leadership*. I am taking one such inspiration from outside my world of business to prove the irrevocable relationship between coaching and winning, between the mentor and his apprentice, between the head and the heart.

First of all, I am a *Roger Federer* fan. Federer is a legend through whose leadership journey, my blend of ten ingredients – self, expression, instincts, emotions, darkside, resilience, fear, creativity, and luck – is a proof of concept.

Beyond Federer, who we will meet in the chapter on emotions, I want to take two coaches behind two world-class leaders in tennis. *Ivan Lendl behind Andy Murray* and *Toni Nadal behind Rafael Nadal*.

One: Ivan and Andy

> **"If I don't practice the way I should, then I won't play the way that I know I can."** Ivan Lendl

The 52 year old Czech man Lendl, an eight times Grand Slam singles champion but never at Wimbledon, is truly shaping the DNA of 25 year old Andy Murray. I wrote this on the eve of Andy's Olympic gold in 2012. Up until end of July 2012, Murray has lost four slam finals, the same number that Lendl suffered before making his breakthrough aged 24 at the 1984 French Open. Such sharp distinction binds the coach and his coachee.

Lendl is playing more with Andy's DNA strands than with skill and technique. Lendl knows it is in the mind, attitude and instincts that he has had to engineer the starkest change in emotional Murray. Where once the

Scotsman, known to subject his self to his own mental games and sink into a strange mental analysis-paralysis mid-match, Andy is now displaying an emotional balance and inner resilience shaped by his mentor.

I would say the Wimbledon 2012 defeat has done Andy Murray a world of good. You need to know your darkest lows, and what it means to be there before you can rise to your highest.

"*The main thing I've learnt from him is to be stable on court and not so emotional,*" he said after vanquishing Jo-Wilfried Tsonga. "*He makes sure that I never get too up, that I never get too down.*" There are common strands in their personalities. Murray has always had a reputation as a complex character but in Lendl he has encountered the master blender of his real potential. For the Czech-born legend has mastered his own blend: on the one hand, he has a dogged, non-quitting focus on the *game*; on the other, he lets his childlike emotions come out to *play*. The difference between a game and play is Lendl's leadership trademark.

Two: Toni and Rafa

"The most important thing is to make sure, that everyday you do something better than how you did it the previous day". Toni Nadal

For all my passion for tennis, here is a unique example of who I have found very inspiring. Often it is about the man behind the player/leader who has shaped the leader as much as it is about the player/leader himself. There is one such man who I watch in the landscape of tennis as much as I see his world famous nephew/coachee play. This is Toni Nadal – the coach behind Rafael Nadal. At CorporateDNA, I constantly use coaching examples from sports to inspire the business world. And Toni is on our leadership slides. So imagine how I felt when I saw him a few feet away from me?

I had the privilege of watching Rafa play in the Wimbledon's Men's final in 2011. My mother who is an avid fan pointed out the man behind Rafa. So my luck extended beyond that to watch a more personal performance, that of Rafa's uncle-coach in the audience, in close proximity from our great seat. His every move, gesture and emotion was visible to me. The involvement, the intensity and the commitment on Toni's face was unparalleled.

Let us take a peek behind the scenes. Because this book is about the DNA of a leader, let us uncode the DNA that Toni has built, step by step, from a four year old boy to a world phenomena today. Being a coach myself, I know the feeling of coaching and shaping someone's life – it is a gift, it is a big promise and it is a huge responsibility.

Toni trained Rafa on poor courts with bad tennis balls just to show Rafa that winning or losing is less about the best tools and quality of courts. It is about attitude, focus and perspective.

"If you want to coach someone, the first thing to do is to make the person responsible. Even as a kid, Rafa had to be the master of his own tennis decisions and set short term goals ". That drove a personal work ethos and responsibility that is at the grassroots of the tree we see standing tall and strong today – Rafa Nadal.

A lot has to do with upbringing. I realise Rafa understood from Toni a valuable lesson on resilience as a child. Childhood is not just about innocence and naivety. It is about learning to expect and face off to obstacles. It is knowing things will go wrong and that's okay. It is knowing what to do when that happens and being prepared and being resilient. That rhymes perfectly with the book and the 6 chairmen and 16 CEOs, musicians, chefs, students and emerging leaders featured in it.

Technique on its own is not everything. Understanding the game is more important than technique, and that understanding comes from knowing everyday we need to be better than the previous day.

"For every player has to develop his own game" Toni Nadal

"For every leader has to blend his own ten ingredients". Rhea Duttagupta

Leadership: It's in your DNA.
A blend of 10 ingredients we all have within us.

ANSWERS

Did I hear three questions?

Everyone asks me "what will be the next big thing?"

I say it is YOU.

Your ability to develop and, yes, reinvent yourself will be the next biggest thing that matters.

---

1. Who should read this book?

Anyone who is a leader, or who wants to be a leader. Or is simply curious about leadership and wants to work with leaders to make a difference.

The world does not suffer from a lack of leaders. It suffers from a lack of Leadership. We all have, in our own way, the conviction of leadership within us. This book, I hope will bring the courage to go with that conviction.

2. Why should you read this book?

No matter who you are – director, CEO, entrepreneur, manager, teacher, student, chef, artist, athlete, parent, maverick, musician – your questions will be similar.

Am I making the right choices? What do I really want? Am I stuck in my career path? How do I conquer my fears? What are my limiting beliefs? How am I perceived? What do I want my legacy to be? What does my team think of me (and why does that matter)? What decisions have I been avoiding? What do I need more of? What do I need less of? How can I enjoy more? How do I prioritise? What are my mistakes teaching me? Am I taking enough risk (and do I understand what it is)?

Or simply, what next?

3. How to use this book

This book is a guide – a coach and mentor to you. It is also a friend and a workbook, where at the end of each chapter it gives you the freedom and choice of your own takeaways, working through your thoughts to answer some key questions and to help you self assess.

There will also be an interactive App which you can use with your smartphone to work on your leadership potential and connect with me.

www.leadership-itsinyourDNA.com

INTRODUCTION

What is this book about?

Some people make things happen,
Some watch things happen, while others
Wonder what has happened.

—Gaelic proverb

Leadership: It's in your DNA. Intriguing title everyone says. I feel a deep resonance to one 'word' in particular – DNA.

DNA is in the title of my book, my business and worldview because it captures the essence of my thinking. *We have everything inside of us that we need ... to do anything we want to.* Deoxyribonucleic Acid may not roll off the tongue, but I am inspired by what it represents. DNA contains the genetic instructions used in the development and functioning of all known living organisms – right? Well, I have a mirror belief that we *also* have certain instructions (or ingredients, as I have termed them in this book) within us to *lead* our lives and once we are fully aware and optimise the blend of these ingredients, we can use them to our benefit much more than we may at first realise.

Now let me deal with the other key word. *Leadership.*

I define leadership as:

Leadership is first an attitude and belief, followed by the ability of one person to stand up and take ownership in walking *taller and stronger* on a new path or an improved current path

My dream with *Leadership: It's in your DNA* was to do one thing well. This was to take the somewhat elitist and seemingly specialised subject of leadership and make it accessible. Real leadership has more emotional and instinctive elements to it than purely intellectual matters. So I have written the book in a way that your **head** could access the power of leadership, your **heart** could relate to the ingredients and your **hands** could take action for the world to witness.

Let me also tell you what this book is not. This book is NOT a step-by-step *manual* to describe how each and every reader can attain the classic leadership positions often associated with leading big companies and nations. Of course, what you will read will help you to attain this role if that is what you desire. But I believe leadership has a far wider and universal reach. Leaders who are smart enough, strong enough, and connected enough know that what worked in the twentieth century won't work in the twenty-first.

For example, how does a golfer who has not had any formal golf lessons and coached on a golf swing, win the prestigious US Masters? How does a novel written by an unknown author end up as a national bestseller? How did a child in South Korea crossing nine kilometres of river water everyday to obtain schooling then become the Prime Minister and an UN envoy? How does the CEO of Unilever transform his team through a shared human experience of terrorist captivation? Why did an Austrian tour guide become the chairman of not one, but two of the world's largest companies? Why did sheer instinct make a chef turn around a failing business into one of the best restaurants? What makes a rising star like Lucy join an investment bank only to derail into mediocrity? Why did an ex banker end up as a homeless guy? How does an uneducated, unqualified group of self taught "lunch box carriers" in Mumbai become certified Six Sigma teachers at Harvard?

I think the answer to all those questions is the same – it lies in the ten innate ingredients in our DNA which we are all born with. I have them. You have them. Presidents, CEOs, the guy on the street all have them. So, what are they?

Your DNA Code for leadership – the 10 Ingredients

The ten ingredients form the ten chapters. Now, quite simply, we all have within us:

1. a **self**: a big inner code which we need to make sense of, believe and develop.
2. **expression**: the way we look, sound, behave *along with* what we say
3. **instincts**: how we just *sense*, and *intuit* without knowing why.
4. **creativity**: taking our innate imagination and building it into muscles of creativity
5. **emotions**: channeling and harnessing our emotions with skill and courage

6. **dark side**: keeping *gremlins* at bay, managing weaknesses or overdone strengths
7. **resilience**: our inbuilt tenacity to bounce back and use adversities as opportunities
8. **fear**: our ability to harness fear as a positive
9. **focus**: dogged determination to prioritise and focus on "what matters"
10. **luck**: our ability to make (and destroy) our own luck

Those are the ten ingredients we are all born with in some shape or form. *Pause*. I know, some of you are thinking ... *but I don't have enough focus*, or *X lacks resilience* or *Y has little creativity*. That is not the point. The point is we have the ingredients whether active, emergent or dormant. The opportunity lies in blending them to their maximum potential and releasing the composite result to the world. So it is not about a missing ingredient, instead it is about turning up (or down) the volume of these common ingredients and channeling them to maximum effect.

I may need more *resilience*, while you may need more *instinct*. Someone may need to manage their *dark side*, while another may need to *focus* more.

The timing of *Leadership: It's in your DNA* is pertinent because we are seeing unconventional patterns of success in this new world. Why do some people achieve so much more than others? What is the secret of their success? Why are some people more driven than others? In what I hope will be a provocative and inspiring book, I have explored everyone from business leaders to students, sport stars to musicians and have studied what inner ingredients they have in common.

I have looked behind their neat covers, the glossy facades, and dug into their stories and myths to show what ingredients really explain exceptionally inspiring people. I have done that with thousands of people. **And this revalidated my instinct of how even the ordinary man and woman on the street, all of us, have the exact same ingredients – we all have ten, whether we know or show it. While that runs against the grain of conventional leadership literature, that is the authentic purpose of *Leadership: It's in your DNA*. For example, the book claims we are all born with a luck quotient (the ability to create circumstances in which what we call luck can occur). What differs between two**

leaders is how prepared one is to seize and attract opportunities to channel that luck. That is different from saying some of us are lucky while others are not.

In case you are wondering – is the book all instinct? *Leadership: It's in your DNA* draws on five contributing fields to support my instinct: psychology, sociology, organisation behaviour, anthropology and neurogenesis. But it does so, above all, with real stories and real experiences – to present a new way of understanding how each one of us can utilise what we already have.

Contrary to popular belief, my conviction is to prove leadership doesn't have to be 'learnt' or 'sourced' through elitist education, expensive seminars and privileged programs.

The book also combines left-brain techniques with powerful right-brain concepts like instinct, emotions, stamina, luck, fear, resilience, and creativity which are made compellingly tangible. We will hear an array of stories ranging from world class corporate leaders on the power of instincts and emotions in the boardroom... to athletes using creative visualization to attract luck... to mastering the art of resilience from the first female police commissioner in a corrupt Asian prison. **A journey into the realms of many leading minds and across cultures to show themes, principles, possibilities and choices one has as a leader. What follows is a book that does not promise short cuts or insider recipes on how to lead. Instead it gives you a key to 'unlock your self so you can build the best version of yourself.' And that process is never complete. Hence the open key ring on the cover.** This book also focuses on diverse leadership "pairings" analysing the dynamics between Chairman/CEO or Child/Adult, Musician/Athlete, Executive/Non executive directors, incoming vs. outgoing CEOs and the highlighted Male/Female facet. **The narratives belong to the author. The interpretation belongs to the readers. I believe every reader should have that choice. To synthesise various pieces from our individual stories and give them meaning is an individual's creation.**

This book is for tomorrow's leaders as much as it for today's. Tomorrow's leaders will come from a diverse range of backgrounds and age groups. They will disrupt the world for the right reasons and make us think, decide and act in different ways. Some now may be just finishing university; some may already be in their career, midpoint and contemplating the next move. Others may just be a step away from a CEO or equivalent leadership point. Some may be in school. Who knows who and where they are preparing themselves? **I hope to spark real adult experienced imagination just as much as fire up yet-to-mature, raw, young potential.**

The Voice of the book.

At any age we are the sum of all our years. For that reason, I have interlaced my own and other people's experiences of 'growing up' with our 'grown up' experiences of leadership. Where I have offered a childhood example, I have sought to convey this through my mindset and voice at that time as a child or a student or a young adult.

I was astounded by the number of times successful contributors to this book dipped into their childhood to make that connection.

Each year that we grow does not replace the previous year, but cumulatively adds to who we are. If my promise is to make leadership accessible, it is vital you feel my narrative derives its authenticity from whichever respective reference point in time I am writing from. The voice, the style and stories are deliberately varied while the messages are universal. I hope you will find this a revitalising approach.

Our formative years, our adolescence and adulthood are quite simply the foundation strands of our DNA. It is what gives us our depth of character. And to the riposte 'Why don't you grow up?' I say 'I hope I never will'. As Groucho Marx said, 'a child of five could understand this. Fetch me a child of five'. Well, we already have that child of five inside us, so just pause and reflect when you are seeking to understand something in your grown up leader self. Just look through your five year old eyes and sometimes that will provide, a clear, strong, simple answer.

Childhood never has an expiry date – our inner child ever leaves us. We not only enjoy reliving pleasant childhood memories, but we happily replicate similar situations in later life that brings that inner child out to play and encourages a healthy, creative disruption. Those of us that relish the child within us are the richer for it. So I would be sad if a bright young student hesitates to pick this up because a voice goes, "it is written by a business entrepreneur who is two or three decades older than me". And I would be equally unhappy if someone already in some form of a leadership position said "but it is late now, I am too set in my ways..."

More about "why DNA?"

As you know from my opening lines, I am fascinated with the human DNA – no wonder I named my business after it. Let me expand on this central metaphor for the book.

At its simplest, DNA is like a unique personal micro chip we all have inside us. It is the nucleus of the cell, made of two strands, intertwined, that contains all the genetic information humans are born with. But the intriguing fact about DNA is, other than being unique, it is capable of replication, thereby producing new cells to repair and replace old ones. Indeed, the ability to replicate is crucial as the new cell replacing the old one has to perform its exact same function. On the note of originality and ten innate ingredients, I believe in thinking that following your leadership DNA is like taking your existing DNA and replicating a richer version of it without losing the original. This means our unique microchip is not static or fixed but can also make copies of itself to help us live, grow, lead and evolve.

Isn't that great? You are not copying someone else's (unlike many people), but enhancing your own to a bigger better version. People I coach often ask me, "but I can't be like X" or, "I don't have Y's charisma ...". **But I say you don't have to be like anyone, just be yourself with a stronger blend of the ten ingredients in your DNA. This notion of building your own version instead of copying another one, is very integral to the book. When a cell reproduces, it must first replicate, or make a copy of, its DNA. While that is an inventible, natural, ongoing biological function, how about you take the inborn biological DNA and nurture it to replicate a stronger leadership DNA? Using the duality of the twin DNA strands one could say we all could have a second 'leadership gene', along with the other "biological gene" we are born with. Whether it develops or stays dormant or active can depend on tapping into, activating and exciting your inner ingredients.**

In conversation with Sir George Martin, CBE, the famed producer of the Beatles, I explored the concept of DNA and his own musical epic journey in relation to this book. Sir George modestly ventured that "*It is possible because I hadn't been 'over-educated' in music, I had a* kind of openness and freshness in my DNA to develop more creativity.....*My father was a fine carpenter, a great inspiration to me in creativity*". Then at 16, in the middle of war-torn London, it was remarkable that a young boy in 1942 had the self-belief and courage of his own convictions to travel into the centre of bomb struck London on his own from Kent to find a recording studio. "I found there was a little studio in Cavendish Square and went there to record my Fantasie in C sharp minor". This is a good example of leadership qualities coming to the fore in an area in which we would not necessarily recognise them operating. But the fact that his guidance, stewardship and the 'this is what you can do' studio environment brought four very talented and very different personalities and created the biggest band ever is inspiring. Sir George has something about his DNA which so appeals to my nature, and to the 'seasoning' of my DNA-and-ten-ingredients metaphor.

Making a big claim on leadership DNA has a phenomenal responsibility laced with conviction. So let me indulge, if you will, into a twin imagery in my mind behind these three letters.

One: The first translates the notion of DNA replication from a somewhat complex biological one to an inspirational, accessible leadership metaphor **'Dormant Neuron Activation'.** You could say this came from a spark in a dormant synapse in my own brain! It was at the very end, in May 2012, when Phil and I deliberated for an entire week, right before the book went to print, on how to translate this notion of DNA replication. After many doodles, ripped up since, *"Why don't we redefine DNA and call it "Dormant Neuron Activator",* he said *" isn't the book meant to be a catalyst to activate and accelerate dormant bits within all of us to be a fuller, taller and better version of ourselves?"* **Yes, dormant stands for the inactive bits that lay suppressed or buried and that's how I feel the ten ingredients can sometimes be. Neurons are electrically excitable cells that spark us to action. So Dormant Neutron Activator, or DNA, serves as an excitable trigger that propels, provokes and agitates you to take action.**

Leadership: It's in your DNA is a self-generated catalyst where I promised myself that if I can spark just one dormant neuron and reactivate a few dormant cells in any leader, leader to be or rising star, then I believe the book will have achieved its goal. Anything more is a bonus.

Two: The second imagery comes from the positive charge – the electric buzz – we get from interactive human connectivity. From our inner selves, the cellular magic of our biology, to our outward expressions of engagement with each other, we are at our optimum best when we **'Develop, Nurture and Adapt'** – it is at the very heart of who we are. **I seek to *Develop* an awareness and understanding of the ingredients I describe. I want you to *Nurture* them and cultivate their use and I encourage you to *Adapt* and optimise their different characteristics in a bespoke way to liberate your potential. Those latent, natural abilities that we all possess in leadership – and beyond!**

These are my two DNA metaphors intertwined like the two strands we know. My combination of bringing about Dormant Neuron Activation with the way to Develop, Nurture and Adapt your ingredients sets the scene for blending that is central to my thinking behind the book and my work. **Stimulus and sustenance, I believe, go hand in hand.**

I hope the power of the Dormant Neuron Activator is starting to capture your imagination for the rest of the book?

Why 'blend'?

Leadership: It's in your DNA is a code which is not fixed or formulaic . It is, instead, a blend of ten ingredients because a blend caters to the individual requirements unique to each reader, who can blend the mix and match of the ten ingredients to suit his or her specific needs (e.g. more emotions for the mature, experienced leader while more resilience for the younger rising star – or vice versa). It gives you choice and empowerment as a reader rather than being prescriptive and clinical.

Why 10?

You may ask, "why ten?". There is a symbolism. The number ten is regarded as the most perfect of numbers because it contains zero, the symbol of matter and chaos of which everything was born; it includes the beginning and the end, the power and the force, the life and the nothing. For the Mayas it represents the end of a cycle and the beginning of another. In China the number 10 is the totality of the numbers before it. In India, it stands for life. I'm also humbled by its inspiration – India gave the world the zero.

Who is in the book?

The book unfolds stories from 6 chairmen, 16 CEOs, 5 leading musicians, 2 sporting athletes, 2 world famous chefs, a policewoman, young Gen Y bright students, young rising stars, high potential managers, principals/ teachers, ministers, social workers, a priest, a poet and film maker. Across twenty nationalities.

To this, I give the reader an unique insight into diverse and eclectic leaders from different geographies (American, Arabic, Chinese, Indian, Greek, Italian, American, Australian, British, Korean, Lebanese) and specialisms (e.g. Chairmen, CEOs, ministers, music maestros, sport champions, investment bankers, social activists, real estate tycoons, fashion pioneers, students) of how they became leaders, what worked for them, their discoveries along the way, the teams they built, the climates they created, mistakes they learnt from and risks they are grateful they took. From boardroom dynamics to pioneering an uncharted vision by a music maestro to the first female commissioner of Asian police transforming one of the world's most corrupt prisons to UN activists and street vendors of Istanbul or the 'dabbawallahs' (lunch box men) of Mumbai, the stories are diverse and the reader is encouraged to choose and mingle the ingredients that play to their strengths, and to work out their own leadership story.

All this is unfolded through the lens of the ten ingredients. I prove that each blend is unique – mixed and matched, if you like to suit everyone's specific needs. For example, why may the mature, experienced director need more instinct while the younger rising star, could be in need of more self belief, and the entrepreneur should watch their dark side? I wanted *Leadership: It's in your DNA* to be one of the few books that is a confluence of voices and choices on leadership, in language that is crisp, clean and compelling.

Mining the intersections of my own narrative with those of the leaders I chose, this book attempts to demystify leadership from a plethora of models, tools, fads, frameworks and theories and proves how leadership is not only about the exceptional and exemplary. It is also very much about those 'real' and 'ordinary' men and women who have extraordinary stories to tell. This book is about those people and how they feel, think, decide and act – about their experiences, their hopes, their fears and their personal discoveries. My endeavor is about demonstrating the "L" word is not a privilege but a right you can earn. It is about stamina, self-belief and determination.

The book asserts that the spirit of leadership and the core human values that underline it are universal, inherent human capacities that "often go underestimated or unrecognized." This book unites boundaries. It will show how the dogged focus of the *dabbawallahs* of Mumbai are just as inspiring as the determination of Nelson Mandela – the 'size of the cause' may vary but size doesn't matter. Inspiration and Impact does. *Leadership: It's in your DNA* is about the everyday people out there and around us, like you and I, who have and can become extraordinary. They are just a touch away. As an author I encourage you to take a journey and discover how some of these everyday contemporary leaders developed into the people that we respect, and to find inside this book the tests, experiments and struggles that make or break us on our own paths to leadership.

So this book is not about traditional superheroes with big and loud projections. This is very much about normal people but with a heightened blend – real people who are capable but flawed, who have got it right but may have failed two or three times, or more, before they got it right. That's why their story in becoming a leader, is so believable.

If you are wondering how the mix of leaders were chosen, it was in two ways. Sometimes the protagonists have inspired the messages through their leadership journeys and at other times I have scripted the message and 'gone out there to find the right protagonist' to bring that message to life. Based on around 50 targeted interviews, *Leadership: It's in your DNA* presents the findings of an in-depth four year journey from the promising peaks of 07, to the recession in 08/09 and back to survival since 2011 where most interviewees have been re-interviewed during those periods, exploring the principles of how a leader's DNA has to unlearn, mould, adapt, relearn in the ever-changing context of the situation. It is real.

Why is this book relevant now?
9 laws for the new world

We live in a world where new rules are replacing old , just like DNA replication generates new cells. For me, *Leadership: It's in your DNA* has to be conveyed in new language, to a new readership, which belongs to a new world with new rules. The *'new normal'* as Paul Polman, Unilever CEO, is apt to espouse. **To get the most from the book, there are some new rules and new non-negotiables which set the scene and to help you get ready to turn to the first chapter.** *So, as they say in taking off to a new journey, switch off your phones, put your mind in an upright position, listen to the instructions and strap yourself in to these rules and non-negotiables* (the exit is on the last page!).

In the new normal:

- **Context is greater than Content** – in other words, rather than the conventional starting point of answering who I am, the answer to "Why I am the person I am" is becoming more relevant now. Context is changing content, our notion of self is both core and fluid – we have multiple adapted selves depending on the context we choose.

- **The world is smaller but with bigger opportunities** – strange as this sounds, this is creating room for more leaders. The world of teams, connectivity, alliances, networks and collaborations is becoming greater than individual heroism.

- **Winning is still important, but the game is continually changing.** The world is rewriting its rules where there is no clear one right or one wrong. It is not about sink or swim or survival of the few and fittest – many can survive and many can swim.

- **Power and decisions lie with the end user** – power is not trapped in the leader but is finding a new centre of gravity in the student, the reader and the consumer.

- **Social mobility is crucial** – More than anything else, institutions – schools, governments and religion – need to let go of stabile, rigid agendas of knowledge, and build a learning experience that encourages DNA development in the 21st century for the many, not the few.

- **Maverick thinking in the new world is good rather than disruptive**. Wikipedia defines the word maverick as "an unbranded range animal", "one who does not abide by rules" or "one who creates or uses unconventional and/or controversial ideas or practices." The new world belongs to entrepreneurs and truthful disruptors. Mavericks break rules, not out of spite but because the rules don't work. They ask more questions than there seems to be answers and do not compromise their standards to fit in, and therefore cannot be managed conventionally. They eagerly make business decisions that fly in the face of business-as-usual. They are tomorrow's leaders, like Guy Laliberte who created Cirque du Soleil.

- **Instinct is often superseding data, in making decisions**. Albert Einstein, who was as much of a philosopher as he was a scientist, said 'the intuitive mind is a sacred gift and the rational mind a faithful servant. We have created a society that honours the servant and has forgotten the gift.' This book will explore the power of instinct from how a chairman of a law firm relies on an use of instinct just as much as a world famous Italian chef (or cook as he prefers) does on food.

- **Diversity is an expected imperative, not just exceptional** – this is about uniting boundaries, and not just with age, colour and gender. Diversity is all about promoting valuable differences to drive better decisions and aid creative problem solving. From children learning a minimum of three languages to adults working with different thoughts and opinions across gender and geographical contexts, diversity will drive productivity, profitability and sustainability in the new world. The book focuses on over 45 diversity touch points.

- **Curiosity will be king (and queen)** – back to Einstein's "the important thing is not to stop questioning...". Our outcomes are greatly determined by the quality of the questions that we ask ourselves and others. We find answers where we least expect. Don't stop looking. Asking the right question is sometimes better than giving a perfect answer, in this new world. We learn more because we have a desire to know more. When we experience novelty, our brain produces more dopamine – an important brain chemical that lifts our mood and increases our sense of wellbeing.

Would you agree with these rules?

Release your Code. Optimise your Blend.

In understanding leadership achievement or success, we normally start with the wrong question. We ask *what is unique about this person* when we should really be asking how does this person optimise his or her DNA blend? That's because I have the same ingredients as someone else but my blend maybe incomplete or mis-blended. The real secret of success comes down to be surprisingly simple and hinges on adjusting and tuning those basic ingredients to maximise their return through people's life experiences. This book will not only change the way you think about your potential but challenge you to make the most of your potential. There will be bumps or little knocks, scars and wounds, moments of truth and self-discovery but that only makes your DNA stronger.

In *Leadership: It's in your DNA*, I want to convince readers that superstar explanations of success do not work. **Real leaders do not rise from nothing. Neither do they rise into success overnight. People standing on stages and platforms may look like they are lucky or that they did it all by themselves but look deeper. Invariably the hidden truth is how they blend their innate ingredients to create their leadership DNA, released that to the world and then drawn the most from this experience.**

Two examples of optimising and releasing my DNA in becoming an entrepreneur – the "why" and "when" of staring my business.

*"**Why I started CorporateDNA**" I could give you many reasons. Here's one about challenging a 'how worthy is my time' assumption. One of the greatest innovations and the greatest curses of the 20th century was the "billable hour". Most professional services – law, consulting, designing – come tagged with the burden or blessing of the billable hour. But I genuinely never understood – infact I struggled a great bit – to crack why a management consultant's billable hour were exponentially higher than a teacher's, or a lawyers over a doctor? I cannot change the system. But I can create a new system, based on value, creativity and earning the right to get*

people's DNA and help them explore it in a new light. I realized that unless the pressure of conventional time-billing was released, my instinct and risk-appetite to deliver on that 'DNA intention' would be compromised. So I released the pressure. This made me poor on one hand but set me free to conceive and shape a business on the other. Once that concept was secure, clients believed. Once they believed, they bought the concept. Once they bought, successful billing was a natural consequence.

*"**When I started CorporateDNA"** I was obsessed by simplicity. If leadership development is my key passion, I need to make leadership simple and accessible. Not complex, jargon-laden and heavy handed. I have got to make people see and believe that the raw ingredients are within them. They just need liberating. Today, my promise to my clients and all my readers is this: whatever challenge, blindspot, and weakness you bring, we can map back to the raw ingredients. Then, whether you prepare a sandwich or a five-course meal is your choice but at least you know that both the cooking ingredients and the methods lie within you. The rest is a choice – do you want to blend your best version? If you talk to the people who truly stand out, you realize that they have a very different way of looking at the world. They do not share the assumptions about why and how leadership happens. Starting anything – a business, an idea or a passion – is about courage. The word 'courage' has its root in 'heart'. 'Cour' = 'coeur' or 'heart' in French. For me, this is the age of the heart hence cour-age. Courage, in the context of this book, is to allow your ten ingredients to play out fully.*

In Turkish, the same connection as the Latin root exists: being courageous almost translates directly to being 'heartful'. That brings us to the word 'encouraging', which also has 'heart' at its core and is about nurturing courage in others to discover and enhance their leadership DNA. When I heard that phrase for the first time I remember thinking – *wow*. What if everyone could better blend what is already within them?

I sincerely believe this book holds universal human appeal and not just for the top executives, global entrepreneurs or star athletes of this world. In fact my own mother – Ma, now 64, who raised me single handedly across two countries, a woman of deep compassion and zeal, sums this up perfectly. Unsolicited, she said this on learning about the blend, "In my lifetime I have practiced tons of emotional courage, resilience and focus, now I wish someone had coached me on instinct and luck!"

Conclusion

Enjoy this book. Read it and believe in it. Take it seriously. Try and practice the ingredients all the time. What was a complex concept will become very simple. What you were avoiding will be attractive and what seemed impossible now will not just be possible but can pleasantly become a beautiful reality. In India and in Native American tribes, a rainmaker is someone who brings rain in a drought and makes it rain. I hope this book helps you dance in your own leadership rain shower. The forecast is good!

> Some people make things happen,
> Some watch things happen, while others
> Wonder what has happened.
>
> —Gaelic proverb

ACKNOWLEDGEMENTS

I could not start without saying thank you to everyone who made this book happen. I have had a series of relationships with the book. It has been a friend, a critic, a coach, a source of frustration at times and yet a mirror. So in all fairness, this book wouldn't be as enjoyable or complete without a certain set of individuals and experiences to which I'm truly grateful. I will also defy convention and dedicate this book to a few places and objects which have offered an inspiring setting or a great stimulus or sustenance to write.

Three key people first.

Ma, my mother – or Shukla to others – who inspired the authorial mind. I still remember a conversation from when we were on holiday in Malaysia in 2008. I shared this growing and seemingly irrational desire to write a book but tagged with a voice which went "but will it be good?" She said, "*Just write it, if no one else believes in it, I will*". Since then over the past few years she has fulfilled many roles ... that of a note taker, typist, coach-on-couch during my writing journey. Her constant love and support makes her the rock that I stand on as an author.

Malcolm, my best mentor, who has championed the work from its earliest incarnation, who has believed in the book during my fleeting moments of doubt, and often helped me find the right protagonist to bring my concepts to life. I am grateful to him for the care with which he reviewed the original manuscript; for feedback and conversations that clarified my thinking. Always reassuring "Rhea, you are on the right track". He has an amazing ability to break down a complex piece of thinking into simple parts.

Phil, my husband who always strikes an exquisite balance between constructive critique and encouragement. Without whom the cover would not have that refreshing dash of energy and the term "DNA" – Dormant Neuron Activator – would certainly never be coined. He came into my world midway through the book and made me apply the ingredients beyond the corporate world to everyone out there ... chefs, magicians, taxi drivers, electricians, shopkeepers and even the homeless. He made me prove the ten ingredients apply universally. I still remember when he first heard of the original title I was then very keen on (I'll save you the humour) he paused for a second before saying in his Scottish accent, "*nah, that won't work – let go of the seriousness and think of it through the inner playful child in you*"

Clients and Colleagues next.

There are many examples. Ray O Brien from HSBC, who said "I always knew you had a book in you!" Or, Kofi Rashid who, in his very American accent, said eight years ago, "girl, when are you going to write a book?" Or Brian Godins, Sundar Bharadwaj, Angela Zinser, Sanchita Baralay, Peter Winall, Jeremy Sutton, Marcus Baker who have been avid supporters. And to my hundred coachees across thirty nationalities to whom I applied the ten DNA ingredients.

Also to Noeleen Louer my friend and assistant who held the CorporateDNA fort while I would retreat into radio silence, in hermit mode, scribbling away.

Bloomsbury, is next.

Lisa, my editor at Bloomsbury who I first met on a freezing December morning in December 2010. It was so cold we didn't take our coats off or free our hands of the hot coffee from Pret A Manger. It took a while to un-glove, before I could pull out the manuscript from my bag. And to the team who worked with my ever creative ideas and impossible diary.

Nine special people who deserve a special mention.

I have their thumbprints in the next page as a symbol of how their personal DNAs have shaped my own. My mentors Paul Belcher, Mervyn Gunn, Sandy Pepper and Malcolm Ransome, my school friend, Archana Saboo, my mother, ma and my god mother Nila, my late grandparents, and my friend Daniel Gallo.

A few special places of inspired setting and objects of comfort.

This book is well tarvelled just like me. It has been my co-traveller to Ghana, India, New Zealand, Europe, New York, Hawaii and Dubai. I would also like to thank the Mitchell Library in Glasgow, my mother's sun clad balcony in the Charmwood village in Delhi, the business suite of my apartment in St Johns building in London's Westminster, the RAC club in Pall Mall and the library lounge in the Cinnamon Club for providing the setting to write. And to British Airways where the first page was born and where a lot of my first jottings took place on subsequent long flights.

And if glasses of wine and cups of coffee had a mind, I would like to thank them, too. And of course my end of evening ritual of a cup of peppermint tea with dark chocolate while reviewing endless print outs of the manuscript. And to my iPad who deserves the most hard-working iPad ever award.

Trust me, all these stimulants came together in creating what you are holding in your hand right now. It all started with a belief and became an attitude to walk taller and stronger through experience.

Thank you.

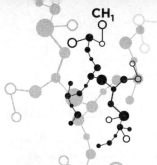

Ingredient One

SELF

— 'I am' —

Self is like the shelf that carries us through life. Instead of loading it with books and tools, as we do, clear out everything and get to know this great foundation for its strong, tall and pure nature. Believe in its strength.

In the beginning...

Let me share a little secret. It may not surprise you to learn I wrote the book in sequence from beginning to end. But I'm only on the second sentence of my book and here's the twist. I set out a mini experiment where after writing the first chapter on the self, I printed the master version, put it in a sealed envelope and marked it, 'do not open'. I then spent the next eighteen months writing and editing the remaining nine chapters. Only after completing those companion chapters, with heightened anticipation, did I go back to my first draft of the self, which is the foundation ingredient of this book. My experiment was to ask myself – did the content of the self chapter still fit? Did the self still tune into the remaining ingredients? Guess what? It did not. That was both unnerving and exciting. I realised my own thinking and convictions of the self had evolved and been informed by the other ingredients. I rewrote the entire chapter starting with the extract below. It felt cathartic. Why am I sharing this? Because in this lies the proof of concept for your leadership DNA. The self is fluid, not static, and evolves with every experience. We need to keep returning to and revisiting the self; with every visit our understanding of our self evolves into a stronger belief in our self .

Writing this book has been as revealing for me as I hope it will be for you. I will make this bold claim and stand by it. **My firm belief is that an individual's ability to win or lead depends firstly upon finding out how one is different from others. That is the differentiated self. Secondly, it then needs to find a way to integrate into society and to be accepted and valued. That is the integrated self. The differentiated self needs to be born first and then be integrated. Human society not only likes success but also needs it. It is not optional, it is necessary to our survival. Equally, though, as our survival is also predicated on our ability to coexist; we win best when our success is integrated, not excluded.**

The book draws on my background in strategy, organisational behaviour, leadership psychology and neuroscience. Much more than that though, it draws heavily on my origins and that of other leaders. That origin is still alive in my core self. At any age we are the sum of all of our years. It is for that reason I have interlaced my own experiences of growing up with the concept of 'grown up'. Where I have offered a childhood example, I have sought to convey this through my voice at that time as a child, a student, or a young adult. If my promise is to make leadership accessible, it is vital you feel my own narrative derives its authenticity from whichever respective reference point in time I am writing from. The voice, the style and stories are deliberately varied while the messages are universal.

Discovering your self – what does leading your own story really mean?

I could perhaps have started this book with a great leadership story from, say, a chairman or chief executive or a great athlete or musician. Or, my own leadership story of running a business. You will soon hear them in abundance in this book. Instead, I'd like to open with a 91-year-old's story to a 19-year-old.

The defining moment

An important personal disclosure first; I can still remember the moment when a curious restlessness was born in me, some kind of an attitude that has served me immensely well in life, and that memory still resonates for me today; it was kind of a Big Bang moment in my own universe.

Born in London in the early 70s, I was an only child of middle-class working Indian parents who moved back to India just before I was two. It was in India that I met one of the most fascinating men I have ever known. He became a great source of inspiration and awoke in me a wonderful sense of the possibilities of life.

He was my maternal grandfather. Men like him were typical of the new professional middle-class that emerged in the nineteenth century under British rule. This class produced lawyers, doctors and engineers – professions essential in a country that was breaking old traditions in search of new ones. There was a wisdom coupled with a relentlessness in people like him that was enormously attractive to the younger generation. I called him Dadu.

Born in 1901 and a lawyer by profession, Dadu had emigrated to Kolkata (then Calcutta) in 1947 after the partition of India. After this enormous upheaval, he had to re-establish his entire social and financial identity in a completely new environment – he needed new clients, a new legal practice and a new identity for his young but large family of ten.

He was a great storyteller. As I grew up, I was lucky to hear Dadu's many and varied tales. Some of the stories drew on his own life (adapted for a child's worldview and mindset, I hasten to add); some were adaptations of plays, novels, movies or epic poems; others were of his own creation. As I walked home from school on long summer afternoons, his stories became an integral part of my mental fabric until well into my teenage years. In fact, I often looked forward to going to school simply because of the promise of a magical story on the way home!

There was something so special for me about the way he narrated these stories. The magic was this: he almost always paid me the ultimate compliment of putting me somewhere in the story. He didn't always make me the lead character, but rather I would be dropped into the story somewhere magically – or it certainly seemed like magic to me. It was as if someone was telling you, as a child, a tale from Mahabharata, Arabian Nights, Narnia, Hogwarts, or anywhere else, and then suddenly making you a character in that tale. Of course, as soon as he did this, his story became my story.

Dadu's mantra was that '**the starting point of believing in any story is to first believe your own story is worth telling. Once you believe it, tell it with passion**. Every event in your life has a piece of you, that may be of interest or use to someone else'

The word 'passion' for me then meant little but it sparked a whole imaginative adventure in me. It did provide me with a wonderful conviction – and confidence – that I had some part to play in the world, a world I could otherwise make little sense of when I was young. I realise now his stories really made me feel I mattered. As young as I was, they gave me the belief that I might be able to script my own story as an adult. This feeling took shape more firmly in my teens, when I understood that I did not want to spend my life merely acting out some part in someone else's view and idea of what my life could be. Doctor, engineer, teacher or...? Nothing seemed appealing and to a middle-class family, that was a worrying sign. Crucially, though, the seeds were being sown for not what I would choose, but how I would go about making my choice. That childhood flicker of understanding from what Dadu meant was growing into a flame of what my life really could be, not just should be.

I am 38 now and that flicker was planted in me three decades ago. I wanted to write and live out the script of my own life story. To this day, I am so grateful that Dadu's restlessness has rubbed off on me.

I think we all have our own Big Bang moments, although of course they come in an infinite number of forms. You might recognise yours for what it is straightaway and be able to act on it there and then, or it may take time. **Big Bangs are like DNA moments; the Dormant Neuron Activation**

moments we explored in the introduction. It is when a dormant, untapped neuron goes 'ping!' and something gets created that did not exist before. The key question for all of us, though, is at these 'ping' or big bang points, what choices do we exercise? The quality of the rest of our lives following our Big Bang moments depends on the choices we make.

Dadu didn't only tell me stories. That amazing old man was the first man to also impress on me a simplified version of Shakespeare's idea that 'all the world's a stage' and we all play a part as actors on it. This widened my outlook forever. I looked forward to coming home to him in the evening and often his stories were more fascinating for a formative mind than the subjects taught at school. He would explain how we are all indeed playing roles on a stage, telling a story to an audience and living a brand (call it, character or reputation) for the world to witness. He told me **learning the ropes of this big stage, in fact mastering the stage, in terms of stagecraft and craftsmanship, was essential. Life is seldom a rehearsal.** Discovering how to leave a footprint (DNA, as I prefer to call it) on this world stage would need to come from mostly outside school, even though a formal education was essential. Contrary to most, he said 'we go to many schools in life, not just one – every transition in life is like going back to a new school. One never stops learning.' Looking back now, that wise man shaped my DNA beyond doubt and I wonder now if he wanted me to do everything he could not and live his dream through me.

Having worked very hard to secure a Masters in English literature from the Scottish Church College, a venerable British institution in Calcutta, I couldn't understand why Dadu became a lawyer. I asked him about his own seemingly conflicting choices. *How could a lawyer be so attached to literature? Surely the two fields engage two entirely different parts of the brain? His reply? 'The legal profession gave me a living and conviction, but literature gave me imagination. Literature provides answers to legal cases I couldn't solve through pure rationale.'* I realise now, that he was trying to train my mind in not only exposing myself to different realities, but seeing the connections and interdependencies between them.

That was a 91-year-old looking back on his life and dispensing advice to someone who had a mirror image age of 19. At the time of our last conversation, he was exiting the stage while I was looking ahead to step on to it, with eager anticipation. The conversations I had with him will always remain fresh in my memory and I suppose the idea of the ten ingredients were subconsciously planted by him. His seventh child, my mother, took the ingredients, like seeds, and rooted them in me for life. That started my journey of self belief and the last three decades have only reinforced the role that *focus, emotions, instincts, fear, creativity, dark side, resilience and language* play in affirming that belief and attracting *luck*.

Writing and living your own story

On that important theme of stage, rehearsal, actor and script, let us turn to the notion of writing the script of one's own life. Societies and cultures have a story of how they came to be, where they are going and what it means to live in that society. In a very similar way, some individuals are said to also have a life story or myth that they believe to be true for themselves. In Transactional Analysis (TA) this is referred to as a script or life script. Created early in life to make sense of our world, shaped by parents and experiences, and often completely unconsciously, we use them unconsciously to explain to ourselves our place in the world and make sense of what happens to us. A positive life script can help us reach our goals, while a negative one can limit us from living our lives to their full potential.

Another way of defining this would be to say that, in one sense, I'm trying to help you be the scriptwriter of your Leadership DNA.

> **"A self that is only differentiated – not integrated – may attain great individual accomplishments, but risks being mired in self-centered egotism. By the same token, a person whose self is based exclusively on integration will be well connected and secure, but lack autonomous individuality. Only when a person invests equal amounts of psychic energy in these two processes and avoids both selfishness and conformity is the self likely to relect complexity."**
>
> Mihaly Csikszentmihalyi,
> Flow: The Psychology of Optimal Experience, 1990

Now, let me plant a few seedlings in your mind in the form of questions:

- What is your biggest achievement in life?
- What have been some of your defining moments?
- Which other lives and stories have you influenced or touched?
- What ambitions do you still have?
- When do you feel truly restless?
- What drives your curiosity?
- Has your self belief been knocked ever and why?

- How much of your potential is unrealised?
- Have you felt at times you have 'walked taller' than you actually are?
- What makes you happy?

In answering these, we start exploring your story. **I always believe leadership is a blend of four Cs. Like a diamond has carat, colour, cut and clarity, leadership too combines Character, Confidence, Common Sense and Capability. We spend a life time building capability but every conversation in this book proves character, confidence and common sense are more inspiring than just capability. You can rarely stand out on capability alone.**

As you explore your leadership 4Cs, picking the decisions and choices that matter, we realise if you can give someone a gift – be it to a child, a student or your team – give them character, confidence and common sense. Capability will follow naturally. **Remember this book is an antidote to mediocrity, which, to me, is a limiting handicap we can have in our path to leadership. It is not that mediocre leaders are not capable, they are, but mediocrity is often about fitting in and staying safe which is neither good, nor bad, but just okay. That 'okay-ness' is un-stimulating. Instead, this book will share with you the people who have circumvented mediocrity – they have written and directed their own scripts: people who have risked stability to stand taller, used confidence and common sense to shape their leadership story, been brave enough to put their characters on stage for the world to watch. These are experienced leaders we follow already or emerging ones that we will follow in the future**. Many of them are leaders in the business world, but you'll also read about social leaders, such as the first female Asian commissioner of police, the headmaster of Eton College, or creative leaders like the producer of The Beatles, sporting athletes and Gen Y rising stars.

The three choices for writing our own story

In practice, we have three choices in how we write our own story:

1. **Be an observer**, a passive recipient and watch your story happen; very likely because someone else is writing it for us.
2. **Be a reporter**, a passive participant recording the events for reflection and recall.

3. **Be an active participant,** shaping the content of our own stories, rewriting the sections that went wrong, safeguarding the chapters at risk and securing safely all the sections that are going well and that you hope will continue to go well.

What is certain, above all, is that whatever that story is, it will be yours, but only truly yours if you shape the script yourself. By all means let others contribute, but you have to be the editor. My aim here is to help you become that third type – active participant – of 'scriptwriter'; to help you become a writer or architect of the one story that is by far the most important of all: your own. After all, you are the only one who has its sole copyright, its licence, trademark and patent – in other words its unique DNA; hence the title of this book. All it needs is willing curiosity, participation and commitment to make your story stand out. To script your story well, you will need to start with the magical four letter word, 'self'.

Back to Dadu's concept of stage, actor and script. Let me take the following examples from different actors on stage. We may call them leaders. For me they are all live performers on stage, living and playing out a script handed to them or self initiated.

The stage, remember, is where you are viewed the most. Stages change; actors with different and unique DNAs come and go, leaving legacies. I chose to delve into the scripts of at least one of each leader type below in this book.

- Chairman is on a shareholder stage.
- CEO is on an organizational stage.
- Sporting athlete is on a game stage – pitch, court and field.
- Musician is on a performing stage.
- Artist is in the gallery stage.
- Student is on an academic stage.
- Film maker is on a cinema stage.

But within a stage, there are differences too. Let us take an example from the musical stage of leadership. Between 1915 and 1955, three legendary musical leaders were born, each two decades apart. The King of Swing – Frank Sinatra, the King of Rock and Roll – Elvis Presley and the King of Pop – Michael Jackson. Each with a phenomenal self-belief in what they were trying to bring to the world. Each with a dark side we will explore later when looking at the dark side ingredient.

While they are performing or playing in the same arena, there is a point to be made about differentiation. Their DNAs are different and each is playing out to a different script they have invented. They are all leaders in their own right and have optimised their blend to its fullest potential. Differentness is the name of the game. Conforming to type can tip you into mediocrity.

Your story – the one that matters the most

The Self

The first ingredient in your leadership DNA is your self and the need to understand your self as well as you can. Let me explain the notion of the self through an analogy. Self sounds and looks almost like shelf. The self is the foundation, which carries us to destinations. Both the self and the shelf are strong foundations; a holder or carrier that often goes unnoticed or uncared for.

Of course, developing self belief is an ongoing process that can never be finite. So, here in this first chapter I look hard at that foundation s(h)elf while subsequent chapters introduce the other ingredients, like the books we place in the shelf of the self, which are:

- sharpening your **focus**
- using your **instinct**
- channelling your **emotion**
- mastering **expression**
- making your **dark side** work for you
- conquering **fear**
- developing **resilience**
- building your **creativity** muscles
- making your own **luck**

The final, tenth ingredient, luck, is something you need to be able to attract in abundance, by making the very most of the other nine. The 'self' is a key concept in several schools of psychology. But what is it really?

For the Swiss psychiatrist Carl Jung, the father of modern psychology, the Self signifies the coherent whole, unifying both the conscious and unconscious mind of a person. More simply put, it is the entirety of who you are. Let me put it differently. To build your Leadership DNA, I would like you to see the notion of self as answering more than 'who am I?' I want you to start with **'Why am I the person I am?'** To this, add **'how have I become this version of me?'** Answering the why and how is pivotal to understanding your self better. When things are going well, we always ask 'What can I do more? What's next?' But as soon as things go wrong, our thoughts turn to 'Why me?' Since starting my business, I realise that context is greater than content and context is changing content. **The 'why' is bigger than the 'what.'**

Understanding your self is, inevitably, the most fundamental and important aspect of understanding all the ingredients that are part of your leadership DNA.

Here's a simple story which illustrates just how powerful the concept of the self can be. You may have heard of it before. It is a story that features in many cultures, one of those tales that transcends time, culture and generation.

A man had been sitting by the side of a road for ten years. One day a stranger walked by.

'Spare some change?' mumbled the man, mechanically holding out his hat.

This carried on for a few months until one day the stranger replied. 'I've nothing to give you, but tell me: what's that thing you're sitting on?'

'Nothing,' replied the beggar, 'just an old box. I've been sitting on it for as long as I can remember.'

'Ever looked inside?' asked the stranger.

The beggar shook his head and gave a shrug. 'Why? There's no point, there's nothing in there.'

'Take a look inside,' the stranger insisted. The beggar unwillingly opened the lid of the box. A moment later, to his astonishment, sheer disbelief and joy, he saw that box was filled with gold.

The point here is universal. We all have our own hidden 'box'; the seemingly unnoticed container or shelf of ingredients that we are all too often either too afraid of, or oblivious to, to open. And so we let it go

unexplored. I call this box the 'Self'. Have you looked inside the box? Examined its contents? Understood the contents neglected thus far? Thrown out the bits that do not fit anymore? Put in some new things?

I believe that to aid the scripting of your leadership DNA, you need to make sense of that box. It contains everything that has passed through your consciousness. All our memories, actions, desires, choices, pleasures and pains are recorded there and self awareness starts with connecting the dots between our different choices, experiences and memories. Taking patterns and insights from one context and linking or applying them to another is a key trademark of a self that is getting ready to lead.

More than anything else, your self represents how you have become who you are – everything there is about you up to this present moment.

Four kinds of people

I discovered this little jewel of a saying tucked in a dusty road sign on a trip to Scotland in 2001. It is an ancient Gaelic proverb which says there are three kinds of people on this planet, I have added a fourth:

1. **Those who make things happen**
2. **Those who watch things happen**
3. **Those who wonder what has happened**
4. **Those who wish things would happen**

This book is for the first type of person, but I hope it will inspire or transition the remaining three types to action. The difference between the types is not of skill, knowledge or experience i.e. capability, but that of character, common sense and confidence i.e. self belief and attitude. I would say the one subject they don't teach in school is a stronger attitude towards your own self; life teaches you that. But imagine if you had greater control over that attitude?

Did you know there are now over seven billion people on Earth? The seven billionth person was born in October 2011. It is a busy world to say the least! This struck an even deeper chord with me when I was fortunate enough to spend some time on the Hawaiian island of Maui recently. Here, forced to slow down and appreciate the beauty of nature, I was somehow drawn to the magnificent rainforests surrounding the Earth's equator. **The rainforests, for example, cover only 6% of the world's surface, but contain more than 50% of the world's plant and animal**

species. A rich and diverse complexity of species struggles for survival in the same place. Some stand tall, towering over the others, some blend in with the masses. Somehow the parallel with leadership struck me in that there are a huge number of potential leaders in a very concentrated space.

If you feel any connection with this natural rainforest image you may even feel a sudden yearning within yourself somehow to stand taller and stronger. I would very much like to walk you through your own leadership rainforest. Embarking on this journey in your company is both exhilarating and daunting; it feels laced with a real sense of responsibility. If you find that this book becomes a companion to your life, pinging a dormant neuron into action, then that will be reward enough in my decision to write it.

The two dimensions of the self

It is useful when thinking about the self to talk about the known constant and the unknown variables.

The known constants in our DNA

These are the fixed, constant and non-negotiable facts about ourselves that are outside our control that we are born into. The known constant includes such basic 'givens' or constants about us like our gender, race, the wiring of our genes, and indeed the culture, geography and time period we are born in. It includes our biological parents and the first school we go to over which we have no control. These aspects are either inherited, or destined and cannot be changed.

The unknown variables in our DNA

These are the changing variables over which we – at least in principle – can exercise greater choice and control. These include the decisions and choices we make, the risks and actions we take, including how we choose to react to situations we encounter.

For example, how does a golfer who has not had any formal golf lessons or been coached on a golf swing win the prestigious US Masters? How does a novel written by an unknown author end up as a bestseller? How did a child in South Korea crossing nine kilometers of river water everyday to get to school then become the Prime Minister and an UN envoy? How does the CEO of Unilever transform his team through a shared human experience of surviving a terrorist attack? Why did an Austrian tour guide become the chairman of not one, but two of the world's largest companies? Why did sheer instinct make a chef turn around a failing business into one of the London's best restaurants? What makes a rising star join an investment bank only to derail into mediocrity? Why did a former banker end up homeless? How does a group of self-taught lunch box carriers in Mumbai become certified Six Sigma case study material at Harvard?

Your unique leadership DNA

We all know that genetic DNA has a specific biological function as the method by which our genes are coded, but what I think of as our leadership DNA is just as personal and one we can exercise choice over.

For me, **developing your leadership DNA is like taking your existing biological DNA and replicating a richer version of it.** In other words, increasing our chances and potential to lead and contribute to the world. Exercising that choice is the best gift of freedom. There is no need to copy other people's DNA, but instead we need to enhance and build on what we have already. This concept is crucial. DNA, as we know, carries the information for all the functions of a living organism and determines our characteristics. When a cell reproduces, it must first replicate – or make a copy of – its DNA. That is an inevitable natural, ongoing biological function. We cannot influence that, but now you know you could fuse the biological with the psychological and add a leadership strand to your DNA and build that version to its fullest.

In the opening of the book, we said DNA is the nucleus of the cell, made of two strands, intertwined, that contains all the genetic information humans are born with. Using the duality of the twin strands, one could say we all have a second leadership gene, along with the other "biological gene" we are born with and that whether it develops or stays dormant or active can depend on tapping into it and exciting your inner ingredients.

Of course it varies from person to person, but the essential elements of your leadership DNA include the vital, formative, early experiences that have contributed to our make-up as a person, including your personality, your natural energy and natural preferences. The people we look at and think about in this book all have different, unique leadership DNAs. Certainly, they often acknowledge the importance of formative experiences in their lives, as we are about to see.

What do the stories of Franz, Willie and Cynthia tell us?

For example, I spoke to Dr. Franz Humer, the Swiss–Austrian chairman of Diageo, an international premium drinks company. Dr. Humer is also chairman of the pharmaceutical giant, Roche, and chairs the board of INSEAD business school.

> **Looking back, I'd say that my experience as a tourist guide in Austria when I was in my twenties gave me really useful insights about how to read people and gauge moods, their instincts and needs. These insights taught me, I think, far more than any leadership book or leadership course could have done.**
>
> **It was while working as a tourist guide that I learned survival skills and developed an innate sense of human behaviour. The job did not come with a salary, but only with tips. Eventually, I could predict – with, as things turned out, a great deal of accuracy – how much I could earn from any particular group. Today, that's the strongest ingredient I have in the boardroom – using the instinctive element in my DNA to read people and their motives better**

And here is Willie Walsh, former CEO of British Airways and now CEO of International Airlines Group (IAG), who shared with me:

> **I spent my childhood taking things apart and rebuilding them – televisions, radios, even my father's car...on one not-to-be-repeated occasion! My father was a glazier in Dublin. He instilled in my family a curiosity and passion for work and a grounded work ethic.**
>
> **I left school at 17, responding on a whim to an Aer Lingus advert for trainee pilots. I followed this career course and I went into aviation. I loved it, and I gave up university ambitions in favour of working in the aviation industry. I was flying commercial jets within 14 months and had my pilot's licence before I got my driving licence**

Willie takes pride in being down to earth and, in a sense, ordinary. As for the people he's been most impressed by when meeting, he mentions former astronaut and pioneering moon-walker Neil Armstrong with great enthusiasm. 'Neil gave me a Big Bang moment'. It is clear that Willie was fascinated, even overwhelmed, to meet the first man on the Moon, but he was equally enthralled by Armstrong's unaffected manner. 'Neil had absolutely no airs and graces,' Willie recalls. 'In fact, I even told him how very 'down to earth' he seemed.' Willie grins, 'of course, later I realised that this was a pretty silly thing to say to the first human being who ever set foot on another planet!'

Or, take Cynthia Carroll, CEO of Anglo American. I was privileged to meet this real jewel in the ground (or mine), so to speak, from the world's largest producer of diamonds. A woman of incredible self belief, fierce resolve and unrelenting grace who has navigated many challenges since assuming her role at one of the world's largest mining companies; from improving relations with South African stakeholders, defeating an attempted bid, inspiring female mineworkers, to raising safety standards for all down to the individual at the mine face. Indeed she lives the script for real, no stunt doubles or stand-ins here, she will don a helmet and safety gear and visit her fellow workers down the mines. Her visionary strategy is for long term sustainability not only in financial performance, but also the mining environment where the company's footprint is viewed not over the short term, but over 50 to 100 years. Her self belief runs deep to steer a global company with over 100,000 employees, generating (2011) earnings of US$6 billion. An inspiration for many, a mother of four, this is Cynthia Carroll, one of only three female chief executives in the entire FTSE100.

We all respond to the world in different ways. We can take in the same inputs, but how these inputs react with our unique leadership DNA produces unique outputs. The way I handle risk, make decisions, connect with others is different from the way you do it, or how someone else does it.

Let us change the business stage to a film stage. Now, when we see a really great movie, it seems to us to have a spontaneous real life quality of life, of vitality, so immense it is hard for us to imagine that the whole movie is based around a written script. There is such a movie within each of us. Our own personal scripts play out every day in the choices we make, in our observations and reactions to people and events around us.

Let us turn to such a movie and see what it can tell us about the role that self belief or indeed self doubt plays in the leadership stage. Sometimes when my consulting work imposes sleepless schedules, I take respite in world cinema which always gives me a dash of creative inspiration. This particular one below is about leadership and the point is poignantly well made, setting the scene for the notion of the leadership dilemma around the leader and the led.

A Pope on stage

'We Have a Pope' is a 2011 Italian comedy-drama film directed by Nanni Moretti. The central character is an ageing cardinal who, after dedicating his life to the Vatican, finds himself put forward for the papal election, only to realise that this is the last thing he actually wants.

The truth is that the new Pope experiences self doubt about whether he can fulfill the role. His frailty unfortunately extends beyond his body, seizing his mind and infiltrating his self-belief. This turns to crisis mode with an inability to answer the question 'Who am I?'. He still believes in God, but not in himself.

The grandeur of the Vatican architecture dwarfs him as he stands by a window, peeking through the heavy satin curtains and watching the crowds outside awaiting the papal election. They, and the world, are waiting for him to lead them. Now, almost a silhouette of his former self, he is suffocating under the pressure of expectations foisted upon him.

The questions of leadership expectations rain down on him. Can he satisfy their expectations? Is he ready? What does he have to offer? Does even God believe in him? His mind cannot conjure a protective umbrella from this personal downpour of doubt and so he withdraws to his room, distancing himself from the thousands of followers who want to be led by him. He is adamant that he will stay in his perceived refuge in seclusion. Hours turn to days and the faithful are tested as they wait for the leader's appearance on the big balcony.

The conclave of cardinals, for their part, is also confined in the building and in desperation to dissolve the stalemate call in a psychoanalyst – a spry, bearded fellow played by none other than Nanni Moretti. It is a clash of two dogmas, as a cardinal warns: 'The concepts of soul and subconscious cannot possibly coexist.' Yet a similar existential crisis might affect anybody who suddenly doubts the value of what they have to offer.

The Pope is finally desperate to break free and lets himself loose on the world at large. He escapes the Vatican stage. This is the wonderful concept at the heart of Moretti's film – a grand Pope let loose in the real world, in the chaotic buzz of the city – anonymous and free of the pressure of his universally known identity

The child within him, for we never lose our younger self, not even the Pope, takes him by the hand into the real world outside. His childlike curiosity rampages in the bustling chaos. He rents a bed and breakfast room. He craves normalcy. He finds himself conversing with his own self on a bus. He chats with a shop girl. He strikes up a friendship with a troupe of actors performing Chekhov. And then... sees a psychotherapist.

This is his cathartic moment. He confesses his passion as a child was to be on the theatrical stage, not the one he has trod nearly all his life. So we see him embrace the theatre and he begins his life anew – it is never too late. As a young man, he already knew all the lines of Chekov's plays by heart. That was when his self-belief was alive and strong. Now we see this belief returning with a smile. 'We Have a Pope' shines a light on self-belief and self-doubt. For example, 'God sees abilities in me I didn't have' highlights his leadership predicament – could he lead? Was he ready? What validation and proof did he need, or thought he sought? It was only when he was on his natural stage that the answers came and then he was ready; he did not have to seek validation he already had it inside him, latent and just waiting to be ignited. Yes, he could lead.

The film also shows us during the election process that each cardinal literally pleads God to pick someone else. Seemingly bizarre, this is a measurement of the deficit of their self-belief. In leadership, there is something about big exposure on a big stage which induces indecision, fear of failure, lack of confidence and a need to escape. Had they measured up they could have taken ownership of their responsibilities and chosen a more appropriate candidate. A sign for boards of the governance kind? Directors and chairmen on nomination committees come to mind.

So as a leader, or one in the making, what do we want? Why do we want that? And how have we become who we have become? How will we get to our ambition?

Self Identity versus Self Reputation

Identity is different from reputation. Identity is who we really are inside of us, while reputation is what the world sees. Identity is the true inner us, while reputation is who, what and how much we choose to make visible to the world. Over time the self can evolve and identities can transition or hidden dreams can resurface. The Pope in Moretti's film had an inner, suppressed identity of being an artist while his firm visible outer reputation was of a cardinal. At some point the difference clashed, his inner identity craved for a release and he simply didn't want to lead the masses anymore. The world struggled to accept him risking his reputation. Do you see the external tension here? Can you relate to that predicament? How often have we heard people say ' ...I became a doctor but I really wanted to be a photographer' or '...if I didn't have a family so young, I would have risked financial stability and followed my entrepreneurial dream'. I have even had a CEO of a bank say, "I wanted (and still do) to be a footballer but my father was a senior banker and would not have any of that nonsense...!"

One of my clients, Kyle Whitehill, is CEO of a large telecoms multinational. His leadership transition went from leading on a mid-sized UK stage, to a COO ship of India with a US$ 5 billion–100 million customer base, to a CEO ship in Ghana where he did a turnaround which tripled revenue. Kyle talks about the **'spine and shoulders' metaphor for leadership. Spine is the vertical specialism of content and capability. Shoulders on the other hand is about the horizontal breath of confidence, character and common sense.** As his leadership stage got bigger, his need to broaden his shoulders became more important than developing his spine. As a CEO your previous expertise as a functional leader expands overnight to being a broader leader dealing with most things outside your core expertise, but the secret is to remain proud of the spine while embracing broader shoulders. What got you to this stage won't get you to your next stage.

Let me share a personal example about transitioning identities. I travel a lot and as a result I am on planes frequently. On long-haul flights, you often get talking to your neighbour. Years ago, I decided to do a little experiment, mainly for my own amusement, where every time the person next to me asks, 'what do you do?' I chose to share just one of my identities, for example, consultant, amateur artist, author or entrepreneur. The different reactions it provoked in people were fascinating.

If you are sitting in business class next to a big corporate honcho, saying you are an amateur artist then that mostly meant the conversation was over in a few minutes. They saw me as an outsider to their world and clearly felt we had little common ground. Instead, describing myself as an entrepreneur or leadership consultant, on the other hand, could mean a renewed interest and a very long, respectful conversation. Notice the word 'respectful.' Changing the opening line of disclosure about what I do charted a completely different conversation and reputational lens through which people saw me. However, the voice inside me, always said 'but I am the same core being, regardless of how many different hats I wear.' Once I even said that my primary identity was that of a 'nomad' – not untrue, given how much I do travel. My neighbour lowered his very expensive glasses, gripped his wine glass and said 'not the backpacking type, I presume, otherwise you wouldn't be here!' Note the unconscious biases and assumptions we all make about perceived identity and real reputation.

But regardless of the identity of the other person – and trust me, I've spoken to hundreds – one thing was guaranteed; as soon as I mentioned the word 'DNA' in the conversation, their faces lit up. Whether they are builders, bankers, teachers, musicians or even poets (it has been my good fortune to have an eclectic mix of seating companions), the focus goes from polite attention to keen curiosity. 'Tell me more.'

On identity, often there is a gap between how we want to come across (intention) and how we are actually perceived (perception). In leadership parlance, we call this gap the 'arc of distortion'. As our leadership stage gets bigger, it is crucial to reduce that angle, by projecting an authentic version of our selves; something we explore in all the chapters to come. That process always starts with self awareness and by projecting your full self, without hiding or masking the self for fear of rejection.

My story – how did I become me?

How did my own DNA evolve? Well, having asked the question, I need to answer that myself first. When I was younger, an astrologer said to my mother 'she is strange, for she is a man and woman rolled into one.' I will spare you my family's reactions when they heard that! Notwithstanding the gender stereotyping, decades later I suspect I am beginning to understand what he meant.

Passages from my life and a few big personal transitions have shaped my DNA. Let us explore these. I was born in London but returned to India when I was two, which had a profound impact on me. I practically didn't remember London, so imagine if I had not been told, I would not register my UK inception. But here is how the power of the subconscious and subtle cues influence us more strongly that we know. I was exposed to several realities. I grew up in Calcutta listening to both Bollywood and the legendary Beatles which had influenced my parents in the 60s. I traveled in rickshaws as well as my Dad's British Morris Minor on Calcutta's pot-holed streets. I celebrated Diwali and Christmas with equal enthusiasm, was made to learn three languages and simultaneously learned ballroom dancing and Bharatnatyam (an Indian classical dance). The points of reference were truly varied. I saw Bertrand Russell and Tagore cohabiting on my parents' bookshelf. I watched Dad's entrepreneurial leather business with Chinese tanneries and Ma's career with Philips, a multinational company, grow in different ways.

Watching Fawlty Towers, the fabled British 1970s sitcom, reading Indian folklore and listening to Dadu's stories all fed in. These contrasting elements extended to my changing family circumstances. When I moved from a large joint family with four cousins under the same roof, to a small nuclear family when my parents separated, I transitioned from a sense of competition to one of individualism. This individualism was anchored in a harsh reality of having very little resources yet making the most of every moment.

So when in 2008, I became a finalist for the UK's Women of the Future Awards, under the corporate entrepreneur category, it made me stop and look back on my journey. How did I get here?

The reality is that while flashes of England were blended into my DNA as I grew up, I never physically touched down on British soil until 24 years later. My first big transition was from Calcutta to Delhi at 17 to study English Literature in Miranda House. This was my choice. Now you may think they are two similar Indian cities but they are as different as Minnesota and Melbourne. Delhi was everything Calcutta wasn't. While Calcutta was philosophical, culturally rich and intellectually minded, Delhi was fast, entrepreneurial and filled with a can-do attitude. It gave me a sense of freedom, self-belief and hunger to work things out for myself. I chose a hard life to commute thirty kilometers each way, twice a day, on hideous Indian buses to get a degree. I used to leave home at 6:30 am and return at 10pm ... all in the attempt to gain intellectual weight while rapidly losing physical! My mother and I had to start a life from scratch. While we had nothing to begin with, we ended up with something far bigger and meaningful – a renewed self belief. That was another passage of re-channelling myself in a new context. The third big transition was Delhi to London at 26, prompted by another repeating pattern of wanting to prove myself in a new context; this time, across the oceans. I still remember as the plane touched the tarmac in Heathrow in September 2000 and I took off my seat belt. It felt alien – like another 'ping'; I didn't know a soul except Auntie Daniel. She is my mother's second cousin's French wife and became a great ally from that moment until ninety days later, when I found a little studio apartment to move into.

Making a name in a foreign land with a last name, Duttgupta, which people either hesitated to pronounce or avoided altogether, presented its own arc of distortion for me to manage.

A new voyage was about to start with a series of mini moves and international immersions – consulting assignments, in other words! These transitional experiences albeit short were powerful and life changing. From Italy to Japan, Ghana to Hong Kong and Sweden to Dubai, I experienced over twenty countries in short stints – my leadership DNA was being influenced by new values, local ways of working, new rules of rights and wrongs. Just when I would work out the 'how to be' code for a country, I was picked and dropped into another! Here is what was most startling though; in between, there was always the annual pilgrimage to India – a strange homecoming where every winter, I revisited India through the lens of a visitor (or a non-resident foreigner as, I sadly felt, when they stamped my passport at the Indian customs). My views of India had altered. As my own self was morphing, I started to appreciate India a lot more. **Transitions taught me that when our 'lenses' with which we view the world change, our reality alters. Even if the world doesn't change, our perspective does, so keep trying new lenses. They may be uncomfortable initially, but give a richer vision.** The other big transition was leaving a corporate directorship to start my own business in early 2007. Leading up to that point, life as a consultant in a big firm really suited me – I enjoyed seeing different clients, tackling different assignments and the variety, creativity and the opportunity to soak up different realities was offering me the best learning curve ever, far steeper than an MBA, but it was all under the 'safety net' of corporate employment.

After ten years or so, my entrepreneurial streak finally took over. Dadu's wish was coming true! I started to believe in my own story. It was time to leave the safety net. The attitude or restless curiosity I introduced in the opening lines of this chapter took over my existence with a relentless 'what if...?' What if I could start my own business? What if I could set my own targets and outreach them? Or, hire my own eclectic team? Handpicked and uniquely bearing the label 'blended by Rhea'? What if I could upgrade my corporate vision to an entrepreneurial identity? We will read in the chapter on resilience about life passages and living in seven-year cycles, including why 32 is a major turning point. Indeed at 32, I gave up a corporate directorship and cleared out all my savings to start my own leadership consultancy. The adrenaline rush was irresistible, but it wasn't just that which drove me to exit the safety net and start on my own. I detected this recurring pattern in my script. Seven years back I had left the safety net of Delhi to move to London and now, the next seven year cycle was itching to uproot me again. The chance to be free to follow my own inclinations, my own internal voice, to immerse myself in practising leadership from the inside out and in doing so, rediscovering myself in a way I would never have been able to otherwise. Had I not taken that leap when I did, I would never have jumped at all. Talking about jumps, I will compare this with a skydive later in the fear chapter.

With every transition, I realised every now and then I was altering a current reality, discovering a new one to make my new reality richer and bigger. Just as rules were changing, the self was re-adapting and channeling to context. With several hits and misses, I realised it was important not to apply old rules to a new context, buy equally important to define some new ones of your own. The more I moved realities, the more I realised the world is much more interdependent and connected than I thought but with bigger opportunities, creating room for more leaders.

Seeing the patterns and connections is essential. I felt the whole fabric of life was being woven from these multiple reference points. In all my transitions it was about upgrading my own version as soon as a current version felt strong and predictable. Restlessness and disrupting the core to discover more and push myself to the edge, continues to give me my edge. Now that may be different for others.

During this intense self-discovery period in my thirties, I also realised that, as strange as it sounds, disruption is a good force for me. I took to extreme sports – ocean rafting, canyoning, skydiving and stunt planes. I only share this to convey how important it is to connect the seeming linkages between our different passions and how the inner free child wanting to be a maverick needed and wanted to coexist with my grown adult role. **A kind of risky experimentation, controlled chaos, the adventure of wanting to control just as impending danger/fear was taking over, gave me a whole new self belief and confidence to push boundaries. It activated many dormant neurons. For me, this gave me an appetite for risk and ability for dogged concentration, conquering fear which I was applying and transferring to my high-stake and high risk leadership business. That may sound utterly bizarre, but it did.**

We all have what I call a 'Play safe' (keeping balanced) versus 'Play risk' (channelling your aggression) quotient. There's no happy medium or a perfect equilibrium in this quotient; how much risk we are ready to take is unique and dependent on your DNA. Risky sports sharpened my mind and helped me find new solutions to work. It may be something else for you – not everyone has to jump off a plane, write a book and bare their soul or even risk all one's savings to start a business – but it will be something. Of course, we all like moments of being safe, but imagine if that is all you ever did. **The point is to be aware of the price of just playing safe. If you play always safe, you will always get safe results.**

Self Detox: your way to leadership

In understanding and believing in your self, I would like to introduce the concept of a Detox. Detox, as we all know, is about cleansing your body and removing toxins. In understanding and believing in one's self, toxins compare to personal interferences such as doubt, fear, hesitation and limiting beliefs. These need to be cleansed too. Let me illustrate toxins through a children's comic series created by Belgian artist Herge and then a Japanese folklore.

In The Adventures of Tintin, Captain Haddock is Tintin's best friend, a multi-millionaire seafaring Merchant Marine Captain with a raft of colourful phrases at his disposal, a key one being (a variation on) 'billions of blue blistering barnacles!' As children some of us were avid Tintin fans but I wonder how many questioned this curious phrase. I didn't.

So, why did barnacles irk the Captain so much? A ship at sea for many years picks up thousands of barnacles that attach themselves to the bottom of the ship impeding its progress and eventually weighing it down, ultimately becoming a threat to its safety. The barnacles need to be removed and the easiest – and least expensive – way of doing this is for the ship to make harbour in a freshwater port. The barnacles soon become loose and fall off, leaving the ship able to move with speed and safety again.

In this book, read port as a new transition experience, the ship as the self and barnacles as interferences.

As we begin looking at our ingredients, ask yourself if you are carrying forward anything that is holding you back? Mistakes, regrets, assumptions or even opinions, handicaps or speculations which act like toxins that interfere with your self belief? Personally, with every freshwater port I harboured in (read experiences), I was getting more and more self aware of the strengths and shortcoming of my own DNA. With every mistake I was becoming a touch wiser.

This anecdote always reminds me of the second example, a Japanese folklore. Nan-in, a Japanese master during the Meiji era (1868–1912), once received a university professor who came to inquire about Zen. Nan-in served tea. He poured his visitor's cup full, and then kept on pouring. The professor watched the overflow until he no longer could restrain himself. 'It is full! No more will go in!' 'Like this cup,' Nan-in said, 'you are full of your own opinions and speculations. How can I show you Zen unless you first empty your cup?'

Link between Happiness and Success

What comes first? Well, up until recently and still for many, success was traditionally defined as a ladder of sequential rungs – good education which leads to good grades which leads to a good job which secures a good life partner, a good house, good family and good retirement prospects. This is a template of linear predictability I disagree with.

Instead, happiness, I now believe is like an inner success, redefined. Let us test this statement. Whilst writing this book, I started a global leadership programme for the most admired global telecoms brand, Vodafone, and its 120 top rising star population – a diverse group across several cultures, earmarked to progress. We asked them half way through the programme; what's most important to you? The answer, across diverse cultures, backgrounds, markets and teams was self belief and happiness. Contrast this response to even a decade ago when most definitely the answer would have been success. **The world is sensing a greater shift to seeking happiness from the inside out. This means first starting with 'what makes me happy and strong' rather than necessarily 'what makes me successful'.**

It is a relief to know some things never go out of fashion. Happiness is timeless. From Aristotle's concept of eudaimonia (the best translation of which is happiness) in the 4th century BC to the Dalai Lama's words today, life's very purpose is seen as seeking happiness. Indeed, 'Life, Liberty and the pursuit of Happiness' are among the 'certain inalienable Rights' written into the American constitution. We are all continually seeking something better in life and the very notion of our lives, what we look forward to – every heartbeat really, if you think about it – is towards happiness. I am absolutely certain this is wired into us.

The link between happiness and success have been investigated by many and in 2005 by a team led by Professor Sonja Lyubomirsky from the University of California Riverside who said: **'There was strong evidence that happiness leads people to be more sociable and more generous, more productive at work, to make more money, and to have stronger immune systems.'** The research shows that while success can put a spring in someone's step, people need happiness in the first place to achieve genuine success. Happiness is intentional – it is decisional. It depends on the decisions and choices we make from how we spend time, what we focus on, what thoughts we entertain versus reject. It is not random – there is a science to happiness. In fact, many studies have shown that happiness leads to a longer life.

Success is different. **I define success as happiness translated into a wider outcome for others to witness. For the board member, when the happiness of annual results is endorsed by shareholders, it translates into success. For the music maestro, when happiness arising from giving a great performance is endorsed by his audience, that is success; for the social worker, when her happiness results in (say) happy and reunited families, that is success; for the surgeon, when a critically ill patient regains life and health, that is success. For a parent, a child's happiness endorses their efforts as successful.**

There is a clear but complex relationship between happiness and success. Happiness, as we've seen, is a personal, internal state of being, but success has become an approval-based, external measure. We almost believe we need others to validate if we are successful or not.

Happiness is when *what you think, what you say, and what you* do are in harmony said Mahatma Gandhi (1869–1948), leader of Indian nationalism, whom my grandfather had the privilege of spending a day working with. In that quote I see a constancy of purpose and alignment between the head, the heart and the hands which affirms that happiness can naturally lead to success.

The story of the (successful) Insurance Agent and (happy) Composer

Charles Ives, a twentieth century American composer who 'was so ahead of his time his music still isn't well known today', seemed to find the perfect balance. For me, he is an inspirational maverick who discerned early on the useful distinction between happiness and success and played out his own life script accordingly. He was an incredible visionary and a rebel. It had been when he was admitted to Yale in 1894 that Ives' first battles with boring convention had begun. He had barely succeeded his non-music courses and was constantly torturing his famous and ultra-conservative teacher, Horatio Parker. **He would insert folk tunes into his exercises or submit pieces with free rhythms, quarter-tones and multilayered textures. His teacher was furious. This caused Ives to be accused of being unrealistic and inconsistent in style, but these strayings are his own style. It became the music we love today. The wildness, humour, simplicity and chaos that are** juxtaposed in his works are all parts of his experience, all part of the world in which he lived.

When told by his father that a symphony generally finished in the same key it started in, he replied that was just as silly as having to die in the same house that you were born in. He didn't want to make his living in music because he would have had to be able to sell what he wrote and he didn't want to fit into conventional taste or lose his happiness to the quest for money. He instead used insurance to get success, so that he could remain happy composing and playing music. So he became a millionaire by selling insurance and didn't then have to worry about selling his music. A young organ prodigy who practiced hard and played baseball, a socialistically inclined businessman who got rich in the insurance industry, a fierce democrat who sometimes wrote fiercely challenging music and a romantic idealist who conceived a music of the future. This was Charles Ives. I love how he integrated the different selves of his identify through the choices he made and found his own link between happiness and success.

> **The fabric of existence weaves itself whole. You cannot set an art off in the corner and hope for it to have vitality, reality and substance. My business experience revealed life to me in many aspects that I might otherwise have missed... my work in music helped my business and work in business helped my music.** One thing is certain: nearly 50 years after his death, Ives' influence is greater now than it has ever been.
> Source: Simon Russell-Beale, BBC 4 Symphony Series

The point is: we all have a story in our minds of the life we want to live. The extent to which we get to live that story is, ultimately, probably the prime measure of how happy and successful we are likely to be. It is then calibrated by our resources and resourcefulness.

Back to the rising star population who clearly validated my proof of concept on the difference between 'great' and 'amazing' leaders. Both are successful, amazing leaders just are visibly more happy.

The story of a Gen Y maverick leader Daniel Gallo

Let us take another example. Daniel Gallo is a thirty three year old talented creative disruptor and that is a compliment. He is a healthy maverick. I can call him that being a dear friend who I have mentored and have been mentored by. If we trace Daniel's nine year journey from starting on a blank page at 24 to where he is today, his story is of a boy who started from nothing as a temporary administrator in Asda, Wal-Mart's Share Schemes department. Nine years on, he is now the Director of Organisational Development and Communications for Manchester Airport Group, with an organic growth strategy to triple its revenue by 2017. His story is of a rapid learning curve which proves the inextricable link between happiness and success. Daniel is my proof of concept for the next generation.

I first met Daniel in an office in Hemel Hempstead eight years ago, a trying assignment, and it was one of those moments where I thought 'this guy has a raw edge, a restless spark about him but he is going to go places.' It is strange how sometimes the first five minutes can tell you if someone has CEO potential. A strong, bright character, with some barnacles in his personality which sometimes made him stand out tall, and at other times, did him less favours. Always curious to self discover, test his limits and be true to himself, his career script line went from: 2002 – Arcadia; 2004 – Northgate; 2006 – Barclays; 2007 – Northern Trust; 2010 – Vodafone; 2012 – Manchester Airport Group (MAG) where he is now. Daniel said his quick moves, at times, were because he was not happy, although he was deemed successful. Note the tenuous link. **'I imagined happiness and kept looking for it till I found it'**. I asked how he was on his 90 day mark at MAG – his answer in true Daniel style, was '3 feet taller.' Finally, I thought to myself, a deserving reward. What has six transitions in nine years taught him?

> **'It has been a steep learning curve but three things stand out – I listen more, I have learnt to be more emotionally intelligent rather than just being emotional and I am more politically astute, rather than letting politics rub against my own morals. I guess I have found what makes me happy – it lies in being given ultimate accountability to spread my wings and deliver. And because people believe in me, I believe in myself and feel happy and as a result I want to deliver even more and make a difference. That seems to translate into success as endorsed by others.'**

Daniel is moulding into the type of leader we need tomorrow, who will break rules to find new and better ones, question out dated norms and find new ways of doing things. He will need a long rope and space to soar, but equally, the heights he will take teams and businesses to, are that much higher. Businesses which can see that as an asset, not a threat, will embrace his DNA to grow their own leadership DNA. He is currently working on a £1 billion acquisition deal. Daniel never went to University despite being accepted by two red brick institutions and started his career instead.

- **Don't confuse ambition necessarily as having direction**. They are not mutually exclusive. You cannot realise your ambitions without first knowing where you are headed.
- **Drop your masks**. The quicker you identify your masks and learn not to wear them, the more authentic your personal impact will be.
- **Have common sense and be smart**. Realise there is more than one way to get to your end goal and that the right way is not always the most direct or quickest.
- **Speed is good but haste is bad**. There is a big difference between speed and haste. As an emerging leader, fastest may not always be right. Try to cultivate patience, even when everything and everyone around you screams, 'right now'

A story of growing self belief, made stronger through bumps, knocks and scars and eventually finding happiness that translates directly into success for himself and his organisation.

Don't aim for success, if you want it; just do what you love and believe in, and success will come naturally (David Frost).

The story of a teacher who became Prime Minister

History shows different contexts have demanded different leaders. In Japan warriors (Samurai) became national leaders through the ability to defend. In South Korea, scholars became nation builders through their ability to offer intellect and wisdom. I had the privilege to meet one such person in Brown's Hotel in London in 2011. Dr. Han Seung-soo was a teacher who rose to become South Korea's 35th prime minister. Sparked by a great chat, I then met him again exactly a year on in the same venue and an amazing conversation unfolded. A Professor of Economics with a Doctorate from the University of York, Dr. Han has also been South Korean Ambassador to the United States, President of the 56th Session of the General Assembly of the United Nations, Special Envoy on Climate Change for the UN Secretary General and is an honorary Knight Commander of the Order of the British Empire (KBE).

On his global leadership stage, leading agendas like national, political, and climate change, Dr Han's humility and quiet presence is truly inspiring.

These incredible achievements listed here are far from exhaustive and proof (if you needed more) that Dr. Han is more than a prolific scriptwriter of his story. What is really astounding, is where he started and how he accomplished them. His rise to the premiership of his country from his humble countryside origins is an unusual story, one he scripted himself through difficult circumstances. He comes from a humble small village called Paksa Maul. He was raised with few resources other than the influence of his grandfather, a Liberan Confucian, who instilled in Dr. Han a strong compassion and upright work ethic.

As a child, he had to walk roughly seven miles and cross two rivers, the North Han and Soyang, twice a day to get to school. He experienced at first-hand the Korean War, which he admits was his biggest crisis and test of resilience. These challenges and learned endurance which have informed his adult life have helped him develop resolve and resilience. Dr. Han has a strong belief in the concept of crisis windows and that people grow in stature for having survived these episodes. He defines these as short bursts of tough opportunity, making the most of which, can teach you more than any formal training.

Dr. Han has led his life in four segments. From teaching self (until his 20s) to teaching others (until his 40s) he progressed to leading on the national stage (until his 60s) followed by currently leading on the global stage. His leadership progression is natural, living proof of the Darwinian evolutionary build.

Ultimately, really the only way to live your life in the way it should be lived is nurturing your 'head' (intellect), 'heart' (relationships) and 'hands' (action) to see, and appreciate, the opportunities life throws at us as invigorating and infinitely worth taking.

Matching children's goals to their imagined potential

'If the next generation is to face the future with zest and self-confidence, we must educate them to be original as well as competent.' (Mihaly Csikszentmihalyi)

Our versions of understanding ourselves, our belief in our abilities and our doubt in our own limitations, originate in childhood. Children grow up with different messages or expectations – be perfect, please others, be strong, try hard, be liked, or even hurry up. Mine was 'have a say.' I grew up with lots of debate, banter, thinking for myself and being given the permission to come to my own conclusions. Sometimes this felt tough and lonely. I am hardly the first to point this out, but because this is a practical book, the implications of the observation about the importance of our childhoods has a major implication for us in how we can put the ten ingredients I present in this book into action in our lives. For me, a grounding in debating, or public speaking as it was called, turned out to be useful. The ability to present, defend and adapt your point of view and the ability to express it well is a sign of recognised belief by the world.

What do you want? **Validating goals and potential requires the deepest form of self-awareness**. Some people begin with unrealistic expectations and become despondent when they fail to reach a goal; some even stagnate because they do not trust their own potential. Some simply set the wrong goal in the first place. Sometimes, children take on the goals directed by their parents and at other times, a child knows what he/she is naturally good at and chooses a path to do more of that.

The more I talked to successful people while researching this book, the more I realised that happiness does not stem from achieving an external goal. Instead, it comes from an internal interpretation of oneself. It is not an activity or an event. It is an inner choice and a conscious state of mind.

Let us take a Gen Y story from China to illustrate happiness.

A Chinese concert pianist's story of living his father's script

I had a jaw dropping moment watching Lang Lang at the BBC Proms in 2009, and my jaw hardly ever drops. I remember coming home and plunging into the creativity chapter in this book. Who is this young man? The world-famous piano maestro, Lang Lang, a prodigy whose piano lessons began at three, was sparked by a Tom and Jerry episode of The Cat Concerto. He gave his first public recital aged only five and was inspired and guided by his father who always wanted him to win competitions and to be the best.

Lang Lang was born in tough, under-privileged circumstances in industrial China. His story is that of a poignant and intense relationship between a boy and his father, who was willing to go to any length to make his son a star. The family was so poor, Lang Lang's mother had to live apart from the family working in the city while his father trained him in a small town where music lessons could be afforded by the very poor. Lang Lang would spend up to eighteen hours a day practising, anxious not to upset his father's dreams. At this point in his life, very clearly, he lived the script of his father's life rather than his own and was being crushed under that script.

Then Lang Lang was lucky enough to meet a teacher who proved deeply influential to him in his life and who told him that **a real performer does not play for winning but in order to find happiness and to delve deep into his own soul to create his own music**.

This was the moment Lang Lang began to understand what playing the piano really meant to him. It is no coincidence that this was the point in his career when he started being truly happy, himself, with the profession that had, in a sense, been forced upon him. Henceforth, his personal happiness began to yield external success.

I witnessed the powerful result of the teacher's advice when I watched Lang Lang lost in ecstasy while performing at the BBC Proms. He is now one of the world's best performers, inspiring business leaders at the World Economic Forum to athletes at the Olympics. He's clearly very happy in his music and how he is using it to bring delight to his audience and success to himself.

Too many people spend a lifetime focusing on what they do not have and trying to justify why they are unhappy – 'my parents didn't send me to the right school,' 'in my day, the career choices available were too limited,' 'I didn't have any mentors,' and so on.

How we feel about ourselves is much less the result of an external event happening to us and much more about how we seek out opportunities and how the mind interprets an event or an experience. Happy people make full use of the unknown variables (their feelings, their thoughts, their drive and their attitude) to control happiness more directly. We actually do have a choice – to be happy or not.

Confidence busters that chip our self belief

The legendary American football coach Vince Lombardi once quipped**, 'Confidence is contagious ...but so is a lack of confidence.'**

Yet, it is often only ourselves that stop us being confident or happy. In particular, here are four 'confidence busters' to avoid.

- **First, we do not live or celebrate in the moment enough.** We perpetually justify our current activities as a means to reach a happier future at some unspecified later date. We study to get better grades; we work hard to have a better retirement; we pray for a better tomorrow. Happiness is too often the unreachable carrot always just dangling out of reach. 'I will be happier when I have the next promotion,' 'I will be more successful when I've got a car like that...' Where is what you want in all this? As the philosopher and writer Ralph Emerson said, 'We are always learning to live, but never living'.

- **Second, we find confronting complexity or not knowing very hard – painful, even – so we often avoid ambiguity.** We see a crisis, or even a delay, as an obstacle and seek to escape. Yet by looking problems square in the face, we give ourselves the best chance of attaining success. We push ourselves and gain a new awareness of what really is possible. The world was never designed to be straight and comfortable. It was, and will always be, random and disruptive so rather than being naive, we would be wiser to develop a strong self belief with its nine companion ingredients, to navigate that chaos more effectively.

- **Third, we place a disproportionate emphasis on measuring our success by socially institutionalised yardsticks, such as class, income, culture , education or external validation.** In other words, what others think becomes all encompassing, and that is where the biggest mistake occurs. We, without even realising, start falling victim to "if only..." Are you doing something because you really do want it, or because you feel the world expects it of you?

- **Finally, fear of failure or rejection – or, you might say being thin skinned.** In all my years of coaching managers and leaders, it amazes me to see how in the face of any seeming or real adversity – even a piece of negative feedback or an intense look from a peer – makes us doubt ourselves or take things personally. Some of us are indeed too fragile. Under perceived threat to our self esteem, we can become over sensitive, putting our self belief under doubt, without reason, where every little knock, scar or bump seems exaggerated. True happiness comes from touching the edge of our fears and overcoming that to move on further. That is success like never before.

A quote from my mentor

Sandy Pepper, a mentor throughout my career, a former consulting partner and now a lecturer at the London School of Economics said the following to a rather anxious me, on an important day. It was the day of my directorship decision in a large consulting firm.

"Every battle, game or performance is won or lost in the head. If you believe you won't win, you most certainly won't. If you believe you will, the chances are, against every opposition, you most certainly might. Manage that belief in your head".

After all, in a very real sense, when you drive the script of your own story you become the pivot point in relation to the world and to your own being. You create a revolution in confidence to yourself and to your belief in your own destiny.

A closing exercise

So at this point, hopefully having sparked many dormant neurons into action, let me, as a final closing question to this chapter, bring together the concept of stage, the script and the DNA.

Step up on your life stage. Stop. Look back and view yourself from the dress circle. If your life drama was performed on stage, where you are the producer, the director and the actor, imagine a huge spotlight beaming down on the floor in front of you. The light beam is about a metre in diameter. Now take a step forward straight into the spotlight. Stand there – see yourself diffuse into all the cast of characters that make up your identity and reputation, and all the roles you play. Watch them act and react in your life experiences and ask yourself:

1. Which, of all the cast of characters you have played, are most predominant in your leadership journey and life drama – does your differentiated self stand out enough?

2. What script theme does your script have – success, adventure, anticipation, failure, series of tests, normal, predictable? Is it a comedy, farce, opera, drama, adventure or a fantasy? Which are the different acts?

3. Be the audience watching your play – are you laughing, crying, applauding, risk averse, bored, curious, confused, pensive or wanting more?

Now look at your answers. How happy are you about the script? Ask, how can the script change? Which new characters are you going to develop and let onto the stage and which, if any, should you retire?

'We make our world significant by the courage of our questions, and the depth of our answers.' Carl Sagan

Self-belief and Leadership

Are you ready to empty your cup, shed your barnacles, look inside the box you are sitting on and even make some room on your personal shelf? **Self-confidence is the sureness of feeling that you are ready for the stage you are already on, or about to step on. This sureness is characterised by absolute belief in your ability and an attitude to winning. We all know people whose self-belief has this unshakeable quality. At this point of having explored the concept of Self and DNA, and layered in the notions of happiness, choices, success, stage, script, self-belief and self detox, it is time to introduce my definition of leadership for this book.**

For me, leadership is the belief and ability of one person to stand up, take ownership in walking taller and stronger on a new path or an improved current path.

I know I have strayed from stylised academic definitions. My definition is fresh with the sincerity of human intent. Being tall gives you perspective. Belief gives you the conviction your self deserves and the ability to sharpen the ingredients we are about to explore. This is what I would like to gift and pledge to you – work with this definition and feel primed to turn to the other nine ingredients.

How tall are you feeling now?

Let me end with another secret. Dadu was only five feet tall, yet the tallest man I knew.

Your code for Ingredient One: Self

Pause. Ask yourself what do you remember from this chapter; list the key takeaways and ideas that had an impact on you – something inspiring, something relevant or something you would like to try.

Now, make a note of the following: the term 'things' below can refer to behaviour actions, conversations, skills or even an attitude

1. List three things you would like to START doing to strengthen your SELF...

2. List three things you would like to STOP doing to strengthen your SELF...

3. List three things you would like to CONTINUE doing to strengthen your SELF...

On an ascending scale of 1 to 10, how robust is this ingredient in your DNA?

Ingredient Two

EXPRESSION

—'I express'—

What others see is more powerful than what others hear. Sharpen the unspoken expression as much as the spoken. In every life there comes a moment which is only yours. Seize it and claim your space.

How do you best express yourself? This is one question I asked everyone in this book. Usually every answer was always preceded by a few seconds, sometimes a few minutes silence. The answers ranged from 'words', 'eyes', 'actions', 'voice', 'energy', 'hands'... some even said through *silence*. The foundation of leadership and life is expression. We are all born with expression. We express our needs, our feelings and our reactions even before we can speak. We express even before we learn how to.

As part of the expression toolkit, language is a big part of what makes us human. Written or spoken, we can't stop talking. Words can inspire us to greatness, drag us down, wound us deeply or soothe our pain. Words have the power to break confidences, build life-long alliances, start wars or inspire geniuses. Yet, language is not all about words. Even when we are not speaking, we are expressing ourselves through our expression and our behaviour. My aim in this chapter is to create a new code for leadership expression. This is to see how your thoughts can translate better into what you say, how you sound and how you behave.

In this chapter, we are going to look at self expression through three CEOs from very different backgrounds (British, Lebanese–Swedish and Italian), an Israeli orchestra conductor, a ten-year-old Malaysian photographer and performance artists.

Before we meet them, let us refresh the three key leadership concepts from the first chapter on self:

1. the actor
2. the stage
3. an authentic presence.

The (Lead) Actor and the (Leadership) Stage

Let us now explore the concept of a stage (where authenticity gets expressed) and the actor (who expresses authenticity).

A stage is where any act of leadership – the play – takes place. With leadership comes exposure and visibility. Expression is instrumental because – admit it – we are being watched and judged all the time through our words, our actions, our energy and our behaviours. **It is as though we are always on stage**. For me, every CEO (read leader), at whatever stage, is a playwright, a play director and the actor. Finally, consider three main ways in which leadership is an honest act of performance:

1. **Leadership involves performance**. Leaders are always on stage, always interacting with their audience who is evaluating the leader's words and actions.

2. **Leadership is about a cast – about teamwork**. Yes, the lead performer on stage may well be the leader, but the play – the performance – can only be as good as the team and as bad as the weakest member of the cast.

3. **Leadership is about impact – performance has a sense of play**. There is a creation and re-creation of reality. As a leader you are never off stage. Even when you are not saying anything, your being and presence is being watched and your performance mode is always on.

Authenticity

What is authenticity? Words such as: real, genuine, sincere and unique may come to mind. For me, the best way to define authenticity is to link it to an authentication code, similar to a secure unique ID code we use in personal banking. Just as without a secure ID, we cannot access our assets, in a similar way; every leader, too, needs that authentic code of self expression on his or her leadership stage.

Authenticity is all about congruence, as this quote explains:

'Watch your thoughts, for they become words. Watch your words, for they become actions. Watch your actions, for they become habits. Watch your habits, for they become character. Watch your character, for it becomes your destiny.'

[Unknown]

Of the several pieces of inspiration in a middle class home in which I grew up, my parents' bookcase in Calcutta comes to mind. That *shelf* was home to a curious selection of 'leading selves' I grew familiar with, from Tolstoy to Bertrand Russell, Ayn Rand to Shakespeare, Tagore and Swami Vivekananda. I avoided these big names and although my Enid Blytons' and Tintins' were tucked right at the end, I would never fail to notice the names of the other shelf-dwellers. Vivekananda, who I then grew to admire immensely, was credited with the revival of Hinduism in modern India. He is well known for his inspiring speech opening 'Sisters and Brothers of America', through which he introduced Hinduism at the Parliament of the World's Religions in Chicago in 1893. He is my inspiration for authenticity and I believe he would have endorsed this chapter with his maxim: **'We are what our thoughts have made us, so take care what you think. Words are secondary. Thoughts live; they travel far.**'

This is the basis of authenticity, a primary ingredient in any strong leadership DNA. We are all attracted to authentic leaders. We admire them, count on them and wonder how we can put our finger on this mysterious quality that makes them seem so special. Yet their secret is easy to discover, for:

- **they are clear about who they are;** *they express that* **clarity**
- **they are in touch with their own inner self;** *they express that* **touch**
- **they are comfortable in their own skin, without any false layers of pretence**; *they express that* **comfort**

That is how simple it is. Lance Secretan, an executive coach, sums this up well: **'Authenticity is the alignment of head, mouth, heart and feet – thinking, saying, feeling and doing the same thing – consistently. This builds trust and followers love leaders they can trust.'**

Professionally, this point about the impact of being on stage struck me years ago. After a successful presentation – one in which I felt I had convinced a client about their employee retention issues through strong evidence and a compelling case, a hard piece of abrupt feedback came my way from Paul Belcher, a senior partner of a consulting firm and my mentor from an early part of my career.

Paul: 'How did you do?'

Me: 'Great, I think. The client is happy. Keen for your feedback, Paul.'

He smiled and took a long pause before saying the following:

Paul: 'Rhea, you were persuasive and good! But remember when you are on stage – you're also exposed to a world watching you. And, influencing on stage has an element of putting yourself out there, where the audience not only hears your presentation, but watches every move, how you hold yourself, the cues you send out through your presence. Beyond credibility of content, think of your impact next time.'

Paul's words hit me hard. I never forgot them. **I realised why mastering that art of self-expression is so vital to our Leadership DNA and so much more important than just mastering the lines you want to say.**

The Brand

We live in a branded world. We have brands too. We 'google' people on our iPhones while listening to our Sony. Leaders have brands too. The obvious way we brand leaders is by achievement, education, promises or pastimes. Melanie is my 'Oxford client', or Sanjoy is 'very Obama-esque' in his style. **Consistent brands are trusted and by that I mean repetition is valued.** Think of a McDonald's or an Apple store experience. From a small town in India to a huge city in the United States, the brand experience never varies.

The point here is this. As a leader, your brand should come from inside you. Without exception, leaning on a borrowed brand to convey your own, does not work. The question you have to answer is: 'Do I know what I value the most about me and can I express that to the world?' **Clear articulation and consistency is key.**

Expressing your Leadership DNA

Paring it back to the very basics, as noted above, we all create impact through four simple channels.

1. **The way we sound, which gives us our verbal identity**

   This is what you convey through the spoken word and your tone of voice. Primarily, this is through:

   - stories we tell
   - conversations and dialogues we share
   - our tone of voice and pace of speech

2. **The way we look, which gives us our visual identity**

   This is what you convey through body language, gestures, posture, stances, eyes and appearance. Primarily, this is:

   - look and overall appearance
   - body language

3. **The way we behave, which gives us our behavioural identity**

   This is what you convey through what we call delivering our intent – decisions and actions that follow our words. Primarily this takes the form of:

   - actions
   - decisions

4. **The way we adapt, which is our contextual identity**

   This is how you read your context (culture, team, purpose of meetings, stakeholders) to tweak and adapt the first three identities. Primarily, this means:

   - adapting your behaviour and style depending on who you are talking to
   - adapting your behaviour by sensing what any situation demands

Throughout this chapter, I will help you define your own leadership expression through tips, techniques and tools to augment your impact through your visual, verbal and behavioural identities.

By means of no scientific research but by means of a comparative to help you place relative weightings and importance to the four channels, I will allocate the following percentages to the three identities:

When our three identities combine, they create consistency, trust and authenticity in how we come across as a leader. In other words, it clarifies the leadership brand we are striving to express.

The more consistent we are, the more likely it is that people will understand what makes us special. The way we express ourselves has to be joined up and consistent so that people admire, respect and – crucially – trust us. It is no good saying we are imaginative if our language is anything but.

Starting with the Mehrabian Code of 7/38/55

A well regarded, but often misquoted, study conducted by Professor Albert Mehrabian in 1971 shows the relative impact of body language versus spoken words and tone through three emotions. He found that:

- 7% happens in spoken words.
- 38% happens through voice tone.
- 55% happens via general body language.

You can see the main point – expression can often be more important than actual words.

Verbal identity through spoken language

What you say

'Your words are the clothes your thoughts wear, so dress them well.'

I saw this quote by accident. Smudged in a piece of newspaper wrapped round some hot samosas I was devouring a few years ago which a young boy handed to me in a noisy market street in Delhi. Since then, I have tried to source the origins of the quote but without luck. Its message, however, is universal.

Language is not a learnt skill but an innate faculty. We are born with a set of rules about language in our heads.

> **Infants are born with Language Acquisition Device (LAD) and exposure to language is all that is needed for a child to discover the system of language.***

We are born to talk. In fact, we can't shut up: around 370 million words are used in an average lifetime, but, when and how did language start? How did our Stone Age ancestors communicate with one another? Could they speak? Did they use language beyond cave paintings? We are truly fortunate to have this powerful gift only if we know to make the most of it.

Leaders as storytellers

Stories are one of the oldest ways for humans to use, learn and remember information. We are story-making machines. We all start out reading fairy tales starting with 'Once upon a time...' as children and before we know it, spend our twilight years recounting life stories playing back real time as 'Once in my lifetime...'. In between the two recounts, we are on a stage, talking about vision, mission, organisation and personal leadership stories.

So what is your story?

'The Universe is made of stories, not of atoms', wrote the poet and social activist Muriel Rukeyser. To the scientific mind, that may sound sacrilegious. Our lives are a series of stories woven together – our own stories and the stories of those around us. Great leaders down the centuries – religious,

---

* Noam Chomsky Syntactic Structures (1955)

political or business – have understood this and have been expert storytellers. Krishna (the *Gita* – the Hindu book of wisdom) and Jesus (in the New Testament) are storytellers who brought their teachings to life through the stories they told. David Attenborough, the world famous naturalist, Bill Clinton or Steve Jobs are first and foremost – storytellers.

They entice us with their stories all the time, sharing successes they have had, mistakes they have made, what inspires them, what they stand for and where they are going.

On the other hand, other top executives, trained conventionally, avoid storytelling and stick to a 'tight-jacketed' left-brain approach. They lay out their vision, goals and results using data points, graphs and PowerPoint slides.

No wonder sometimes they are criticised for turning the boardroom into a 'bored' room.

Types of Stories – Stuart Gulliver, Group CEO of HSBC

Let us explore what kind of authentic stories leaders can tell in different contexts. There is one such leader, a storyteller who is also a personal role model for me. This is Stuart Gulliver, the Group CEO of HSBC.

This is why I chose Stuart. For, I have seen, felt and believed his impact for a good two years before I even met him. That may sound strange but given HSBC is a client of ours, I have been working with the bank's DNA on embedding Stuart's values into the troops, so to speak, and seen the impact he has on them. For me, it was like a film, where I was working hard on the script but hadn't met the lead actor. Now, the timing is important too. It says something about HSBC's strength in the wealth-creating economies that, despite the problems of the Eurozone, sluggish growth in the UK and the painful legacy of trailer park lender Household in the United States, it is still the most profitable bank in the Western world. **What is this CEO's story to the world?**

Before we answer that let me just say I have a nostalgic affinity with HSBC. Three generations of my family bank with HSBC. Secondly, as I said, they are also a client. And, from a chance third link, I realised, after my business made it to the national semi-finalists in the 2008 small business awards, that HSBC was the awarding sponsor. There is a respectful reciprocity to this relationship. So, it was only natural curiosity to meet the lead actor of the global HSBC stage on the 42nd floor of HSBC's headquarters in Canary Wharf, London.

Stuart, or STG as the bank and I fondly refer to him, is a rock. This is the story of a career banker whose DNA has grown with HSBC for 32 years. Let me play back the exact conversation I had with him in early 2012. He had no script and neither did he know what I would ask him, but his conviction has a clarity and crispness that truly stands out.

Being in the business of leadership narratives, I decided to begin with a whopping opening question on identity, let the silence hang and watch him handle that. Over to STG, the trader turned CEO on one of the biggest banking stages.

Rhea: Stuart, who are you as a leader and what's going to be different under your CEOship and where is the bank going? Do people know what you are thinking and about your values in action?

(When a leader starts leading on a big stage, a 'who I am' story is the first point of reference to build trust and break down walls.)

Stuart: My original intention was to enter the legal profession, but my parents weren't able to support me financially to join the Bar. So I decided to defer my entry for a few years to build my resources, gain some business experience in the bargain and then return to study law. I joined HSBC. I feel this ties back to being grounded and living in the real world. Little did I know that my first 30 years at HSBC, specifically sitting on a trading desk, would stand me in good stead. People thrive in the market, in the community – it is the cluster theory, it is what gives cities the edge. Having trading targets kept my feet firmly on the ground. I had my own profit and loss account – colleagues would know if the 'big guy' was full of bullshit. I had my trading screens, my phones and my coffee(s) amongst everyone else. In the trading room, the air is filled with banter, the noise of the market and this audio backdrop provides enormous insight into what is going on around you – a plethora of opinions, views and real-time deals. I now have my first office, having moved up 38 floors to the top of number 8, Canada Square, Canary Wharf in London Docklands. I'm happy to say, before you think I have 'crossed over to the other side (of walls and doors)' that I have simply traded my trading floor to tread the floors of all HSBC offices.

I noticed he was playing to my leadership stage metaphor of trading in an open and big market, from large boardrooms to down to earth access stories like the Indian dabbawallas and Turkish market vendors we will meet in the Focus chapter. And there was a sense that STG had seamlessly moved from operating in his open trading market to a group-wide CEO platform. In that moment there were no walls or doors in any HSBC building – only an open plan bank across an intercontinental stage. It was fascinating and in my mind the differentiation – integration balance was playing out restlessly.

Rhea: with this step up from trader to CEO, your stage has become bigger as have the expectations, right? What continues to shape your leadership DNA?

Stuart: Travelling and trading are two life experiences that have shaped my DNA and my values. While trading is immensely exciting, it is very similar to being a lawyer – standing up in court and making your case, giving and taking the arguments and different opinions; travelling opens you up to these different geographies and cultures. My itinerary of training took me to Malaysia, Hong Kong, back to Malaysia, Japan, then again to Hong Kong and Japan, to London, Hong Kong once more and finally to London. I visited China every month from 1989 onwards. The first time I was in Beijing, there were no streetlights, coal carts were being pulled along in the streets by oxen and there were already widespread smog. I have always been fascinated by different worlds and have an endless enthusiasm to know and understand different cultures and religions. Maybe HSBC was always destined to be my home, given my love of trading and travelling. After all, the bank was set up in 1865 in Shanghai and Hong Kong to finance trade.

Rhea: as a leader, what's the balance between past roots and future direction?

Stuart: I openly share how important roots are to me. If you can't remember and respect where you have come from, it is hard to drive where you are going. I never forget my roots, which certainly weren't privileged.

Stuart grew up in the southern English city of Plymouth and went to an unexceptional state school. He took himself to Oxford and has remained refreshingly down to earth.

In 1980, an HSBC executive serving in India urged him to join HSBC's elite 'International officer' programme (as it was called at the time), which paved the way for his banking career. He rose through the ranks in the bank's Global Banking and Markets division and held a number of key roles in the Group's operations worldwide, including postings in London, Hong

Kong, Tokyo, Kuala Lumpur and the United Arab Emirates. During the 1990s, STG built HSBC's investment bank in Hong Kong and turned HSBC's Asian markets business into one of the group's major money-spinners, even in the aftermath of the Asian financial crisis.

Rhea: In leadership, how important is winning?

Stuart: Well, let me use an analogy. Believe it or not, I was a boxer – although not a great one (Simon and Garfunkel's song 'The Boxer' comes to mind as it begins 'I am just a poor boy though my story's seldom told' and I think STG could now say he has resolved the former part of this opening line and can now rectify the latter). I hasten to add that, as the absence of my name in lights in the boxing world testifies, I was not in the same league as Muhammad Ali or Sir Henry Cooper. It did, though, teach me that, contrary to sometimes wishful thinking, winning is everything. You either win or lose in the ring. There is no team. There is no taking part, rather than winning. Not for one moment am I placing winning and the individual above all else. I just feel it is instrumental to remember certain human endeavours require this personal focus and single-mindedness. One could say the essence of this could be distilled in the word intensity and this is a good companion to integrity. Through trading, travelling and boxing, resilience, obsessiveness and passion also populate my DNA. And I believe these character traits stood me in good stead throughout my career as a trader. You have to really want to do these jobs. That desire and application creates, if you will, the 'stage' in which your ingredients can freely flow and mix. Not wishing to overly dramatise the point, but this concocts the elixir to sustain you in such vocations.

Rhea: Getting to the top is almost easier than learning to 'stay on top'. How does a leader on a global stage keep a balanced perspective of winning, humility and responsibility and sustain their leadership over time?

Stuart: I am a steward before I am CEO. That is a 24/7 responsibility – it stops being a job in today's vernacular and there isn't a place for reflections like 'Crikey, I haven't had a weekend off', but this is also a privileged position of stewardship. I hold the stewardship of a company of 280,000 people across 80 countries that also happens to be worth US$160 billion. So, yes, you have got to believe that this is 24/7, there is intensity for a cause and a burning commitment. I am not here forever. The bank, the institution, is bigger than any one individual. Stewardship is key and I hope to pass on the bank in better shape again. This keeps you grounded. It is not 'I am the firm'. Glamour is lauded in the trade press or criticised in the daily press.

For star leaders, every joke is colossally funny and every idea is colossally bright. This gives you an inflated self worth which can become self fulfilling and make you remote from the world. You forget your role has an expiry date. My roots keep me real.

Staying grounded in that reality is important and for me, (not forgetting humour), there is the pleasure [and Stuart does have the most infectious sense of humour]. Not taking yourself too seriously, having a laugh and staying grounded are essential seasonings in my blend. Self deprecation and self empowerment are good bedfellows; letting you rise to your aspirations on the one hand, whilst keeping you down to earth on the other. For me, humour helps cope with stress and it is far better to deal with stress and pressure this way than attempt to ride over these on a wave of arrogance. Society wants normal people, not arrogant people, running banks or any other organisation.

Rhea: Your focus in the first 18 months has been a tough period of doing the right thing while risking popularity. For most leader's being liked provides a huge sense of security. Instead you have cut costs, downgraded high achievers with only mediocre values (your filter for integrity before ability), taken out layers in the bank, got rid of private jets, conveyed hard tough messages. How did people react?

Stuart: With a lot of trepidation. I like a challenge and I like being challenged. I surround myself with people who can challenge. It is crucial for you to hear the reality – not what people think you want to hear. The key is how to stay grounded and not somersault to the flipside of celebrity, where it can be so easy to lose touch. To trust that in your immediate circle and to distinguish it from platitudes with others is key.

Politics and bureaucracy are like weeds that need to be stripped out first before any good seeds can be planted. I had to remove a chunk of the cost base in the first 90 days. The way we have run the firm as 80 different banks has given us diseconomies of scale rather than economies of scale and made it complex. Against the backdrop of a hostile environment (laughs), isn't it always hostile and 15 months into this, if you analyse the profitability of HSBC the two home markets, UK and HK, account for about 1/3 of the profit. The two home markets plus the next 20 countries account for about 92% of profit. If 8% of profits come from the remaining 60 countries there is a management issue of risk versus reward. That's not sophisticated maths, that's simple common sense. I am in love with one expression made of two words – 'courageous integrity'. Every morning when I brush my teeth, I chant the two words – courageous integrity – importantly, as conjoined. It is about leading, or acting, with courageous integrity. It is not being courageous and having integrity. The combined expression is deliberate – it is not about being courageous and flying really close to the wind... and hoping no one catches us.

I realise in the face of tough decisions, significant resilience is key for a leader, because you are accountable and you are the public figure...you need to stay reasonably positive but not foolishly optimistic in your attitude. Realistic optimism. You can't be gutted every time you get slammed in the press. Thick skinned is one way of putting it.

Rhea: I think your authentic brand is all about 'bold yet simple'. Why does simplicity matter so much to you?

Stuart: 'Simple' is my chosen style. Just saying the word is scary because it is so simple. In a complex chaotic world, it is important to be able to talk simply and passionately about our role as a bank, not loaded in jargon and fancy promises. In simple words, I simply want to give the bank back to itself.

That was momentous!

Language and the brain

Notice the way STG plays with language and how it appeals to the head, heart and gut. To get to his heart of storytelling as a gift, I am going to delve a little into NLP.

NLP is Neuro-linguistic Programming. Neuro means relating to the brain's information-filtering process. Linguistic means the language we use to assign personal meaning to information and events and Programming is the set of responses that occur as a result of this filtering and subsequent linguistic map.

There are three main ways through which stories can be told through and each of us has a bias towards visual, auditory or kinaesthetic expressions.

Visually – I see
Examples of visual language:

- Let us see what we can do
- We need to focus on what is ahead
- I'm clear about what we discussed

Auditory - I hear

Examples of auditory language:

- I hear what you are saying
- That sounds good to me
- This really strikes a chord

Kinaesthetically - I feel

Examples of kinaesthetic language:

- That feels right
- I sense this is going to work out fine
- That's a real weight off my shoulders

We have used language for only a quarter of the time since modern human beings evolved 200,000 years ago (2 per cent since the genus homo appeared 2.5 million years ago) and have used writing only for some 4,000 years. To add a few more minutes to that timeline, please read on and let us tease out how language impacts stories.

Let me use an old joke about a group of journalists who arranged an international competition to present an essay about elephants. The titles were as follows:

- English   Hunting Elephants in British East Africa
- French   The Love life of Elephants
- German   The Origin and Development of the Indian Elephant from 1200 to 1950
- American   How to breed bigger and better elephants
- Russian   How we sent an elephant to the moon
- Swede   Elephants and the Welfare state
- Spaniards   Techniques of Elephant fighting
- Indian   The elephants as a means of transport before railroads
- Finnish   What elephants think about Finland

A good creative dig on how stories vary by cultural stereotypes, for example: French lust, German seriousness, American bragging, British colonialism and a punch line with the Finns being what others think about them. Language can be contextual.

The Plot

Now, in storytelling, a plot is central to all stories – from CEO keynotes to bedtime stories.

The definition of a plot and its principles originated in Poetics by Aristotle. For me, it still holds just as true. According to his definition, a plot has to have a beginning, a middle and an end. The end must have a logical outcome resulting from the beginning and middle events. Tied together are the elements of action, time and place. Leaders' stories are built on the same principle.

The beginning provides the introduction of the story, the background information the reader needs in order to know (and care) about what is happening. This is where the characters, the setting and the conflict are introduced. This is also where the inciting incident takes place; the trigger for the conflict that drives the story.

The middle section builds action that eventually leads to the climax. This will often also include actions in subplots and minor conflicts that propel the protagonist and antagonist along. During this phase the tension builds, the pressure increases and the consequences become more significant. It includes a climax – the watershed moment when the rising action reaches its peak. At the climax the decisions and actions of the protagonist determine the outcome of the story.

The end has resolution –the conclusion of the story. There is generally a release of tension and anxiety, a catharsis and the point where the audience/reader sees the final outcome of the conflict.

Here is another in depth example of how leaders and CEO influence through authentic storytelling.

Vittorio Colao – the global CEO of Vodafone group

There is a man who brings together Stuart Gulliver's drive with Antonio Carluccio's Italian passion. This man is Vittorio Colao, global CEO of Vodafone, the UK's most valuable brand, whose profits exceeded £9 billion in 2011. At the time of writing, he looks set to add to this year's growth with a US$1.04 billion bid to acquire Cable and Wireless Worldwide. I am also pleased to say that he is one of our top three clients.

His passion, when we secured the assignment, was to 'home grow' a group of over one hundred rising stars up two levels below the Senior Leadership Team. 'Why not?' he said, 'now is the time we need our own people to grow the business and to grow with the business.'

So, what does developing these hundred plus leaders, who have been earmarked for growth under a sponsor like this, look like? He clearly knows the culture he wants to breed and the leadership he wants to grow. Famed for the Vodafone way, the seven values he sketched on a napkin as the Group's DNA, principles like Simplicity, Customer Obsession and Innovation Hunger. These have become the lifeblood of Vodafone and we are developing them in every rising star in 19 countries. We work with a lot of values in many companies and trying to get these embedded in the company's DNA inspired me to name my business CorporateDNA. What I have loved about the Vodafone Way is the raw passion behind their aspirations; they do not resort to bland management-speak like other companies do. Since Vittorio came on board in 2008, he has tried very doggedly to make a stronger link between the company's relationship with its customers and satisfying shareholders. **'You can't have shareholder value or customer friendliness – you have to put them together or else capitalism can produce problems.'**

Sometimes when I meet people at the top of a major corporation, it is not apparent what makes them different. They do not stand out in any obvious ways, but here is a bold Italian who clearly does. I first met with Vittorio in October 2011, in London's Millbank Towers. He is slim and tall – lanky, even. So much so that when he sits in a chair, there is fun to be had seeing what he will do with his legs. One minute, he is leaning back and one of them is draped over the arm. Then, his legs are folded under, then it is the turn of the other one to hang off the side of the chair. I was amused by his seated choreography.

The opening words of his speech to a group of eager rising stars were very unusual:

'I have to be honest, I am not prepared for this talk. But I can talk about anything. [Long pause]. Well, this is a leadership programme, but my advice is don't follow a model – be yourself. If you look at people who have made mistakes, often it is because they haven't been themselves or have tried to follow a model or a recipe. I realise that's because they worry a lot about making a mistake. But why hide a mistake? Most people have enormous energy and strength to achieve what they want if only, if only, if only, they tried less hard to copy or clone others and just were themselves.'

His second piece of advice was: **'Try things yourself. Don't rely on others for second-hand opinions to form your view. Whether it is a phone, a service, or a skill, respect your own opinion enough to give something a try and form your own view.'**

Vittorio continued. He was lucky to meet Steve Jobs, who said to him **'Market research? At Apple, we watch people and how they think and feel. That drives our product development'**. Vittorio raised his passion at that point and said– **'so, just try yourself, watch yourself whether you like or don't like – be yourself.'**

He grew up in northern Italy, in Brescia. His mother spoke six languages and worked in publishing; his father was an oil executive at Total. After studying business at Bocconi University and acquiring an MBA with honours from Harvard Business School, he went on to acquire valuable experience in the investment banking sector and then proceeded to hone his strategic skills at the Milan office of McKinsey & Co in 1986. He soon became a partner of the firm, covering media, telecommunications and the industrial goods sectors and he was also in charge of office recruitment. **'It might look as though I planned it but I did not. In my career, I always wanted to stay with people I liked. So I joined McKinsey because of the quality of the people who interviewed me. They were tough interviews, selective. I thought, if they're this selective, it must mean there is something good on the other side.'**

McKinsey gave him his grounding, **'They taught me the fundamentals, how to analyse before you have the ideas, how to establish parameters. And about business integrity and ethics. And hard work.'**

Over the years he claims he realised that you have to **'adjust what you have learnt to your situation. It is often a 60/40 balance. 60% of what you know may be right but 40% is wrong – either outdated or irrelevant. Don't hold on to "this is how I did it" and "this is what I know".'**

Before reaching this position ,Vittorio took a detour. He left Vodafone in 2004, demonstrating that a straight line career path within the same company is not the only way to become the CEO. He joined RCS MediaGroup, an Italian media conglomerate. Two years later, after a row with their main shareholders, he returned to the Vodafone fold. His single-mindedness and reputation for not giving up easily were given free rein and, arguably, contributed to the parting from RCS. The experience was, however, instructive in other ways as he learned telecoms and media companies are culturally very different.

He admitted his own mistake straight and out loud to the group in October 2011: **'of course I have made many mistakes – we underestimated the iPhone when it was at its development stages; we over-relied on our knowledge and research. Guess what? We underestimated a couple of billion customers' usage'**

Vittorio is a pragmatist, knows what he wants and is direct – his English is perfect, too. His wit is dry and he does not miss any nuances. Authenticity runs through his DNA.

Authenticity in other forms

In my work, I often hear questions like these:

- **How can I stand out?**
- **How can people feel my presence?**
- **I want to be authentic. I want people to remember me beyond my performance. What can I tell more of?**
- **How can I tell it better?**

At their heart, those questions are all searching for authentic self expression.

People's inherent, yet flawed, belief is that words are all encompassing. This world, after all, does talk a lot and very effectively so. There are other techniques of storytelling. For me, how you make someone feel could be so much more than what they hear. Impact can equally be created through other mediums. Let us look at an incredible orchestra conductor who creates an incredible impact on a thousand people without a single word, or a photographer who does the same through his images.

Where do we start on authentic impact? Connecting something you are passionate about with something you want to do is the main step to creating impact. The day your job, business, or cause emanates from your passion, you are on the sureshot road to fulfilment. In all of the examples below, we will encounter some key truths about authenticity.

'People will forget what you said, people will forget what you did, but people never forget how you made them feel.' (Anonymous)

Hence, a primary ingredient in any strong leadership blend, is authenticity. We are all attracted to authentic leaders. **Authenticity is not about hero worship. Authentic leaders are not perfect, but they are genuine. They are flawed but sincere. So then people ask, how can I be authentic? I say, it is a combination of six traits – letting it out, letting go, tuning in, daring to win, being congruent and leaving a legacy.**

1. **Let it out**

   Self expression and presence is the starting premise of authenticity. Expressing oneself is all about giving voice to or externalising what is inside you, be it an idea, a thought, a dream or a passion. We can all feel inhibited about putting our idea out to the world, but courage, pitched from your inner believing self, should encourage a reciprocal response. Voicing your idea frees it and gives it a chance to connect with the outer world in which we live with others.

2. **Let go**

   The leader delivers, but the audience interprets. No matter how much one has prepared, planned, rehearsed before the event and re-scripted behind the scenes, once you are on stage you sever the link. You stay responsible but keep transferring ownership to the audience to respond constructively. Authenticity is about creating that relational agreement with your audience. Candour, channelled with empathy, can really take authenticity to a rewarding level.

3. **Tune in**

   Attunement should not just be between self and your chosen instrument (or message), but between self and audience. Sir George Martin whom we will meet later in the book believed that authenticity is not what you hear, but what the audience hears. Tuning into the same frequency to broadcast to your audience that you initially used to connect between self and your instrument, establishes trust.

4. **Who Dares Wins**

   The courage to do and be different , this motto, with acknowledgements to the SAS, is about 'I dare to be different, to stand for what I believe'. Pivotal to the point I made in the opening chapter on the self's need for differentiation versus integration, the challenge is to explain, persuade and deliver even when no one else understands or engages, to transfer that belief and principle into action, while maintaining the authenticity throughout from concept to execution. Dr Kiran Bedi, who we meet later in the chapter on

Fear, invokes this masterfully in her achievements at the Tihar Jail in India while no one understood her.

5. **Congruence**

   Congruence is the connectedness or complete congruence between our head, our heart and hands – in other words, between our thoughts, our relationships and our actions. Cynthia Carroll epitomises this, as CEO of a global mining company, others see her congruence as both real and believable. When someone says to me 'this congruence stuff is hard work', I reply, 'the incongruence stuff is even harder' – as it consists of sending mixed messages, building false hopes, layering presences, where we end up deceiving ourselves and others.

6. **Legacy**

   Always ask yourself what your authentic brand will leave behind after you. This is not about status. This is about reputation and gravitas. What you leave for others should be organic, a concept that confers longevity to your belief, so your influence lives on, even after you do.

I do believe it is all about the choices we make. Authenticity, in the way I have illustrated in these six points, happens when we make the conscious choice to be true to ourselves, when we are committed to our hidden passion, to let out that little bag of gold we all have, into the world, to see it grow and touch other lives. Make the right choices and even when you make a few wrong ones, embrace the learning from them and move on.

For all of the above, authenticity has a great prize – it leaves a legacy. Now, legacy is not just being in the hall of fame. Legacy is how your actions continue to impact others after you are gone. Just like great lives inspire us, those who pass away also inspire us by reminding us of what is important and the legacy we leave behind. In 2012, the world lost a real inspiration. The death of Steve Jobs inspired many, including Bill Gates, to push on with his philanthropic work, reminding him that we only have a limited amount of time on the earth.

Guided by a billionaire CEO's passage of leadership in philanthropy, the Bill & Melinda Gates Foundation works to help all people lead healthy, productive lives. Being guided by the motto that **'every life has equal value',** he made a heart warming revelation about legacy during an interview with Bill Weir on Nightline where he talked about his last visit to Steve Jobs' home in the weeks before the Apple founder's death.

'He (Steve Jobs) and I (Bill Gates) always enjoyed talking,' Gates revealed. 'He would throw some things out, you know, some stimulating things. We'd talk about the other companies that have come along. We talked about our families and how lucky we'd both been in terms of the women we married. It was a great, relaxed conversation.'

Gates went on. **'Steve had a very different set of skills than I did...He was every bit as intense, believed in revolutionary ways of using computers. But not in an engineer approach, [but rather] a design approach and that had huge strengths, particularly the last episode where he ran Apple. He was able to do incredible work.'**

'It is very strange to have somebody who's so vibrant and made such a huge difference, a constant presence, to have him die,' Gates said on Steve Jobs' passing. 'It is a huge milestone, very sad not to have his talents helping out. Very sad for his kids who I've gotten to know a little bit. Great, great kids...It makes you feel like, wow, we're getting old,' he added. 'You look back and think about the great opportunities we had to have a big impact.'

With a pledge to give away 95 % of Gates' personal wealth, the Gates Foundation claims to have granted more than $26 billion since 1994. While some of that money is devoted to improving U.S. education, roughly 75 percent goes to the poorest countries in the world. A chance encounter connected to the Foundation, through a very good American friend of mine, Kofi Rashid, with whom I worked in Dubai during his tenure with Dubai Holding. He moved back to America after the crises and is now advising the Gates Foundation. I caught up with him and it was fascinating to hear about the guiding values at the Bill and Melinda Gates Foundation. It so reminded me of Stuart's and Vittorio's values. Notice the language and the intent behind the values, it is about using fresh, straight talk in spelling out your leadership authenticity; examples of which I have set out from the principles of The Gates Foundation below:

- **Optimism**... we are impatient optimists by nature: we see the glass as half full and are motivated to confront problems that others consider impossible to solve; our success will be measured over years and decades – not days and months.

- **Collaboration**...We recognise that our resources and abilities are only a small part of what is needed to achieve our goals, so we hold strong the belief that our ability to achieve impact is greater when we work with others. We are self-aware, while mindful that we do not have all the answers.

- **Rigour**... Our conversations are open, honest and sometimes tough for all concerned. We take responsibility for our actions and seek to rectify our mistakes.

- **Innovation**.... We believe that many of the most intractable problems can only be solved through creative and innovative solutions. In pursuit of these, we embrace risk and learn from failure, helping others to avoid the same pitfalls in future.

Of the many value statements I work with, I regard the above as authentic for the guardians who espouse them.

As we know, entrepreneurs and CEOs are only two kinds of leaders. Let us explore other types and look at the common elements of how creating impact is about authentic expression and ultimately being connected with your passion.

- Through code, a programmer tells a story about new ways of doing things
- Through a painting an artist tells a story about a new visual interpretation
- Through a performance, a performer tells a story about new possibilities
- Through a sport, an athlete tells a story about new way of winning and teamwork
- Through images, a photographer tells a story about stirring imagination and the desire to see, experience and discover new places, new lives and new ways
- Through a building, an architect tells a story about design and legacy
- Through a piece of music, a conductor tells a story about harmony

The conductor who inspires us about leadership storytelling

Itay Talgam is a conductor with some of the world's best musical ensembles and orchestras. He has assisted great maestros such as Leonard Bernstein and Claudio Abbado.

'As a young person, I often experienced the transformational power of music, listening to my beloved Brahms or Beethoven. That made me want to conduct, to have direct access to "the force". But as a conductor I often sensed a strange discrepancy between the nature of my own experience and that of my players: even when we joyfully shared the interpretation, their engagement in the music was different than mine. Having to physically create the sound while infusing it with spirit, they knew the secret lies in balancing control and letting go. I am still learning today how these two faces of creative work are best combined, working with different groups of professionals, in music and in other fields, in search for ways leading to magical infusion'.

As a native Israeli, he studied at the music academy of Jerusalem and Philosophy at the Hebrew University. Later Itay continued his studies in Italy and the United States. His approach to the understanding of music-making and conducting as a metaphor for leadership, communication and relationships is unique.

Itay Talgam finds metaphors for organisational behavior and models for inspired leadership within the workings of the symphony orchestra. Imagining music as a model for all spheres of human creativity, from the classroom to the boardroom, Itay created the Maestro Program which aims to help everyday people develop a musician's sense of collaboration and **a conductor's sense of leadership: that inner sense of being intuitively, even subconsciously connected to your fellow players, giving what they need and getting what you need. It is this art of listening and reacting in the moment that makes for a swinging jazz combo, a sublime string quartet, a brilliant orchestra and great teams at work.**

'A conductor's happiness does not come from only his own story and his joy of the music. The joy is about enabling other people's stories to be heard at the same time.'

As Sir John Elliot Gardiner will say about emotion, creating perfect musical harmony through one tiny gesture without saying a word can be the hardest thing to do. An orchestra conductor, with that single little gesture in the air (the right hand tracing a fleeting shape (less than a breath long) can bring enormous harmony and clarity. Itay talks about doing without doing. I call that being. **The primary duty of a conductor is to unify performers, set the tempo, execute clear preparation and beats, listen hard and shape the sound of the ensemble. The parallels to what a CEO like Stuart or Vittorio are doing is striking, like a chief conductor of business who keeps everyone together to an end outcome of a crescendo.**

The young photographer who inspires us about legacy

Every year I try and go to the Veolia Environment Wildlife Photographer of the Year exhibition, in London, owned by the Natural History Museum and BBC Wildlife Magazine. For me, it is a great source of authenticity through nature.

'While there is no magic formula for winning and no hard and fast rules to explain why one photograph wins and another doesn't, all winning shots have one thing in common – originality. The judges are looking for something that stops them in their tracks. The competition plays an increasingly crucial role in raising the profile of wildlife photography and generating awareness of conservation. Nothing speaks louder than an evocative photograph that stirs the imagination, tugs at the heart strings and engages the mind.'

[Mark Carwardine, Chair of the judging panel].

Last year, the one that leapt out of the frame was called 'Alien' by Hui Yu Kim (Malaysia). Hui Yu is very young, under ten years old, making magic with her Nikon D300 + 105mm f2.8 lens!

Hui Yu photographed an imposing portrait of a tropical flat-faced longhorn beetle on a family photography trip to a tropical rainforest at Gunung Jerai in Malaysia. A light bulb in a mosquito net attracted local invertebrates during the night and in the morning there were lots of them to look at. Hui Yu is keen on macro-photography and chose the most colourful animal to take a portrait of, but look at this young leader's words *'It had a strange look, like an alien, but it wasn't angry. It sat still on the branch all the time,'* she says. *'I want people to know that all creatures, even small ones, count. So don't destroy the forest.'*

That is authenticity – it can start as young as that. For me, that is a wonderful tiny piece of legacy left behind through a tiny creature photographed by a tiny person.

Presence – the power of voice!

One last but very important thing about presence. This is one of the most powerful instruments we are born with which we do not exercise and make use of enough. The voice and its tone. All of us are born with a particular voice. It is our trademark, but very few of us create impact through voice. This is a hugely important aspect of communicating with influence. As Benjamin Disraeli said, **'there is no index of character so sure as the voice'.**

I was recently addressing a group of people on motivating teams and at the end of the session decided to take a few questions from the audience. After a few usual suspects around the topic, I had a man raise his hand and ask me a question. He was in the back of the room and I could barely see him, but I heard him and the power of his question was exceptional. When I asked him to show himself, he stood up – there was a tall, athletic looking gentleman but with a very feeble voice, almost seeking permission as he repeated the question for the group to hear. The tone was not in congruence with the power of his words. Somehow his impact felt compromised.

That takes me back to my favourite maestro. Even in his quiet moments, Beethoven always seemed to be on fire. In the string quartets, all of the symphonies, the piano sonatas, his energy is explosive. Have you heard the Moonlight Sonata? When he is calm, he still manages to inject a shaft of troubling seriousness and sometimes of menace. That is his authentic trademark. His passions were influenced by events and his life was affected practically by the ideas and changes that were swirling around him. They were his passions still. That is authenticity.

That shared feeling is a gift of leadership.

From music, photography and voice let us return to business.

Samir Brikho, CEO of Amec Plc

Samir Brikho, the CEO of Amec Plc stands out for me with a strong international DNA in his leadership story. So where does this spark originate? With Samir, the starting point is cross-cultural and international. Our conversations grew with the book's evolution.

Regardless of time, location or mood, Samir is bright-eyed and focused with a crackling energy about him. He is also very open in sharing how he is feeling – 'sad, mad or happy' as he says! I could say he is a living example of where a leader's identity is no longer set or secured by one origin, or a defined place in a family or society. Today, a leader's identity, through the journeys traced by different roles, is in a constant state of change and evolution. Samir's identity itself has travelled a varied geographical route to this juncture. Not least, beginning in war-torn Lebanon which is not, as the saying goes, a place, under those conditions, from which you would wish to start – but it does give you a whole new set of different ingredients to kick off with. His sobering statement that he was always grateful to have survived each day, taking nothing for granted, really brings this home, especially **'not knowing whether you are going to survive tomorrow makes you see what are the most important things in life and to focus on the right priorities. Later on, that focus itself gave me an edge in business'**.

The civil war broke out in the mid-1970s and the family moved to Uppsala. Samir was then 19 years old with an International Baccalaureate behind him. In Sweden, the Brikho family worked hard to adapt to Scandinavian society. They quickly learned the language, made Swedish friends and adopted Swedish habits. Samir, with his quirky humour and observations, confirms **'to be adopted by a new country, you have got to think the way they do – not just dress and eat like them'**.

Samir joined Amec in 2006. Amec then was a UK-centric conglomerate; a diverse collection of businesses, straddled across a broad mix of industries/sectors. It could be said that AMEC struggled to articulate its vision and strategy to its employees, to its shareholders and to the City. The share price underperformed but since then, he has achieved an extensive recovery – the company has reported eight quarterly results that have all set records and placed the company on the FTSE 100 list on the London Stock Exchange. The vision is to lead the market in consultancy services, project management and mechanical construction focused on the energy and power (oil, gas, alternative energy and nuclear) industries.

After ten minutes of his story, I was dying to know how he defines good leadership. His summary was brief: **'Good leadership encompasses real emotions and an ability to dream the future.'** I was relieved none of the usual suspects such as strategy or planning made an appearance and that vision was replaced by the dream. He reminded me of a pearl of wisdom my grandfather gave me as a child. **'After fleeing a war-struck nation, despite being a good lawyer, I realised while intellectual ability and education are important, they are by no means the secure key to the future. The most important is being able to convey a dream and get others to believe in it, but there should be no distance between the dream and the dreamer. Both should be believable together.'**

Dreaming, or imagination, imbues leaders with the ability to provide direction to their employees and enables them to project and create a company where people want to work. It allows parents to instil an aspiration in their children so they can dream to fulfil it. To sit in the present and imagine the future is something we have probably all found ourselves doing in a quiet moment, but it is a rare ability for a leader to do it with grace, ease and conviction. Samir does that. **When we read about human history, we find it presented from a variety of perspectives. We hear about humans as explorers, politicians, warriors, inventors, artists and so on, but we seldom hear about humans as dreamers. Yet so many of the significant advances of civilisation have been inspired by individuals who simply had a dream.** They are the ones who lift their heads up high to perceive the heights of dignity, inspiration and creative fulfillment that truly define what it means to be a human being.

So, what is a leadership dream?

'Good managers must have the ability to create a vision for the company and think 3, 5, 10, 20 years into the future. They must also know how people behave and be able to see an individual's capability even if they do not understand it themselves. Many people today are very involved and innovative in their leisure time; a good manager must be able to inspire the same level of commitment at work.'

His childhood, although fraught with the violence of war, included experiences that etch the memories into adulthood. From the early pleasures of diving for shell fish and sea urchins to the difficulties of living in a war zone and leaving the security of his home as a teenager, it was an unusually formative start to his life.

As Samir shares his stories, it struck me that speed, pace and agility are trademarks of his too. He thinks fast. Speaks faster. Acts faster again. Last year he said, with real zeal and hunger in his eyes, '**when a company is growing fast, its key players need to be able to step out of their size 5 shoes and start running in size 9 immediately – there is no time to get comfortable and try how a new pace feels or if indeed the shoe fits**'. In 2006, Samir set out from his first Monday morning on October 2, at 8.00am, with the whole management team to establish a 60 day agenda to analyse the company's strengths and weaknesses. His aim? To secure the transition of the company from its construction roots to its main markets now in the oil and gas, nuclear, renewable energy and water. The analysis work that predated him had one thing missing – decisions – so he judged this timeframe would now concentrate everyone's mind in this direction. The exercise was successfully concluded and on the 60th day he presented to the board and on the 73rd day he informed the new corporate vision and strategy to the market.

In such exercises there is resistance to change so to take the heat and emotions out of the discussions, he provided data which clearly underlined the need for changes (and the nature of it) and which led to the board's buy-in to the new thinking. **It still needs courage, dogged determination and human emotional resilience to declare the future before others can see it, to then stand by it and project your self-belief without hesitation. He shares with me the view of his mentor, Ferando Flores, a 55-year-old philosopher, former Chilean minister of finance and former political prisoner under Augusto Pinochet's rule who 'took me as a rough diamond and polished me well'.**

He reminds me of how a great leader makes room for something more, something extraordinary with rich and new possibilities for the future. Sometimes it is simply down to such a leader, once the dream has been articulated, to make the (safe) space for others, unfettered and uninhibited, to craft and build the desired objective hand in hand with subtle, intuitive, but always passionate, guidance. This is history making and Samir Brikho may well be on the path of making that history big, bold and exciting! (Disclosing New Worlds, Spinosa, Flores and Dreyfus)

Samir says, **'Now, I always ask "why" more than I ask "what"** – because why someone does what they do is more important than the act itself'.

Having discussed life and leadership to some extent with Samir, I would say this statement sums up his DNA as a leader for me. It is this curiosity and relentless zeal that gives him a real spark.

Have you enjoyed the journey so far? We have after all been to Israel, Malaysia, Italy, UK and Lebanon. Shall we proceed now to an act of brilliant leadership conceived by a Canadian entrepreneur?

Cirque du Soleil – redefining the stage of performance

In 1984, an assortment of 20 street performers put together a show in the small town of Baie-Saint-Paul in Quebec, to celebrate the 450th anniversary of explorer Jacques Cartier's claiming of Canada for France. Few could have guessed that this ragtag bunch of French–Canadian hippies, calling themselves the 'circus of the sun', would soon set off on a journey of world domination. Now, they have redefined circus.

Twenty-five years later, Cirque du Soleil's big-budget, animal-free circuses are Canada's largest cultural export, employing more than 4,000 employees from more than 40 countries and pulling in close to an estimated C$1 billion a year in revenue. Its founding member, Guy Laliberte, has gone from being a fire-breathing street artist in the early 1980s to a billionaire. Guy is an amazing example and a true inspiration of originality.

Sir George Martin inspired me to go see the *Love* show in Las Vegas which he hand crafted with his son Giles and the Cirque du Soleil team celebrating the musical legacy of The Beatles through their timeless, original recordings.

Cirque du Soleil have changed the world of non-verbal performing arts (circus) and taken it to a whole new level. On my 38th birthday I went to see *Corteo* in Paris and three months later I saw *Totem* in the Royal Albert hall in London. Totem traces the fascinating journey of the human species from its original amphibian state to its ultimate desire to fly. Inspired by many founding myths, Totem illustrates, through a visual and acrobatic language, the evolutionary progress of species.

Somewhere between science and legend Totem explores the ties that bind Man to other species, his dreams and his infinite potential.

'Everything the Power of the World does is done in a circle. The sky is round and I have heard that the earth is round like a ball and so are all the stars. The wind, in its greatest power whirls. Birds make their nest in circles, for theirs is the same religion as ours. The sun comes forth and goes down again in a circle. The moon does the same and both are round. Even the seasons form a great circle in their changing and always come back again to where they were. The life of a man is a circle from childhood to childhood and so it is in everything where power moves.' – Black Elk, Oglaga Sioux, 1863–1950

Life is one big balancing act. That is the key message for me in every Cirque du Soleil show.

The common theme across all shows is a delicate balance, because it must tie the various acts together without a prescriptive narrative. The Cirque team avoids a straight narrative in order to allow room for the audience to interpret the show any way they want.

This itself is as an ultimate example of man's ultimate potential and the power of human expression.

As Bernard Petiot, Head of Casting and Performance (I love that title!) describes their selection process for artists:

'We have two distinct approaches. With artists from an entertainment background, like singers, musicians, clowns and actors, our approach is based on respecting the strengths they already have. They are professionals who come to Cirque with special skills and abilities and we

treat them as such. Our role is to help them apply their expertise in the Cirque du Soleil context.

With athletes, their arrival at Cirque means they have chosen to reorient their careers. We therefore have to respect the skills they've learned, but we also start from the premise that those skills are insufficient to meet all our needs, whether in terms of acrobatics or show-specific aspects like stage presence. As a result, we teach them what they need to know to make the transition a success'.

The biggest challenge of creative expression, across forty nationalities, is language and expression itself – understanding artists, making yourself understood by them and making sure they get along with each other. The solution lies in helping artists from twenty nationalities adapt to a shared DNA and become active participants in one performing stage at Cirque. In other words, making the most of each person's individual colour and unique personality and cultural traits.

His advice to the numerous applicants is not to put up any barriers or cling to preconceived notions. **'In a word, candidates should open their minds to getting in touch with their inner artist!'**

That is not different from my role in getting leaders in touch with their inner, untapped genius to perform on a chosen leadership stage – from reorienting careers to building on existing identities.

A final word.

To create an authentic presence – whether via your business, art, photography , performance or music – you need to delve deep inside you to find that 'bag of gold' we all have inside. Add passion, purpose and energy to unleash your authenticity. **Don't just do something because you have been told that is right, don't adopt a life view because your parents espoused it or because your team wants you to. Differentiation for the right cause, may cause you some discomfort, sometimes even pain, but the reward is well worth it.**

So, let it out and leave a legacy. Remember, who dares, wins.

Your code for Ingredient Two: Expression

Pause. Ask yourself what do you remember from this chapter; list the key takeaways and ideas that had an impact on you – something inspiring, something relevant or something you would like to try.

Now, make a note of the following: the term 'things' below can refer to behaviour actions, conversations, skills or even an attitude

1. List three things you would like to START doing to strengthen your EXPRESSION...

2. List three things you would like to STOP doing to strengthen your EXPRESSION...

3. List three things you would like to CONTINUE doing to strengthen your EXPRESSION...

On an ascending scale of 1 to 10, how robust is this ingredient in your DNA?

Ingredient Three

FOCUS

— 'I do' —

If belief is about I can, focus is about I will. No distraction or interference can be powerful enough to get in the way of translating strong belief into even stronger action.

This ingredient is all about being smart in the art of managing your energy. Being fully present, and determined in the pursuit of your goals, avoiding distractions and prioritising what matters most. Focus is about applying the right choices to our goals and leaving a legacy. We will tour through Turkish and Indian traders, learn from CEOs, COOs and CFOs of private banks, fashion houses, and technology companies and be inspired by an ancient Chinese school teacher.

The street vendor of Istanbul and the dabbawallahs of Mumbai

When visiting Istanbul's Grand Bazaar a few years ago, I was drawn to an over-zealous street vendor selling vegetables in a busy part of the market. His English was good and he was eager to tell me about his work. Here is a great lesson he taught me on focus.

Picture this. The Grand Bazaar sells almost everything you can imagine: it is an eclectic menagerie of tiny cave-like stalls and as you wander about, you feel overwhelmed with a sense of being in a strangely timeless place. Erdal, the street vendor I spoke to, was surrounded by competitors and customers from dozens of nationalities milled around. His barrow — the main tool of his trade — was only about six feet by three.

This self taught trader, who never had an education, earned his living amidst chaos and competition by applying himself to a range of tasks. Tasks that are carried out by several departments of large organisations on a much greater scale, were conducted by one man. Every morning he had to work out what to buy, how much of it and the precise product mix based on an anticipated daily sales forecast. He also needed to price it and work out a marketing strap-line which he would shout out to persuade people to buy from him rather than from his rivals. All the while he was watching his competitors without blinking an eyelid, adjusting and adapting as he went, while continuously gauging customer reactions – who smiled, who frowned, who walked away and who stayed and bought.

Talking to him and watching him in action, I realised that the one ingredient that helps him run his trade is his unremitting focus.

His concentration on his business was laser-sharp and he displayed a wonderful single-mindedness that would probably be underestimated (or indeed ignored) by the highly-paid business people working in offices, only a few blocks away. I was left wondering what blue-chip executives could learn from him.

Despite the vast difference in context, the street vendor's attitude is similar to that described by Stuart Gulliver, HSBC Group CEO, whom you met in the chapter on Expression where he says: **'the mental state when we trade is called "the zone": it is our ability to focus as if nothing else existed. That is our trademark.'** What we learn from elite bankers and Erdal is the dual tasking of focusing both on the job in hand and the bigger picture. This, then, is the marvel of our street trader who, albeit on a smaller scale and without any sophisticated infrastructure, covers both singlehandedly.

In the market theatre of Istanbul we have seen the individual focus of Erdal. Now let us meet an entrepreneurial team from the Indian sub-continent which is so focused that they act as one ingenious human machine – with stunning resourcefulness, astounding productivity and impressive accuracy.

We take our leave of Turkey and travel to Mumbai, another city of contrasts and a place where earning a living needs the utmost dedication, application and focus. Mumbai offers many fascinating examples of human focus and a passion for wooing and constantly delighting customers. One of the most interesting examples of this kind of focus at work comes from the city's 'dabbawallahs' – The Mumbai Tiffin Box Suppliers' Association, an association of some 5,000 lunch delivery men. It is not just me who is inspired by them: the international business community has awarded them one of the highest and most widely recognised standards of excellence in customer satisfaction — the coveted Six Sigma Award. Here is their story.

The business started with one great but very simple idea. With roughly 20 million inhabitants (more than 19,000 people on average per square kilometre), Mumbai is India's most densely populated city. To get to work on time and combat the intense traffic congestion, workers leave for the office very early. There are, of course, an abundance of cafés and restaurants in Mumbai, but men working in the city tend to prefer their lunches to consist of a precise array of dishes, catering to their own, precise tastes and cooked precisely by their favourite cooks: their mothers and wives.

With workers having to leave home around six in the morning or earlier, their wives and mothers would need to start cooking their lunches in the middle of the night for them to take it as they left for work. From 11am every workday, the dabbawallahs stream off the city's railway network into the downtown business district to deliver an army of hungry office workers their favourite hot, home-made meals. Carrying 'dabbas' or tiffin boxes lovingly packed in nearly 200,000 suburban kitchens, the delivery workers are part of one of the world's most admired distribution systems.

Around the middle of the morning, the 'dabba' is collected, usually on bicycle, by a collecting dabbawallah. Each dabba has some sort of distinguishing mark on it, such as a particular colour or symbol: this is important because many dabbawallahs cannot read or write.

The bundled dabbas are loaded onto trains, with other sets of markings used to identify both the railway station where the boxes are to be unloaded and the actual building where the boxes are to be delivered. They then travel 15 miles by public transport and across six miles of road with multiple transfer points in a 3-hour period. At the appointed station, the dabbas are unloaded and handed over to a local dabbawallah, who delivers them to their hungry recipients.

The scale of the operation is, by any standard, remarkable and the service is growing at about 5% a year — not even the infamous monsoons hold them up. The service is also incredibly accurate: after more than a century of fine-tuning, the dabbawallahs make only one mistake in a staggering 8 million deliveries, an accuracy rate of 99.9996% and all this for £2.00 a month. It is not surprising they have drawn attention from leading business schools around the world, including Harvard, whose Six Sigma accreditation* has produced a case study of the dabbawallas, urging its students to learn from the organisation, which relies entirely on human endeavour and employs no technology.

For Paul Goodman, a professor of organisational psychology at Carnegie Mellon University who has made a documentary on the dabbawalas, this is one of the critical aspects of their appeal to Western management thinkers. **'Most of our modern business education is about analytic models, technology and efficient business practices,' he says. 'The dabbawallas, by contrast, focus more on "human and social ingenuity"',** he says.

Fans of the Mumbai service include Sir Richard Branson who joined the dabba-rounds in 2005. The dabbawallahs' focus on offering great service is unwavering and they guard their routine jealously. After all, when HRH Prince of Wales visited them in 2005, for example, he had to fit in with their schedule. He was so impressed, he even invited some of them to his wedding to the now Duchess of Cornwall. About 85% are illiterate, making the fact that — like shipping companies — they employ a 10-digit

---

* a business management strategy, originally developed by Motorola in 1981, which seeks to improve the quality of process outputs (delivery of a product or service) by identifying and removing the causes of defects (errors) and minimising variability in manufacturing and business processes.

alphanumeric code to track deliveries all the more remarkable. Yes, the ingenious system of markings used to identify dabbas and their destinations, coupled with the well-organised system for conveying dabbas by rail, plays a vital role in maximising the reliability of the service they offer. However, what really makes the dabbawallahs' system so effective is the sheer pride that they take in their work and in belonging to a world class team.

Ironically, the dabbawallahs themselves do not see what all the fuss is about. In Vasant Bacche's words, a dabbawallah packing a cart outside Churchgate Station: 'I don't know about management schools. I can't read and write. That's why I've done this for 15 years.'

At heart, the reason for the dabbawallahs' tremendous and extremely accurate performance appears to be a matter of mindset, of focus, of the almost fanatical devotion that the dabbawallahs have towards their work.

Today, the power of their unique system and loyal customer base is being harnessed by top multinationals. Inspired by 'message-in-a-box' (dabba), Microsoft, the world's largest software company, tapped into the dabbawallah distribution network to promote awareness for its Vista operating system. Every sale earned a 100 rupee commission (£1.20) and Microsoft India claimed the unique promotion as a far-reaching success.

Why am I sharing these stories of street traders?

People with 'limited' resources often have one incredibly 'unlimited' tool at their disposal – a willing mind and its ability to focus. This applies with equal resonance and impact to whatever the task is: whether it is making a living selling fruit and vegetables in Istanbul, or reliably transporting lunches in Mumbai from homes to offices, producing some major creative work, running any kind of organisation or pursuing a dream or plan of any kind.

Each person also directs their energy in a certain manner and for a certain pay off – an extrovert will channel it externally to get energised by the world, an introvert will focus internally to energise inner thoughts. A worrier will focus on any impeding danger or what won't work, while an optimist will channel it to positive actions and what will work.

If the dabbawallahs are creating magic on Mumbai streets, let me take you to a mirror establishment 7,000 km away but in what is regarded as a successful corporate institution that many may view as a sophisticated western version of the dabbawallahs. Sir Roy Gardner is the Chairman of

Compass Group, which, as the world's largest catering company, serves around 4 billion meals a year and employs more than 428,000 people in 50 countries. Despite the sophistication and advancement of Compass, Sir Roy said exactly the same thing when we met: **'if you get the details right when you are developing a new idea or service, deliver it consistently every time, and you can't go wrong. You don't always need great new strategies; you just need excellent focus.'**

Focus: a leadership must-have

'God is in the detail,' the German-born architect Mies van der Rohe remarked in an interview with the New York Times in August 1969, not long before he died.

Focus on details lies at the core of all human achievement and major advances. Just take two from the modern world; a Boeing 747 jet has roughly one million parts, all of which need to be precision-engineered and fitted, while the Saturn V rockets that took the Apollo astronauts to the moon had about six million components and are said to be the most complex man-made machines ever built.

There are two further examples within these. In 1965 the focus of two men, Bill Allen President of Boeing and Juan Trippe Founder of PanAm, sowed the seed for the 747. Juan said 'if you build it, I'll buy it' and Bill said 'if you buy it, I'll build it'. A simple handshake underpinned the agreement that would lead to one of the most impressive developments in aviation history. As Kathleen Clair, who was Assistant to Juan Trippe, recalls: 'that handshake was better than a written contract, so they went ahead and did it.' Number 13 in the Apollo program saw life threatening damage occur to the command module enroute to the moon that reduced their oxygen supply to a critical level. When asked by the scriptwriters of the movie whether anyone panicked, Gene Kranz, the NASA flight director famous for directing the successful Mission Control team efforts to save the crew of Apollo 13, said **'No, when bad things happened, we just calmly laid out all the options, and failure was not one of them. We never panicked, and we never gave up on finding a solution.'** That became the origin of the screenplay line **'failure is not an option'**, so although he never said it at the time it definitely captured the sentiment, which was confirmed by Gene using it as the title of his autobiography.

The mission to the moon is not the only example of focus.

The flexibility of attentional structures is even more obvious when they are compared across cultural or occupational classes. Eskimo hunters are trained to discriminate between dozens of types of snow, and are always aware of the direction and speed of the wind. Traditional Melanesian sailors can be taken blindfolded to any point of the ocean within a radius of several hundred miles from their island home, and if allowed to float for a few minutes in the sea, are able to recognize the spot by the feel of the currents on their bodies. A musician structures her attention so as to focus on the nuances of sound that ordinary people are not aware of, a stockbroker focuses on tiny changes in the market that others do not register, a good clinical diagnostician has an uncanny eye for symptoms because they have trained their attention to process signals that otherwise would pass unnoticed.*

Over the past sixteen years, I've spent much of my professional life working with leaders and successful people across twenty cultures and doing my utmost to **climb inside their their minds** to find out what makes them tick. If I were asked to name a trait common to them all, I would say it was a clear, consistent and constantly demonstrable ability to focus.

I would define focus, for the most part, as the absolute and unwavering intention to stay in the moment when applying oneself to a goal.

Today, though, by understanding more about focus and its context, application and relationship to the other nine ingredients detailed in this book, we can take it much further. For example, our own ability to focus can be broken down into elements of concentration and determination.

The elements of focus

What are the elements of focus? The equation, I believe, is:

Focus = Concentration <u>plus</u> Dogged Determination <u>minus</u> Interference Traps

Let us take each in turn.

Concentration

Good leaders do one simple thing really well. They concentrate. They concentrate completely on the challenge before them at any one moment and tackle it head on. In my own experience, whenever I've lost an opportunity, a client assignment, or fallen short of a goal, I can trace the

---

* *Mihaly Csikszentmihalyi, Flow: The Psychology of Optimal Experience 1991*

problem directly to moments when I've not concentrated on what is important and missed reading the small shifts in a client's energy, or spotting the momentary pause where they were trying to formulate a thought which would have given me a cue or a breakthrough. The opposite is true as well: every time I have won, achieved or succeeded is because I have chosen to make focus a habit by wholeheartedly concentrating on the one task or goal at hand.

There is, I think, a physicality to concentration.

Determination

Determination is concentration multiplied exponentially. I see this as applying concentration with consistency and energy, even in the face of adversity.

There can be concentration without determination (or persistence, if you prefer), but there can be no real focus without it. In most types of success, one can suffer many failures (lost battles) on the way to success (winning the war). It may well be that most successes are preceded by failure.

Ray Kroc – the businessman who built a small United States burger chain called McDonalds into something rather bigger – used to have a placard hanging above his desk with the following words on it, words believed to have first been written by Calvin Coolidge, the 30th US president.

> **Nothing in the world can take the place of persistence. Talent will not; nothing is more common than unsuccessful men with talent. Genius will not; unrewarded genius is almost a proverb. Education will not; the world is full of educated derelicts. Persistence and determination are omnipotent. The slogan 'press on' has solved and always will solve the problems of the human race.**

My own journey from a large corporate entity to creating a start-up taught me how to press on the hard way. From playing to my natural strengths of innovation, building strong relationships and selling, I realised – after a number of mistakes – that in the early days vision and innovation was not everything. At the start up stage, the details mattered even more: often a big ugly risk could lurk behind slipping a small, tiny detail. Staying in business requires more than starting the business – I soon realised I needed a team to help me play to my strengths while the details could be addressed by reliable colleagues. Margin, and profit, comes from the details just as much as from the one big idea – as ever, focus is at the root of it!

Why is focusing so hard?

After all, why when the human brain can process 7,560 bits of information per minute, which means something like half a million bits per hour, do we find focusing hard?

The culprit is our competing choices. On one hand we seek and value instant gratification – we want everything sooner, faster and right now. On the other hand, we are also continuously bombarded by distractions from multiple choices of competing interests and demands.

As Mark Twain aptly remarked in his autobiography: **'Life does not consist mainly – or even largely – of facts and happenings. It consists mainly of the storm of thoughts forever blowing through one's mind.'**

Hence it is vital to know what matters and what can be influenced.

Some distractions are environmental – where they stem from your immediate physical environment – and are usually fairly easy to overcome by using a moderate amount of will-power. Others are internal 'thinking' distractions, and, are much more difficult to ignore.

Nature of distractions

Take this example of a coaching client of mine; a senior executive director who was about to make a sales presentation, decides to check his blackberry just before entering the room, and spots an email from his builder who has just upped his quotation by 20% for some extension work. You could say that's something comparatively trivial in the context of an about-to-start all important client pitch and its potential return. However, received at the wrong time, that kind of e-mail triggers an anxious response from him that easily distracts him from the key task at hand, never mind the fact that if he delivers a great presentation and wins the work, the pay off will be in multiples of that 20% uplift. When my company provides leadership sessions to individuals or groups, every single phone, smartphone or laptop must be switched off to enable the session to start, including mine! Distractions are costly. A 2007 study by Basex, a management science business, estimated that distractions cost U.S. businesses $588 billion per year and similarly high costs are likely in other countries around the world. This high cost is a likely estimate for other organisations around the world. In a recent programme in Romania, I physically collected the phones and put them away. While delegates were shocked and paranoid that something terrible would happen during the course of seven hours of phone-less-ness, any initially anxiety about being out of touch soon evaporated once they realised how liberating it is to be able to focus in the moment without distraction. It is about investing in some quality time with and in yourself. For not so long ago, the world never came to an end if you were in a session and uninterruptible for an hour or two and guess what, despite our perception of our pace of life today, it still doesn't.

A vital point to make about distractions is this: **the scale of the impact that a distraction has on us is very often completely out of proportion to its importance.**

Interference Traps

These distractions – often referred to as cognitive distractions – are best described as thinking traps. They distract us fundamentally from our ability to focus on the one goal, person, event or activity that matters to us.

We will all have heard sports commentators say that **the most important space to an athlete is not on the pitch, course or field, but instead the space between his or her ears.** Building on that concept, the following six categories summarise the most common thinking 'viruses' that enter that important space of our mind. There is some natural overlap between them, but take a step back and see which you commonly fall victim to.

These six traps kick in especially when the stakes are high or we perceive some kind of ambiguity or threat. Take a coachee of mine, at senior manager level of a large energy company, who after being turned down for a directorship six months ago, has just been put forward for a second opportunity. She finds it very hard to secure a positive focus in preparing for the upcoming promotion process. Notice the types of thinking traps she falls into over a period of six months:

- **Black and white thinking. 'I'm not going to try again. If it had to work it would have worked the first time. Not again'.** This all or nothing stance leaves no room for coping with the shades of grey.

- **Over-generalisations. 'I knew it – just my luck, something always goes wrong'.** Taking one fact and turning it into a general rule. In other words, this is a kind of gross magnification ('that's always the case! It is all over'), an exaggerated sense of gloom, or minimizing ('never ever does it work') and a lack of perspective on the real extent of a particular problem.

- **Mental filtering. 'I told you so'; 'see, I knew it wouldn't work'.** Allowing a negative state of mind to disqualify the positive.

- **Mind-reading. 'I noticed my boss was always tense on my promotion topic – that must mean he didn't rate me anyway'.** Second-guessing and jumping to false assumptions is one of the worst draining thinking traps ever.

- **Blaming and labelling. 'That's me. I tried my best. I know my manager simply didn't try hard enough to push my case,'** A refusal to take responsibility for something and assuming someone else is always the cause.

- **Personalising. 'The business missed its target. It must be because I am a failure'.** Here we inject a disproportionate personal responsibility even when the wider context has little or even nothing to do with you.

Haven't we all succumbed to most or all of these thinking-traps at some point? We form false emerging beliefs as to why something has happened and what might happen next. These in turn hamper us, weaken our resolve and dilute our energies. Think back to the box and the shelf in the first ingredient – self. Consider your thoughts as individual entities. They can be rearranged in order and in content. You can therefore make a conscious effort of what you keep, take out and what you put into them. As I say that, what thoughts are entering your mind now? What thoughts do you wish to exit? Gauge the mood you are in before and after this process and take inspiration from Star Wars 'Always remember, your focus determines your reality.' [Qui-Gon to Anakin, Star Wars Episode I] Or for a wiser reference point, turn to Buddha who said **'All that we are, is the result of what we have thought'.**

You can control what enters your mind. Even though new thoughts will always enter, you can learn how to ignore them or use a virtual parking lot to capture them for later. Not every thought is worth indulging or investing in.

Let me introduce you to someone who is a star at focus, who is adept at not only avoiding, but neutralising thinking-traps.

Stacey Cartwright, CFO of Burberry Group

We all know Burberry, the British luxury brand famous for its iconic trench coat, widely coveted for its timeless style. Stacey Cartwright is EVP and CFO of Burberry. I met with Stacey on a sun-dappled afternoon at Horseferry House, Burberry's global headquarters in Westminster, a block away from where I live.

The conversation started with her roots and the people who have influenced her choices. 'My dad was a great role model, but he had a harder start than me. I had an easier start so I strove to go higher'. This is arguably a measure of her perspective of both where you come from and how you should always challenge yourself to achieve more.

For someone who became a Group Financial Controller at 27, this mother of three has a relentless focus and clarity that is undeterred by experience and responsibility.

I was keen to see Stacey for a number of reasons. Women have been pouring into the finance pipeline for decades, yet, the drop-off at the top is dramatic.

Breaking into this select group and constantly delivering stellar performance takes a lot of determination and stamina. Stacey has plenty of both. Her guiding principles on focus are clear:

1. **'Exposure to complexity early on helped me focus – you sit around the top table with senior people and learn by absorbing what's around you, seeing what works but equally what doesn't. You learn a healthy business is not just a profitable business but a growing business, lead by a connected senior team'.** This highlights Stacey's clarity of thought on the impact of culture in driving growth – valuing 'right-brain', or non-finance-like skills in combination with the precision and analytical 'left-brain' – has pushed Burberry into the FTSE 100.

2. **'Ability is a necessity, but finding the right opportunity and focusing all of one's energy into that moment is what drives success. It is taking a door that's partially open and relishing the challenge to push it wider than it has been before.'**

3. **'Clarity on what you don't want is as important as knowing what you do. Whether it is standing my ground in a business situation or prioritising putting my children to bed, knowing one's values and choosing a business which respects them, is integral to long-term performance.'** Stacey conveys a calm integrity that confirms the clarity of what she wants is underpinned by the knowledge of what she doesn't.

We then discussed how her partnership with CEO Angela Ahrendts is driving the success of Burberry. Considering that the CFO is often the CEO's closest confidant, the nature of the CFO/CEO relationship can be the biggest enabler or obstacle to delivering your role succesfully. 'Angela is my alter ego. Her balance of EQ and IQ is what inspires me', Stacey says. Playing that partnership role with natural flair and charm, Stacey infuses her work with an intelligent approach and practical management to achieve challenging goals. In a self-effacing style, so accomplished is her delivery that it is arguably one of the most successful CEO/CFO pairings in business today. Later on in our adventure with this ingredient, we will discover another focused partnership: Bob and Al's from CommVault.

We heard about the Big Bangs in the first chapter, but let us now look at an example of the Big Rocks needed for focus via a story I heard in Hong Kong some years ago. Its roots lie in Confucian thinking.

The three big rocks of focus

One day, a wise teacher was speaking to a group of his students. He pulled out a large wide-mouthed glass jar and set it on a table in front of him. Then he produced about a dozen large, fist-sized rocks and carefully placed them into the jar one at a time.

When the jar was filled to the top and no more rocks would fit inside, he asked, 'is this jar full?' Everyone in the class said it was.

'Really?' he asked. 'Let's see.' He reached under the table and pulled out a bucket of gravel. Then he dumped some gravel in and shook the jar, causing the gravel to work itself down into the spaces between the big rocks.

Looking carefully around the class, he smiled benevolently and asked again, 'Is the jar full?'.

His students were catching on quickly. 'Probably not,' one of them answered.

'Very good!' he replied. He then reached under the table and brought out a bucket of sand. He started dumping the sand in and it seeped into the spaces left between the rocks and the gravel. When he was finished, he once again asked, 'Is this jar full?'

'No!' the class shouted.

'Excellent!' he replied. Then he grabbed a pitcher of water and poured water in until the jar was filled to the brim. Once again, looking intently into the eyes of each student, he asked, 'What is the point of this story?'

One student raised his hand and said, 'The point is, no matter how full your schedule is, if you try really hard, you can always fit some more things into it!'

'Very good,' the teacher replied, 'But let's look a bit deeper. This story also tells us something else: if you don't put the big rocks in first, you will never get them in at all!' Big Rocks, in our life, are the most important priorities and goals.'

What are your Big Rocks? Financial freedom? A project that you want to accomplish? Time with your loved ones? A dream or a hidden passion? A business? A particular cause? Teaching or mentoring others?

In your life jar, remember to put these Big Rocks in first or you'll never get them in at all. The gravel, pebble and sand – in other words clutter – will always get in the way.

Focus is all about prioritization. It is the intentionality to be in the present no matter what and directing the course of your mind to stay on track.

You need to recognise that time is finite but your energy is not. The way you can do that is by choosing to control the time, energy and emotion you give or spend on each idea, goal or thought that enters your mind. This is where the two variables of 'time' and 'focus' converge. This converging path enhances concentration.

David Arkless, President of Corporate Affairs, Manpower Group

In my discovery of leaders across the world, there are a few I will say are leaders by pure nature, as opposed to nurture. David Arkless is certainly in the top half of that short list. **'I know I'm not very normal'.** This confession in true David style sets the scene for our conversation. **'One cannot be normal when they travel 320 days a year from a refugee camp in Angola to positively intimidating the United Nations on human trafficking, and then from convincing a stubborn Chinese government on labour market trends to driving behaviour change in UK plc boards.'**

Before I formally introduce David and you get swayed as a reader by his remarkable, sometimes enviable credentials, to do any form of justice to David's story, I must first anchor it in its humble beginnings. Born in underprivileged circumstances, the son of a miner, David says: **'When, you have nothing, you often don't think of aspirational stuff, you just focus on getting through the day.' In his somewhat lonely childhood there was a seeming strength in not having much as a child. Without much external** or familial stimulus, he ' got used to building and creating things to keep myself amused.'

Fast forward a few decades, David Arkless is the President, Corporate Affairs for the Manpower group, the world's largest employment business. This function includes responsibility for Governmental and International Affairs as well as various strategic relationships with high-profile organisations such as the World Economic Forum, The Centre for European Policy Studies, The European Policy Centre, the U.S. Department of State, the government of Shanghai and the United Nations High Commission for Refugees. He has also been at the forefront of ManpowerGroup's involvement in the Ninemillion campaign, a UN initiative to provide education to the 9 million young refugees all over the world. That is impressive to say the least; I feel privileged to have known David for seven years and witnessed his own DNA grow. I asked him, 'how on earth do you sustain your focus , given all the things you are trying to achieve?'

We talked about how the 2008/2009 economic crisis has morphed leadership behaviours. David's clarity and precision as the conversation unfolded convinced me he was speaking from a position of personal experience, emotion and a sense of deep personal realisation. Eight insightful reflections followed:

- **A crises tests a leader's ability to focus.** The one thing that should never change is how a leader sticks to his or her principles, values and what they have committed to. It is fundamentally important that the followers recognise the leader standing in front of them in his or her authentic being; someone who has not become a different person because of the crisis.

- **Consistency is key.** 'As a leader you do not have to come up with new and exciting ideas or messages every day. So long as you are consistent in the core messages you cascade, including the core values you stand for, people will always gravitate towards you'. I deciphered David's message stripped to the bone, as simple yet powerful. The biggest crisis we have recently faced is not an economic one but one of greed of the human psyche affecting a detrimental consequence in the economy, the market and the boardroom.

- **Reputation is like building a perfect house made of hay.** It takes time, perseverance and skilful mastery to construct a structure that provides shelter, security and identity. The tiniest force of wind, it does not even have to be a gale or storm, can topple this delicate structure in minutes. The power of the current crisis is strong enough to be considered a hurricane. So the key is how you construct the shield you use to deflect the storm – which derives from your consistent core values, the mainstay of your decision making ethos. In such times, leaders who understand the delicateness and transitory character of reputation will outride the storm. 'Protect it for it is only as strong as your last good decision and as weak as your next bad one'!

- **An enemy to focus is knee jerk reactions.** Cost cutting, losing people, closing offices, crushing creativity and compromising on values are symptomatic of the basic emotions of escape, avoidance and survival. The panic struck firing of these five emotions, fear, anger, disgust, shame and sadness, result in short term gains for longer time pains. David's phrase is a mantra I have heard from him over the years 'settle for the longer game'.

- **Preparedness is the single biggest determinant of good executive decisions.** Ask Dr Han Seung-soo, who we met in the chapter on self – he is a proponent of preparedness 'Always be prepared' in Korean is; 항상 준비돼 있어라. From the pre-recession world where too much was invested 'in the here and now' or 'as experienced leaders, we will get into the room and figure it out together', Dr Han and David brought home another extremely simple but overlooked point about 'if reasons make the lists, emotions make the decisions.' Most conflicts are misunderstandings blown out of proportion and if time and effort is invested in the pre-decision stage, good decisions are bound to flourish.

In CorporateDNA, relational transparency in the boardroom is a key focus. People, regarded as leaders, need to focus on open and truthful relationships with others as to their real motives, desires and opinions; not just what looks, reads and sounds good. Relational transparency requires an ability to demand trust by giving trust first, through personal disclosure, as echoed by Stuart Gulliver earlier in the language ingredient. Of course, in ego infused boardrooms, going astray is easy. Leaders like being accepted and liked. To this end fear of rejection and loneliness can motivate these leaders to engage in hiding and deception. With David, I have discussed the pressing issues of corporate fatigue. Isn't it really easy for leaders under pressure to stray on focus while fighting the inherent fatigue that comes with the role? According to David there is no choice in this. Energy and positive infection is a non-negotiable part of responsible leadership. I agree.

A Tokyo tale

We've touched on Asia by way of the Grand Bazaar in Istanbul and the streets of Mumbai. Let us now take a long-haul excursion to the Far East.

A decade ago. I was 28 and in Tokyo. It was my first work trip to Japan with a large Big4 consultancy firm and I was, as you'd expect, slightly nervous and anxious to make a really good impression.

After a 14-hour trip and a very delayed flight, I landed at Tokyo's Narita Airport. The first thing that happened? My BlackBerry stopped working and inevitably as is with blind reliance on modern technology, all travel and venue details were technologically trapped! Faced with a two-hour ride into central Tokyo for my meeting, I had to change at the airport and go direct to the client's offices. Jet-lagged and stressed out by my exhausting journey, when I arrived, I saw an impeccable queue (I mean geometrically flawless) of 12 people waiting for me. The chief executive asked me a few questions about the flight; I answered politely but didn't see much point in saying anything about it being so badly delayed. The next 10 minutes were taken up by the time-honored 'meishi' exchange. In Japan, business cannot begin until the business cards (meishi) are ritually exchanged with both hands and a small physical bow. The CEO then asked me if I was ready to proceed.

I was but to my surprise, he led us out of the building and across the road. Tokyo in May is hot and extremely humid. In a formal silk-lined business suit, I was becoming increasingly uncomfortable and wondering how far away the training venue was. Much to my surprise (soon to morph into shock), we walked into an open green park with tall, over-grown grass. To make things worse, the CEO stopped, bowed, smiled and said 'let us begin'. I dropped my bag containing all of life's essentials (or so I thought) – my laptop with the slides, Post It notes, and so on – and tried to keep calm.

Was he serious? He wanted me to start now, here, in the open air? Yes, he was serious! Much as I tried to mask my reaction, he said 'Ms Duttagupta, we Japanese people embrace new concepts in open spaces. Do you need anything?'

All I know is that out there out in the open, jet-lagged, confused, anxious and now flooded with adrenaline, I managed to focus and spent the next five hours instructing them in techniques of the balanced scorecard, a performance management tool first designed in the 1990s. I still carry photographic evidence of people sitting on newspapers on the summer grass as I stood there teaching, using two natural tools – hand gestures and voice!

I survived and that evening, we rejoiced the training over some serene sushi and green tea as a group. I then came back to the hotel and fed my over anxious appetite with a glass of red wine and a good steak; at the time the best treat for me wiping away the exertion of the day and toasting to what was my first master class on focus. I realised that sometimes the best way for the mind to get concentrated is for you to acknowledge there is no choice when the stakes are high. This is why many of us often find ourselves able to focus and concentrate wonderfully when we have no alternative. It can be done – simply for that reason.

Sarah Deaves, Managing Director of Royal Bank of Scotland

I bumped into Sarah Deaves at a fashion event in London's Sloane Square, and we did our own meishi of swapping cards. We then met in the last few weeks of her tenure as CEO of Coutts & Co, shortly before her move to the Royal Bank of Scotland (RBS) as head of affluent banking, now termed private banking. This transitional moment provided a great opportunity for Sarah to look back at the multitude of leadership roles she has held within the maze of the banking industry. As banker to the Queen, Coutts can trace its origin from 1692, two years before the Bank of England was formed. In association with NatWest, it became part of RBS in 2000. Interestingly though, in 2011 the RBS prefix was dropped from its international business and it is now known as Coutts again worldwide, in recognition of its singular brand and standing.

Her career started in 1983, stamping cheque books by hand and looking after customers bringing in piles of notes, some full of fish scales – they were fishmongers, a big trading segment then, I hasten to add. A year on, when I visited Sarah in her new office at RBS, I could sense that Sarah had jumped on a wobbly, moving train with RBS with a large number of changes going on. There was a new CEO to replace the person who recruited her, a new team in a new culture, within a fast-changing regulatory agenda and changing market economics.

I could sense how Sarah's focus had changed from Coutts to RBS, and there was a palpable sense of it as she told me the story of the first hundred days in her new role. 'Focus is the only thing that gets me through,' she said.

With recent negative headlines still surrounding RBS and in one of the most volatile markets in modern times, she took on a new high-risk role. As Head of Private Banking & Advice, with 4,000 staff, she is creating a brand new private banking proposition for 600,000 of NatWest and RBS group's most affluent clients and she is relishing the challenge. 'It is really about trying to reinvent things for the future,' she explains. 'And it has been tremendous being able to lift and shift some of the knowledge I've gained at Coutts to use in a slightly different context.'

The position has also brought a set of personal challenges. With half her team based in Edinburgh, Sarah is away from her husband and two young children (now six and nine) in Islington, north London. 'It is not ideal', she admits, but then she has never believed there is a perfect balance. **'I don't think anybody has it all,' she says. 'I think people make choices and the reality is you give some things up to have other things'.** At least the choice is there. Describing her settling-in phase in RBS as a true baptism of fire, Sarah shared what she has taken on was laden with ambiguity: **'what I'm given is a black and white wire frame from which I have to build a fully functional house. At the start, without fully knowing what the house will look like, all I can do is focus on making the foundation strong.'** Sarah's calm and anchored style, which is essentially her leadership trademark, inspires abundant belief and focus among her colleagues.

Sarah's leadership stage has changed as has her script and her audience. Sarah's time at Coutts was a massive chapter in her life and she was there for long enough to see how the innovations she put in place actually came to life and took their own life cycle. The private banking division within RBS is a more complex challenge as it entails her leading a part of a business where all the dimensions are not under her influence and the dynamics are more fragmented. Sarah is fully aware of the bigger opportunity that these seeming crises offer to her own leadership growth. The challenge is bigger, as is the potential power of what her new story can become. The one thing that connects the two chapters is Sarah's ability to focus and concentrate on what is important, keeping away the gremlins of doubt and confusion.

Sarah's words to me, were, **'I always like to understand what I have got. By understanding the stage I am working on I am better able to reduce the arc of distortion between how I want to be perceived (intention) and how I am actually viewed (perception). When you are on a new stage, people on the ground always have a view of the previous stage you have come from and it is important to focus on spelling out who you are on the new stage and why that matters so much.'**

Good at many or great at one?

There's a key question that most of my clients bring to our coaching sessions at some point or other. Is it better to be good at many things or great at one?

I realised watching many leading examples around me, in starting your leadership journey, being known for one thing is what will help you find your stage and voice. It helps you build a legacy, a trademark, a footprint for others to see.

Once your footprint is known, your interests can diversify into many great things. At this point, you need others to give those new ideas life, blood and energy. As the late Sir John Harvey-Jones, the outspoken industrialist well known for the BBC television show 'Troubleshooter' said, **'surround yourself with better people than you'**. He surrounded himself with experts, those great at one thing, but the one thing he was great at was leading them.

This combination is also neatly summed up by David Ogilvy, the renowned British advertising executive who was an industry pioneer on Madison Avenue, the New York centre of the advertising world. He said, **'First, make yourself a reputation for being a creative genius. Second, surround yourself with partners who are better than you. Third, leave them to get on with it.'**

As many things take your fancy, retain passion as your secret compass. There will be times when the path you've taken is more difficult or longer than you anticipated. That's where passion comes in. Passion can keep you from quitting when you feel like there's no end in sight. Passion can help you enjoy the road to your destination however hard the ride on that road is.

Watch one devil though in your focused road to success – procrastination. Putting things off, or waiting for-a-better-tomorrow is a disease, which sabotages focus. In talking to leaders with different experiences, I realised procrastination is less about lack of time management and planning; it is often a deeper form of insecurity which manifests itself in the form of avoiding decisions and wavering commitments.

To sum up, real leaders are ordinary people with extraordinary focus. The other concept I want to explore in this ingredient is 'being smart'. Let us take an inspiring example.

Bob and Al – the power of smart thinking

Think of two young, driven boys from the 1950s. One from Brooklyn, responsible for working in parking garages and golf shops masters and the other, the son of a mid-country Iowan farmer. What happens when a chance encounter brings them together in 1988? Well, wherever your imagination takes you, what you certainly don't expect is them to build a US$ 400m technology business in ten years, called CommVault and become the leaders in data management software. However, this is exactly how a great business is sometimes born; two like-minded people meet through destiny and translate a simple idea on paper to a great business. This is the story of Bob Hammer, Chairman and Al Bunte COO and this duo's magic mantra – smart leadership and relentless focus. They met in a data room in 1988 when Bob had come to buy a portable computing business and someone said to him 'You should meet this Bunte guy'. As Al said to me during our conversation 'Bob didn't know what to do with me but we hit it off straight away.' They established their own interpersonal DNA, building their first business together for the first decade which then helped them to leverage the strength of their DNA in starting their second business, CommVault.

Often in my experience of working with large boards, most CEO/COO relationships are strong, healthy partnerships but socially distant and not really visible to the troops in an everyday sense. In this case, the direct impact of Bob and Al's partnership is transparently down to earth. Their chemistry rubs off on others and their impact is felt by every employee as I directly witnessed in their annual infinity club – one of the best recognition events I have witnessed, hosted for their outstanding high achievers, joined by spouses and partners. Here typical power points and long speeches were replaced by Bob and Al's personal touch and message of belief – a human 'Point of Power' in every sense of the word! It was so much more powerful than a PowerPoint presentation. Bob and Al said, this was about reinforcing the play and work culture for which the ROI is huge!

Something unusual attracted me to CommVault. Compared to the big names of big businesses in my world, here is a crisp and phenomenally successful story of a relatively small business and the power that lies in the simplicity of focus and relentless execution. It is a smart business run by two very smart people. As I walked into their summit in 2012, my eyes fell on a large artwork of a rock climber perched of a cliff with the words 'in the zone' below it. That immediately spurred me to think of the El Capitan or Half Dome – rocks in Yosemite I visited in 2003, which are symbols of character and confidence that bring out the best and the boldest in people, including a Zen-like concentration people practice in these ambitious ascents. 'In the zone' is something that Bob and Al, as lead climbers, have perfected for themselves and for the organisation and its 1,500 plus fellow climbers. It is an intensive and a relentless drive, a sort of transcendence where the reason for climbing and wanting to do the best 'comes from the heart' as Bob says. It is a sense of accomplishing your challenges and taking on your competitors, the market and rewarding your shareholders through a paradigm shift of making the impossible, possible!

Bob and Al play to all those metaphors. They are the rock, they are the rope and they are the climbers, while also being the guides helping others climb. Their DNA vibrates strongly in the CommVault story. For me, a somewhat cynical consultant having seen many clichéd ways of organisations recognising people, their 14th anniversary was refreshingly different – a sincerity of intent reciprocated by the whopping 40% who met their targets as outstanding climbers now joining that journey Bob and Al started.

I'm an avid fan of smart thinking. Taking the company share price from three cents to fifty three dollars, these smart leaders are 'plugged in to the zone'. What do I mean by this? With our earlier analogy from investment traders when someone is in the zone, they cut out every distraction, every noise and clear every obstacle through dogged intensity to the goal. These are nimble and astute people, creative and savvy – they actually 'think up' new ideas by seeing a connection or a pattern someone else hasn't, but they also know what their 'blind spots' are which helps them use others to plug their gaps. They build great teams and inspire a whole entity to action, for they have made a conscious choice to replace the power of routine with the power of focus.

In conversation with Bob and Al, I asked them what 'smart' meant and how was it different from clever or intelligent?

Smart for them is quick thinking, connecting the dots, seeing patterns and the ability to learn through common sense, not just knowledge. There a two types of smart – intellectually smart and street smart. Intellectually smart people know lots of things while street smart people make things happen. Education is technical while leadership is practical. Bob and Al's story is all about smart leadership. They didn't invent anything new and revolutionary. Instead, they spotted a gap in the market and created a smart holistic approach to data management over the disparate solutions that were variously available and made it a success through smart execution. The trick though was to layer this with a 100% organic growth.

So I asked Bob, what are your principles, what really matters to you?

Bob: Firstly run your business as you would run your life; respect it, have ambition and execute your goals. Secondly, if you've a vision and you are really, really clear about it, never compromise on it. Thirdly, have the vision but realise you don't have to do it all yourself, have teams who can execute it. Again, focus on your strengths.

This American duo have gone beyond the talk and proven their philosophy. In 1988 on sharing their idea, the response from analysts in the industry and gatekeepers was disheartening. Several analysts told them 'forget it – the barriers to entry are too big' but that storm cloud prophecy did not dent or dampen Bob's belief and focus in creating a single data management platform.

Cutting across big phrases like strategy and game plans, Bob's steadfastness lies in his simplicity and real clarity of getting the basics right; he is known for cutting through long, impressive PowerPoint's and asking questions like 'What are you trying to do?' What are you trying to say here – just say it simply?'

For Al, smart is simple. If two people read the same piece of information and one comes up with something more interesting and unpredictable than the other, that guy is smart; we place a greater premium on smartness compared to intellect.

With Al, while I didn't share his farming context, I did share his consulting background. Al went to Andersons Consulting and I went to PricewaterhouseCoopers. Al reminded me of my own career with a big consulting firm. We both shared pivotal early lessons that have honed our focus: focus is not a linear sequence from a to b to c. It is all about throwing yourself in, not getting comfortable, and learning the ropes and secondly always believing doing nothing is not an option – you can't just watch, you must have a say. Focus is about having a say and taking action beyond just thinking.

Similar in thinking, they are complementary on their focus of execution. Al focuses on getting creativity right, while Bob focuses on executing it commercially.

The world belongs to smart leaders – Bob and Al know how to capitalise on emergent micro-trends, leverage opportunity, discern insight from competitors and design a future of choice for their organisations as well as themselves. In short, they have focused their attention on how to seize immense unforeseen opportunities while others react to things and watch the space.

Smart leaders have reconciled the seeming paradox between supreme confidence and profound humility. They have confidence in their inner convictions – they know who they are, they know where they are going and they have figured out how to get there. Yet they are also mindful of their limitations. Bob and Al humbly share examples of mistaken assumptions or mis-hires they have made but learnt from. Their authenticity inspires others and their moral compass sets a direction that others can both trust and admire. They also carry on being real and human, having a life outside work. Bob still drives his Harley; Al goes back to the farm and harvests.

As Al and Bob said 'after every success, never put your feet up.'

I would add to that: always have itchy feet because itchy feet take you places. They stop you from becoming complacent and stagnating. Here's to itchy feet and a smart partnership in solving forward through sheer laser sharp focus.

Unusual in this book, I had a rare chance to talk to the two women behind these two leaders. Ann, Bob's wife said, 'I did not marry a CEO, but I am not surprised he became one. He always knew what he wanted right from the age of five when he wanted a boat.' They have been married 46 years. Dianne, Al's wife, said 'we met at university and at heart he hasn't changed the core of who he was then.'

Here is a story of focusing on your passion. Bob had after all, as a teenager, scribbled 'I will run a big company' in an envelope and handed over to his dad as his declaration of intent. **Passion is simple – take something you really love and focus on it with a real intensity. You are bound to succeed.**

Focus, focus, focus.

Your code for Ingredient Three: Focus

Pause. Ask yourself what do you remember from this chapter; list the key takeaways and ideas that had an impact on you – something inspiring, something relevant or something you would like to try.

Now, make a note of the following: the term 'things' below can refer to behaviour actions, conversations, skills or even an attitude

1. List three things you would like to START doing to strengthen your FOCUS...

2. List three things you would like to STOP doing to strengthen your FOCUS...

3. List three things you would like to CONTINUE doing to strengthen your FOCUS...

On an ascending scale of 1 to 10, how robust is this ingredient in your DNA?

Ingredient Four

EMOTION

CH$_4$

—'I feel'—

Good emotions are great allies. Bad emotions are saboteurs. Know the difference and channel your emotions to context. Emotional courage lies at the heart of our existence.

The one-inch almond

This ingredient comes from nothing more than two one-inch long, almond-shaped, neuron-packed structures in our brains called the amygdala.

Our two tiny but powerful amygdalas sit right behind the ears. Responsible for regulating emotion, behaviour and long-term memory, they have given rise to war, conflict, organisational failures and family breakdowns. They have, however, also given rise to creativity, optimism, success and romance!

My aim with this chapter is simple. To strengthen your leadership DNA, it is critical to unpack our emotions and explore those emotions which act as allies and those which act as saboteurs.

Emotions play out everywhere – from playgrounds to boardrooms, big stages to busy markets, families to politics. We will go on a journey and invite chairmen, CEOs, a priest, a famous composer and sporting athletes to join us on the way and share their emotional lessons.

Is emotion an intelligence?

Psychologists and scientists have identified many different types of intelligence over the years – social, financial, political, military etc. The most recent addition to this list is emotional intelligence, which has its roots in the work of Charles Darwin who first pointed out the importance of emotional expression as a key to survival in human evolution. In 1990, Mayer and Salovey attempted to develop a more scientific way of measuring different individuals' emotional abilities. In his ground-breaking book, Emotional Intelligence (EI): Why It Can Matter More Than IQ (1995), Daniel Goleman brought the concept into the mainstream. EI is commonly thought to be the ability to identify, evaluate, manage and master the emotions of oneself, of others and of groups to positive effect in both one's business and personal life.

However, in this book I have chosen to extend intelligence into courage. Let me explain. Step for a moment from the word intelligence into being emotionally aware and more emotionally courageous.

Emotional courage

Time and time again people ask:

- How do I sustain high levels of energy?
- How do I avoid getting emotionally and mentally overwhelmed?

- How do I get a stronger sense of self and purpose without losing myself in the rollercoaster of shifting business targets, people's feelings and constant expectations?
- How do I stay centred and anchored?
- How do I balance my energy across today's activities and tomorrow's needs?
- How do I read and leverage other people's emotions better?

My answer? You need the courage to artfully balance emotion and energy. But the truth is in my own case. Little did I appreciate this as much at the start of my career.

I genuinely believe that courage lies at the heart of our existence. The word itself derives from coeur – the French word for heart. In that sense, I am a believer that we live in the Age of the Heart (coeur) – Cour-age. Emotional courage begins by accepting yourself. Believing you are worthy of happiness and acceptance by others are the first two elements in laying a secure foundation for the self. It is also about being emotionally robust enough so sabotages and manipulations do not happen.

For me, that involves a willingness to be truthful in facing emotion rather than suppressing discomfort, guilt, emotional pain, disapproval or insecurity as well as the positives, joy, happiness, pride.

My first 90 days as a management consultant

In my early days as a consultant in a large global consultancy, it is true that in any given working week I could experience anything from fear, anxiety, doubt, happiness, pride, despair or frustration. All of that within a 60 hour week, with its residual emotions drip-feeding into the weekend. That experience base was a great grounding, as much as I struggled, to find a fitting balance. From doing deals to board presentations, analysing data, research, market testing, contingency planning, learning business models and solving complex problems – all within a high-pressured and fast-paced environment of strong egos, ruthless competitiveness, constant change and a controversial regulatory environment. Nothing in my earlier years had prepared me for emotional courage. So it was good to discover that I was not alone. 15 years later, my CEOs and coachees are asking the same questions.

'The human body can experience a vast array of emotions. Daniel Goleman, author of Destructive Emotions, written in conjunction with

the Dalai Lama, documents an estimate by Tibetan Buddhists that they can attain 34,000 distinct emotional states. To put that in context, research undertaken by Cardiac Coherence on CEOs indicates rather worryingly* that an average CEO will manage fewer than 15 of these states in a typical 24-hour period. It seems clear that there is much for CEOs to learn about emotions.'*

There is a strong and tenuous link between emotion and energy that is crucial to leadership and we will explore this later in the chapter.

Ctrl–Alt–Del

Enough of science. Let me simplify this through a light-hearted reference. Remember the famous three key combination we press on PCs to restart, reboot or shut down a computer? Put lightheartedly, I recently received a text from a family friend, which said:

'... just three steps to enjoy life: CTRL + ALT + DEL'

I have another three steps to suggest:

1. *Control* your 'blind spots' and negative emotions.
2. Look for *alternative* solutions.
3. *Delete* the baggage or negativity which causes conflict or unhappiness.

Emotional courage is a bit like that – of course the three keys here will take a bit more experimenting.

Examples of emotional courage that I have explored through my own experience and the other people in this book could include any, or all, of the following:

- Saying no, which can be so hard for some people
- Listening to your heart even when the world seems to disagree with you
- Being courageous enough to say 'I'm not ready for this promotion'
- Calling out a negative behaviour of someone senior and powerful
- Forgiving an enemy
- Allowing yourself to show tears as a sign of strength, not weakness
- Regulating one's own negative emotions

---

* Tappin, Steve and Andrew Cave. *The Secret of CEOs*. Nicholas Brealey Publishing Ltd 2008.

- Thanking and appreciating
- Always remembering where you have come from – your roots

Researchers such as Paul Ekman and Antonio Damasio list approximately ten core emotions: anger, fear, sadness, enjoyment, disgust, surprise, contempt, shame, guilt, embarrassment and awe.

'We can only be said to be alive in those moments when our hearts are conscious of our treasures.' — Thornton Wilder

The almonds at work

Can you see how emotion cuts across as the common dominating factor influencing these six examples from the fields of branding, films, calamities, folklore, sports and business?

1. **Emotion in brand.** A brand such as Apple, which focuses primarily on emotional appeal, drives how we all think, feel, act and make decisions. Apple, of course, is the archetypal emotional brand. It is not just intimate with its customers; it is loved. That love or emotional worth had a reported brand value of $153 billion in May 2011, giving it a market capitalisation of more than half a trillion dollars – more than the estimated GDP of Poland in 2011 at $532 billion. Yet we know this brand almost went under only a decade ago. The goal of emotional branding goes beyond customer satisfaction into customer loyalty. For example, in the back lanes of London's Chinatown, Lilly, the girl at the till in one of the supermarkets plugs Apple earphones into the inexpensive Chinese mobile phone in her pocket so that it looks like an iPhone. For her, it is a badge of honour.

2. **Emotion in film**. A poignant, emotional epic is *Bucket List* featuring two of my favourite actors. Two terminally ill men meet as utter strangers in a hospital room with three months to live and decide to live out their bucket lists – the list of things they want to do before they kick the bucket. Edward Cole (Jack Nicholson) – corporate billionaire with no family, is hospital room mates with blue-collar mechanic Carter Chambers (Morgan Freeman) – poor but with a loving family. Realising the incompleteness of their lives, they take off across the globe relishing nature, history, taking risks, eating caviar and indulging in adrenaline, giving up their egos and making amends in relationships. They realise their biggest chance for personal change can only happen against a time bomb of ninety

days of life with each other as mentor-friends. Here they discuss the meaning of life, ambition, love, responsibility, faith, philosophy, dreams, repentances and regrets. Dialogues come as universal messages: 'If life has taught me anything, it is that 95 percent of the people are always wrong', or 'the last days of his life were the best days of mine', or 'You measure yourself by the people who measure themselves by you' or 'So, what do you believe?' ... I resist all beliefs....No Big Bang? Random Universe? ... We live. We die. And the wheels on the bus go round and round.' While the plot is about coming to terms with death, the message to both young and old is universal – **find happiness in life before it is too late**. As with the opening chapter on self, this message is central to the DNA of this book. We all get caught up in the mundane grittiness of life so that we forget to unlock our inner dreams and enjoy life. Devastated by the hard-hitting reality of terminal cancer which is worse than any possible crises – financial, social and moral – two real people chose the *king of all emotions* – happiness, which no money can buy. Like this film, happiness never goes out of fashion and whatever our age and stage, we all seek it.

3. **Emotion in calamities**. When I watched the appalling scenes of the 2011 Japanese earthquake and tsunami, the one vivid scene I distinctly remember was of a dog, rescued from drifting ocean debris, jumping up to its owner and wagging its tail at their reunion more than three weeks after the tidal wave hit. The power of that emotion in the dog and the owner had an emotional impact on me bigger than the reported number of fatalities. **The power of actually seeing an emotional reunion tugged at my heartstrings and somewhere the happiness of a reunion was more moving than death.**

4. **Emotion in storytelling**. Emotion is the fast lane to the brain's development. Right from Aladdin and the Magic Lamp in the 9th century Arabian Nights, firing a child's imagination and ability to dream the impossible, to Barack Obama's 2004 Democratic National Convention keynote address, emotions tell eternal stories that inspire us all. A day before his Boston speech, Obama was an obscure state senator from Chicago. After his electrifying address, he was a national political figure. Four years later, he was elected President of the United States. **Emotional storytelling evokes imagination, inspiration, participation and empathy in people who are so keen to follow and find meaning. It is the same for a President as it is for a small child – the 'almond' controls it all.**

5. **Emotion in Sports.** Fresh off the emotional headlines of success are the two momentous weeks of the London 2012 Olympics. As I stood in St James's Park, on a hot and humid day, watching the 105 runners, I wondered what the winning recipe was. After winning his second gold medal on Saturday, Mo Farah was asked if he could explain the secret of his success. 'It is all hard work and grafting,' he replied. Well yes, but I wonder if that is everything though? We have heard the winners talk about teams – their coaches, their partners, their family and friends. We also heard the losers apologising to people they 'let down' and shouldering all responsibility for failure. Across every sentiment was a sense of pride and belonging to something bigger; a palpable group loyalty.

   That moved me immensely. A DNA of deep belonging – not fame for fame's sake. Athletes who have worked for years to win offer us the best inspiration to apply back in our lives– years of early rises, years of endless gym routines, years of restrain and self control; years of fighting every set back, and years of keeping the dream alive.

   As I saw the sweat stream down the throbbing veins of these marathon runners, I saw in front of my eyes living personifications of deferred gratification and of pride and belonging to a cause bigger than themselves or the sport. 'I was not known. Now I am known,' Gold medallist Stephen Kiprotich of Uganda said, smiling with pride, not arrogance. 'Determination matters. I'm happy.' In his happiness, I felt an inspired surge of belief. Leadership is in our DNA. We can do anything if we really want to. It is a matter of choice.

6. **Emotion in business**. The 2000 merger between Time Warner and AOL never worked. Much trumpeted at the time, the $360 billion deal faltered because the two key participants – Steve Case and Gerald Levin – knew little of each other (and arguably, of one another's businesses) before they struck the deal. Levin, a lawyer by training, had worked his way quickly through Time Inc's corporate ranks and, while aware of the need to have an Internet strategy, had little idea of the best way to get one. Case, 20 years his junior, could not have been more different having worked first in marketing for Pizza Hut and then GameLine (a business which initially delivered computer games down telephone lines) which eventually grew into America Online (AOL). According to Nina Munk, whose book *Fools Rush In* (HarperCollins, 2004) is the authoritative account of the merger and the subsequent fall-out, 'even before the deal was announced, it was clear to just about

every insider that this was going to be a fiasco.' The argument is that the US$ 360 bn deal may have been motivated by logic or strategy but destroyed by egos.

The Story of Emo

For the purpose of illustrating the power of emotions in leadership, I will chart a real client's story through a fictitious character called Emo. Emo could be any CEO – Emo could be you. Starting at a specific point in time, let us put Emo through the motions of this story. The story goes like this.

Emo has just been promoted to a CEO. Delighted, he still can't believe the promotion which arrived more than a year before expected as the previous CEO left on health grounds after a successful five-year term. Without a succession plan, the board had to quickly search for a new leader in a difficult market. Emo was chosen, beating one strong internal favourite and two external contenders. Not only that, what made it interesting was the fact that Emo was two levels below the previous CEO; in that sense he had outpaced the level above to get this role. He had built a stellar reputation on leading a recent transformation project reporting into the previous CEO and that meant he had board visibility for the last eighteen months. Both the past history and future expectations to Emo's succession were big.

We will track his first 90 days as a CEO.

As an aside, this fascination with 90 days, or 100 days or 120 days of any major experience is about initial impact. First impressions in the first three months count. With relevance in many life experiences including parenting, schooling, career, marriage, that initial period is all about excitement coupled with the apprehension of 'let us see how this goes'.

I met Emo just after his 90th day as his coach and this is how he recounted Day 1 and the period after:

Day 1 (Emo): *That morning, though, was different. I woke up acutely aware I had gone to bed as an executive and woken up as a CEO. The shift felt large. I needed to prove to the board their decision was right. I left home earlier than usual. As I took the lifts up to the 35th floor, at 6.30am, I wondered did the liftman know of my change? Could he sense anything different? A wave of anticipation washed over me as I walked past my old desk into the new office. I started my morning rituals – checking email, picking up voice messages, reviewing daily project status over a strong,* *black coffee – then... I felt a throbbing anxiety. Is this what a CEO does? What next? The rest of the day went by.*

The next 89 days went by – fast.

Day 90: Emo had achieved good results which were published in the company's first quarter. The press, shareholders and the board were happy. His team was less so and Emo himself was 'knackered', as he admitted. We had a two-hour coaching session where we plotted his 90 days week by week. Every event, emotion, trigger, dilemma he felt over the last three months was framed and reframed – no matter how positive or negative.

'I am happy on one side, but glad this period is over. The truth is I have also felt terribly lonely. Old friends are not friends anymore – they are direct reports. Overnight, people looked at me in a different way. The language... even the jokes seem different. For all the glory and power that comes with a CEO's role, I have also felt helpless and confused – [he then took a long breath] – and sometimes even a bit scared. But I believe the board is happy. So, I guess I have done an okay job...' (in a reflective tone)

What had happened was Emo's inner self was seeking validation. He needed to get a perspective on his emotional self through friends and family, peers, the board and the wider business. Finding the right support network was missing. In our first coaching session, which happened immediately after the 90 days, I realised a pattern: to every stumbling block in Emo's first 100 days, based on feedback and growing self awareness, there was a trapped emotion that needed dealing with.

Below we see the proposed remedy against every piece of feedback Emo received; note his worry, or trapped emotion:

- He needed to listen more than tell **[Emo: 'but won't I embarrass myself and look vulnerable by not telling people my views?']**
- Ask rather than pretend he knew the answer **[Emo: 'but won't I risk contempt by revealing I don't know']**
- Wait and be long term **[Emo: 'but won't I disappoint others I am not showing immediate actions']**
- Mentor rather than befriend his team **[Emo: 'but won't I disappoint people I have been close to or worse, feel I have distanced myself']**
- Define goals rather than execute expectations **[Emo: 'but won't I embarrass myself by not telling people what is needed']**

He realised his first 90 days as a CEO was a successful but lonely period. In connecting with his own emotions in a non-judgmental and honest way, we agreed he would now look at being more emotionally courageous and allow other people get to know his CEO self.

We unlocked the new internal voice that was always telling Emo: **You are in the spotlight, everyone's looking at yourself. Prove yourself and don't look needy or unsure.**

What Emo can teach us: Two truths about Emotions

Firstly, feelings are normal and natural. We all have them. Secondly, we can't reject them, but we can learn how to express, manage and channel them.

One minute Emo was finishing a shareholder meeting, the next minute he was taking a call from an unhappy board member, or being thrown a curve ball by a market analyst reporting negative forecasts, while returning back to his desk to see a former colleague leaving a curt memo stating a need to see him. The brain shuts down, the heart starts racing and emotions run high. So, these two suggestions are invaulable:

1. **Find your feelings. Find out where they live.**

    The seat of where our feelings live is important. Is anger hiding behind self-doubt? Or is resentment from yesterday's meeting being carried to the next, where there is no need to bring that personal baggage?

2. **Explore your emotional map.**

    As we grow up, each of us develop an emotional map. This is influenced by our early sharing experiences: how did our family handle emotions? Were feelings discussed, if so which ones? Which do we still find hard to discuss? Is it time to change that footprint? Is your footprint different in different relationships (work, home, society)?

Emo was the youngest of three brothers, the oldest was in the air force and the other in engineering. His father was a retired army general. Emo was trained not to show emotion but to work hard and prove himself.

Today Emo is a CEO of a large organisation. **He needs to unlearn his rules and change his emotional map to adapt to his new context. Through his journey, we realise good, able people can have tough emotional learnings. We should not confuse the person with the problem just as we should not confuse being emotional with emotional intelligence and**

courage. Able leaders can also feel angry, hurt and doubtful. There is an Emo in all of us.

This leads me to someone I admire immensely.

Sir David Lees, the Chair of the Court of the Bank of England

I have had many conversations with Sir David who became a good sounding board for my leadership beliefs. A seasoned, soft-spoken gentleman who looked a good decade or so younger than his 72 years and for his seniority, more gentle in manner than one would perhaps expect. From the first minute, I sensed Sir David's immense impact was refreshingly un-chairman like. An exceptional honesty sat neatly with real humility. I soon discovered Sir David's career has been an eclectic mix of roles. He was a director of the Bank of England for eight years and held chairmanships of FTSE 100 companies like GKN and Tate & Lyle. He was taken aback when his predecessor John Parker called him out of the blue one day and said David, why don't you go for Chairmanship at the Bank of England after me?' His first reaction was 'Me?'. After a twenty-six year career at an engineering group like GKN and 35 years since he did his last ever interview, Sir David confessed his first emotion was emotional. Careful emotional and mental preparation led to his appointment as the Chairman of the Court of the Bank of England in April 2009. In a sense, it was a first appointment, not a standard succession; the role had never existed before. **'It was hard preparing for it. It surprised me that I got the role; I was not a technical banking expert. I was soon to realise one of the greatest leadership facets. When you are in the field of experts, you can lose the common touch, the common experience, the common sense of what makes people and markets tick, the emotions behind the decisions we make. Maybe what I bring is connecting an old iconic 450-year-old institution to the reserve of its own everyday energy.'** Indeed, maybe that is the instinctive touch he brings to chairing the Court of the Old Lady of Threadneedle Street, as the Bank of England, the second oldest central bank in the world is referred to as.

Reactions are learned responses

We are not born with emotion hardwired into us. We learn emotional responses as a reaction to our life experiences. Here is what the Russian psychologist and Nobel Prize winner, Dr. Ivan Pavlov with his famous dog experiments, in 1890 teach us about emotional conditioning.

In his experiment, Pavlov and his lab assistants would ring a bell and introduce a variety of edible and non-edible items to measure how much dogs would salivate. However, after a while, Pavlov noted the dogs would often begin salivating even when the bell was rung but food was missing, just at the sight of a food bowl or the lab assistant's white cloak. Based on his observations, Pavlov suggested that salivating upon the expectation of food is a conditioned reflex. It represented the triggering of a biological reflex (salivation) by learning (in this case, by the sound of bell or sight of the bowl).

An emotional response is a conditioned, learned response to one's environment, wired through permissions and rules from upbringing and reinforced through repetition of a set pattern of life associations.

Let us say two managers, Jane and Janet, with similar experience and potential are put up for a promotion. Neither of them get promoted and both express intense emotion. Jane as a blocker: she becomes angry, blames the system and shuts down. Janet as an enabler: she is determined to work even harder, learn from this experience and get promoted next time. Janet's emotional response is healthier.

Emotional blindspots – they trip us up

Blind spots are emotions that we have not felt completely or ignored because we are afraid of where they might take us. By avoiding them, we never really get to genuinely understand them, which is vital for learning how to detach from them in a healthy manner.

When I was learning to drive in India, my driving instructor would (annoyingly, to my impatient adolescent self!) curb my urge to drive off by asking me to do the ritualistic turn-back-and-watch-the-rear. **He called it a blind spot: those areas that are so close to us that rear-view mirrors cannot pick them up. We must therefore get out of our comfort zone, turn our heads around and ensure that it is safe to stop or make a necessary turn.**

Despite his drills, I failed my first driving test – can you guess why? I forgot the crucial blindspot check in my urge to get started and pass the test; an important lesson in the role blind spots play for success. **We can apply this metaphor to our own lives and in leadership especially when things are too close to be properly seen: when, in our rush to take action or respond to a situation our emotions take charge, we cover up shortcomings,** especially those that only a close support network can notice. It takes courage to ask for feedback on our blind spots.

The new CEO – Chief Emotion Officer

Acronyms for Chief Executive Officer are a popular discussion and the one that recently attracted me was the 'Chief Emotion Officer'.

CEOs are leaders who need to use, express, manage and master a range of emotions from optimism, hope, inspiration, joy, excitement to sadness, despair, disappointment and fear of failure. There are different metaphors for how leaders master emotions. As Goleman says, **CEOs are the emotional thermostats of their businesses**.

As Sir David said in his first ninety days, **'One has a brain that is instinctively very powerful in sorting out what matters from what doesn't. Walking the floors of the Bank, I realised as I spoke to people that the bank needed to get in touch with itself and allow its reserved emotional energy to manifest'.**

No one had said that so clearly before throughout all my consulting work in the banking sector. If you consider what banks actually do, they predict outcomes for the future, which in turn affect nations, markets, businesses and families. No matter how rational and calculated these forecasts are, to me, banks and economists are financial astrologers bearing upon masses of emotions at ground level generating hope, optimism, relief, confidence or despair, sadness or regret. I have every belief these mega buck forecasts economists make are impacted by their own emotions, their moods, temperaments and their optimistic or pessimistic personalities. Sir David continued, **'Leadership is NOT only about first over the top with the best answer. It is also about the art of collecting the thoughts, ideas and emotions of others and giving it a voice.'** The Bank of England has its own emotional footprint which needs re-hauling for the future.

Let us extend that point further. **Throughout the journey of this book, I have been consistently struck by the ways in which a handful of leaders can articulate the relationship between where they come from and who they are. Comfort with origins is one aspect of people who combine self-awareness with the ability to disclose. Their emotional courage is the hallmark of their leadership, as you are about to discover.**

Emotional Lessons from 3 Johns: A Chairman, a World-famous Composer and a Priest

John Heaps, Chairman of Eversheds law firm

A chance meeting with the Auxiliary Bishop of Westminster led to me meeting his school friend, John Heaps, the current and recently appointed Chairman of Eversheds, a large law firm in the top 60 worldwide on revenue in 2010. As I sat waiting for him in his offices just minutes from St Paul's Cathedral, my thoughts turned to the novel idea of a priest introducing me to a lawyer, as well as that of a priest having been a lawyer himself, which we will explore further later. As John walked to meet me, I was struck by the sense of humility and integrity that surrounded him. An unspoilt humanity about him which on one hand makes him the ideal organisational man with company blood coursing through his veins and on the other, his Evershedian self is a detached yet keen observer, quietly sensing his new role and its landscape. His 25th year anniversary as a partner marked his appointment as Chairman.

One doesn't meet many of these. His inaugural speech as Chairman at the Partner's Conference in May 2010 reminded people, **'History is important. It helps us understand our DNA.'** That is John. Comfort with origins. He admits he is strongly influenced by his own personal experiences. One of five children brought up with strong values of love, care and support, he then arrived at a moment in his teens when he had to find his own way. A series of adventures came his way in different guises. Also, as part of this unfolding self-discovery, two seeming knockbacks struck hard. Not getting into Oxford and not getting a partnership at Freshfields. However, John says this gave him an edge he may have otherwise not secured. **He called it 'determination through disappointment'.** In John's words, **'There is nothing pre-ordained in life, and no set view of fairness but if you have the will and desire, despite the setbacks that get strewn in one's way, you will find a better way, a stronger more determined route through disappointment.'**

The full story unfolds. From a grammar school in Leeds, followed by chance bumping into a red book, rekindled a desire to go to Ratcliffe College and explore rugby as a game in which he discovered natural talent. **John admits he suddenly went from 'being okay' to realising 'I was capable of more'.** That was a very empowering feeling. Then, undeterred by the shock of not making it to Oxford, in February 1972 our protagonist found himself on a Greyhound Bus with his friend John McGlashan on a tour of the United States. Free. Uninhibited. He was 18 and he was discovering the world. Somewhere the picture in front of me was of a law firm Chairman as a liberated 18 year Yorkshire lad, letting go of pre-set views and jumping in to the flow of life to discover what possibilities lay ahead. Following a degree in Law at Liverpool University and after an intense six years with Hepworth and Chadwick, the second setback came when he was all set to go for partnership at Freshfields (part of the 'Magic Circle' of leading UK law firms) and **'I didn't get it'.** That was a big blow for him. Today, this man is none other than the Chairman of Eversheds, one of the ten largest law firms in the UK however you measure it – revenue, fee earners or number of offices. **Those affecting setbacks gave him the impetus to hone his mindset beyond the rational – to read his context better – to tune in to his instinct – to exercise choice much earlier in life which. Choice, as John says, may sound like 'an illusory concept' but it does come a lot earlier than you know or realise it. The trick is to connect with that choice via instinct. The rational may not always help you see it.**

The role of Chairman is an interesting one for me. You are a leader but you are a different type of leader, not a hands-on, CEO type leader. As a leader of a board, you are a bit like an orchestra conductor (who we will meet in the third story). Basically as Chairman, John is there to lead people to a crescendo but he has to bring that whole orchestra to where it wants to go; not necessarily where he wants it to go. As a leader, he is an enabler.

Navigating between the roles of the detached facilitator, to the unbiased thinker and integrator, a Chairman is the wearer of many hats. My meeting with John in September 2010 was at the milestone of his first 90 days of his tenure.

'The actions one takes during their first three months in a new role will largely determine whether they succeed or fail. No one inherits a green field. You have boarded a bus already moving at speed. Transitions are periods of opportunity, a chance to start afresh and to make needed changes in an organisation. But they are also periods of vulnerability, because you bring change to established working relationships and a detailed understanding of your new role. If you fail to build momentum during your transition, you will face an uphill battle from that point forward.'

So how does one accelerate these transitions? And what are those lessons he would impart to aspiring chairmen?

In John I also hear a younger version of the wise words of Sir David Lees, who we met earlier: **Leadership is not only about being the first over the top, although that is part of being a leader. It is also about the art of collecting the thoughts and ideas of others and channelling them to action.**

John certainly promises the potential to become that and more. No wonder in the 2010 personal feedback he received from others, the comments ranged from 'a gentleman' to 'a man of the highest integrity' and, of course, a 'quality lawyer and partner' and 'he has Eversheds right in his heart'. As an author, I have proof of that Evershedian spirit in a man who radiates humility, consistency and integrity. Of course there is also that fourth dimension I saw on day one: **emotional courage with authenticity to continue being himself at the helm of a powerful legal firm.**

John Arnold, the Lawyer turned Priest

My next conversation took place in neither a boardroom nor a seat of political power. It was neither in a flash corporate building nor a library. It was at the seat of the Archbishop of Westminster, Westminster Cathedral, the great edifice designed by John Francis Bentley, inspired by the early Byzantine architecture of the Mediterranean.

I was meeting Bishop John Arnold, an auxiliary of the Roman Catholic Diocese of Westminster. I am not a religious person in a traditional sense but I nurture a sense of spirituality for which I am grateful to my parents. Spirituality, for me, is more personal and intimate than religion. It is more about a connection with the universe and a bigger force through which I identify with myself, how I view the world, interact with others and make decisions. Spirituality does not need religion to define itself.

Spirituality has a place in leadership and in this chapter's context of emotional courage, it lies in the importance of the leadership spirit of the leader, as either being able to inspire followers, or not. With that mindset, I was curious to find out more about lawyer-turned-priest, John.

Born in Sheffield in 1953, John was convinced, between the ages of 8 and 16, that he wanted to be a solicitor. After all, his father was a successful solicitor and John was used to going to his father's law office from a young age. In 1975, he graduated with a Law Degree from Trinity College, Oxford and completed his legal qualification by being called to the Bar in the Middle Temple in 1976 after studies at the Council of Legal Education.

However, in the autumn of the same year, he felt a strong and strange urge to enter a religious order and, after a two-year initial period of formation, he made simple vows in 1978 before beginning studies at the Gregorian University in Rome. In 1981, he transferred to the Venerable English College and continued his studies for the Diocese of Westminster, completing both a Licence and a doctorate in Canon Law. Things did not stop there. He was ordained by Cardinal Basil Hume as a deacon in November 1982, and as priest in July 1983. With the completion of studies in Rome, he was appointed to Westminster Cathedral as a chaplain with responsibilities for the Westminster Hospital in 1985.

Here is a story of emotional courage on how to know and act on when your inner compass points to a new Plan B. His father was upset for many years by the deviation from Plan A but John stuck to his guns.

As John gave me access to his world, seeing him in his black clerical suit and seated in a dark brown leather chair in his room in the cathedral, he looked incredibly 'at one' with the environment. The room. The cathedral. The city. London had adopted him in 1985 at the age of 32 and, according to John, the city brings together so many strands of life and diverse identities. A centre of monarchy and government, it is the religious, political and commercial nervous system, and a home for educational establishments, culture and the arts.

A large part of his pastoral work is to help people slow down in pace and remember what is important for their lives. In stillness and reflection comes self awareness and from reflection comes wisdom. **That is at the heart of experiencing the difference between superficiality versus spirituality.**

The more I explored this lawyer-turned-priest's thinking, there seemed parallels between his world and the leadership world. A leader's spirit of leadership is no different. It needs to be connected with the organisation's best interests while staying tuned in to his own spirit – to ensure that one's own spirit is guiding the organisational spirit in the right path. Alignment was a strong message.

'My only fear is that I may fail others'. That should be the fear of every leader. They may fail the organisation. Fear, as we will explore in the book later on, arising from a sense of responsibility, in a good measure, is a healthy, justified fear. Always know what you are responsible for and who you are responsible to and how to be responsible in changing contexts.

So how can spirituality be applied to leadership?

John's words were: **[The leader's spirit lies in his instinct. Using instinct as a strong partner to experience is key. Sometimes with the best will in the world, the end decision will be wrong. Learn to use your instinct to validate every decision before acting on it, because the world we live in so vast, updating our own views on the rules of the world with changing times is beyond any single human intelligence.]**

His wisdom left me reflecting more and more on how the corporate world could promote leadership based on respect and empathy rather than fear and greed. **Mistakes will of course still be made, but rather than allow the regret of making a mistake to sap our energy, we just need to turn a mistake into a lesson and fears into hopes.**

I remembered reading somewhere **problems are like washing machines. They twist us, spin us and knock us around but in the end we come out cleaner, brighter and better than before.**

Sir John Eliot Gardiner, Farmer and Conductor

If the last John was a lawyer turned priest, this John is a Cambridge-trained historian turned musician and latterly farmer. Sir John Eliot Gardiner is a leading light in the music world.

I met him on a misty early June morning in 2011 at his 500-acre farm in Dorset which is surrounded by his own woodlands, beef cattle, sheep and wheat fields. We did most of the interview in his kitchen, where he seems most at ease, in a homely and informal manner with frequent visitations from Biscuit, Cuddles and Hector, his three golden retrievers who accompany Isabella, his wife, as she goes about her work. At the end, we proceeded to the library, where an entire bookcase is taken up with his 250 recordings, many of them made with his own performing groups, the Monteverdi Choir and the English Baroque Soloists. No stone in 'early music' is left unturned: Schutz, Purcell, as well as French Baroque composers such as Rameau and Charpentier and Bach, Handel and Gluck are all there. John Eliot went up to Cambridge to study history and Arabic but became more and more convinced that music was his real destiny.

I had to ask him the obvious question, what, if anything, was common across his music and farming identities? He immediately dissolved the two into one by saying: 'in both music and farming, the audience (read world) sees the artistic end product not always realising the hard graft, technique and science that sit behind them. Art and science, for me, are

**not either/or options: they are symbiotic and harmonious (potentially).'
With farming you have the unpredictable variables of market demand
and weather, both affecting the viability of the livestock and arable
enterprises. With music you have still more intangible elements to factor
in: the different moods both of the works you are performing and of the
musicians you are working with, as well as constraints of time and
money.**

Well, I thought to myself, business and leadership is also like music and
farming. Behind an appealing product or service, sits a whole apparatus of
science, skill and discipline. I spoke out loud and said, **'So, are you saying
artists are scientists as well and vice versa.'** He agreed that the modern
leader needs to find a balance between technique and intuition in the
process of finding your own style of leadership: it is all about blending the
art with the science, the right hemisphere with the left, the (practical)
context with the (ideal) content.

Next we took the continuum of performance and rehearsal. John Eliot said:

**'After I had finished my studies, I was appointed apprentice conductor
to the BBC Northern Orchestra in Manchester. In a typical concert
programme beginning with an Overture I would be allowed a nine-
minute rehearsal, for a twelve minutes piece. This was great training in
prioritizing. You have to be ultra-prepared and hope that this will guide
you towards finding the moment when everything ignites in performance.
But that's life – you cannot rehearse as much as you would like (too
expensive), instead you have to run every scenario in the unfolding of
every piece through your mind beforehand. A lot of performers panic,
fearing the worst and thereby attracting nerves or negative energy,
risking their own performance as well as their team's. Negativity is,
contagious in its most virulent and destructive form'.**

**I strongly believe in the analogy of the stone and the stream: by shifting
it a couple of inches left or right you can alter the whole direction of the
flow, turning negative energy into positive in a trice.**

In both business and drama, sometimes, not always, we are able to rehearse
our world before we experience it. We call it role play before real play.
Read on.

Rehearsal and leadership courage

**The three Johns are all on different stages – corporate, faith and music,
each playing out a different script to a different audience, whose**

happiness in turn is being driven by three different stimuli. Each script involves an element of performing to the public; they all rehearse their scripts and no matter how experienced, they often sense anxieties and worries before going live on stage.

The concept of an emotional rehearsal, beyond the mental one, is fascinating for me.

When I started CorporateDNA, my primal instinct was to bring drama-based learning into leadership work in practising emotional courage. Popular in Ancient Greek theatre, public performances used to be an integral part of life from triumphal processions, aristocratic funerals to public banquets. Within a large stage or theatre, people watching, actors performed for emotional effect – joy (comedy), intrigue (drama) or sadness (tragedy). The leadership world of stage – actor – impact is not that different with themes like change announcements, leader departures or celebrations.

In both business and drama, rehearsing our world before we experience it is likely to increase our chances of a more successful emotional and inspiring response from the audience – emotion and inspiration being our two most effective channels of engagement.

While mental rehearsal is mainly a way of remembering what we have got to say, emotional rehearsal helps experience new beliefs, create new neural circuits in the brain and develop new habits of thinking, feeling and behaviour before we engage in physical practice. You can even imagine something going wrong and rehearsing how you'll cope with it.

Leaders in organisations face the same problem. How, for example, do you rehearse an upcoming and potentially painful conversation with a difficult boss or an underperforming employee?

When participants role play and eventually get stuck at a difficult point, I often invite someone else from the audience to step in, almost in a 'let me wear your shoes' capacity which makes it a safe experiment. The new player relaxes and steps into the situation from the outside. By watching a peer step into your shoes, you are better able to see their world through someone else's eyes, pick up on faulty assumptions you may be making and understand the impact of your own chosen behaviours much more readily.

In a recent such role-play at a pharmaceutical company, we encountered what I would say is saw a very common scenario. Roberta, a rising star and head of the sales team, was stunned to learn that her mentor and ally Kyle had told the executive team that while he believed Roberta had great potential, she wasn't yet ready for promotion. Roberta was shocked and told us she wanted to role-play this incident with one of our facilitators. 'I felt so betrayed,' she said. As we discussed the issue in some depth, she felt comforted by our neutrality as facilitators. Recognising she was in a safe place to admit her own self doubt she said, 'Maybe I am not ready yet – but I feel Kyle betrayed me.'

This is how the role play unfolded:

Roberta: I heard you told the Senior Leadership Team that I couldn't handle the new responsibility of leading the new offshoring team in India.

Kyle (played by an actor): Wait a second! I didn't say you couldn't handle the responsibility. I simply said I thought you were being promoted too fast. I don't want them to set you up to fail.

Roberta: Well you should have come to me first if you had doubts.

Kyle: I was going to talk to you about it. But I also have an obligation to discuss such points with the management to get their view.

Roberta: You have an obligation to talk to me first. I can't believe you would jeopardise my career like this.

Kyle: Roberta, get a grip! I have always supported your career! This is a question of 'when' you should be promoted, not 'if'.

Rather than share her feelings, Roberta provoked an argument because she is hurt. But at no point does she actually share her feelings or say to Kyle that she feels hurt, angry or even admits her own confusion about not being ready. These unspoken feelings can colour a conversation, leading to false conclusions and resentment. This is a common problem where managers and leaders feel they must frame problems exclusively as logical, left-brain business rationale. Using their hard problem-solving skills will, they think, lead to a better outcome. False, I say! When emotions are at the heart of a situation, it is crucial to focus on them and work with them – ignoring them is what can turn a small problem into a disaster. Logical reasoning can do little here.

The law of emotions

This law is simple. There is a positive and a negative.

The law of attraction is simply a new label for an established philosophy or theory, that 'like attracts like'. What you think most about is what you get.

Both neuroscientists and behavioural scientists have clearly demonstrated what you focus intense emotion on can be self-fulfilling and tends to attract your attention to more of the same by physically strengthening the neural pathways dedicated to that 'thing' you want. Remember, this law is neither negative nor positive. It just is!

The ratio of neurons that govern unconscious thought compared to those governing conscious thought is roughly 10 million to one. In effect, we are primarily unconscious beings on auto-pilot. Some of those unconscious reflexes have a priming role. For example, as soon as some people see a large group of people – in fact, long before we're consciously aware of them – our unconscious brain goes to work getting us ready for fight or flight. And because we have got neurons in our head that pick up on the emotions of everyone around us, once one person in a group goes into fight or flight mode, the whole group soon does.

Remember, bad results are not just a matter of bad luck! It may be about negative emotions, such as worry or anxiety, attracting negative results. Positive thinking attracts positive results. We will explore this more in the final chapter on Luck. So if this is how our neural pathways are built, why not populate them with the positive, with strong feelings of self-confidence and anticipation?

Let me show you how emotions transcend from business into the world of sports. Emotions are even being funded in research. Did you know, Emotion Regulation of Others and Self (EROS) is a £2.1m project being supported by UK's Economic and Social Research Council (ESRC) over a four year period (Nov 2008–Oct 2012) to establish the role of emotions in success? Surely, as we can see, emotions matter immensely. The following insightful question is illustrative:

'Can the psychological skills used by top sports people be used to prepare us for other moments of intense pressure? And if so – which ones are most effective? These are just two of the questions we are hoping to answer with the data generated.'

Professors Andy Lane and Peter Totterdell from the EROS network.

The Corporate Athlete: Lessons on emotion from the sporting world

High Performance and winning for that matter, is highly emotionally charged. In the year of the Olympics we know the difference between a gold and silver between two athletes is less likely to be practical skill, but more about the skill of emotional and psychological management under pressure.

For me, leaders in corporations performing on a high-stake stage are like sporting athletes. Consequently I'm keen on the idea of the corporate athlete. The similarities and differences between sports and business are fascinating. In both, competition is fierce, results matter, winning or losing occur in small margins, resilience during adversity is essential, as is an ability to decide and act under pressure. Both need clear targets, the ability to manage energy, combat negative emotional reactions to the smallest failures and so on.

There are differences too: athletes invariably work with a great coach. Coaching in the business world, however, is sometimes either discretionary, a privilege or, at times, remedial. Athletes get practice time before performance, unlike in business, where rehearsal is rare. Athletes are better trained on how to balance work or stress with recovery. People in business may experience burnout due to over-work and stress, which causes them to experience the 'crash – burn – recover' cycle.

Emotions are the common ingredient across both performances.

Energy is at the heart of everything: Energy and emotion

Right at the start we talked about the tenuous link between energy and emotion. Let us explore that here in the context of sport and business.

It is now proven that energy, not time, is at the heart of performance. Each individual represents a cell of potential energy in the larger company body. Yet what do we take for granted? Energy! Productivity, as well as health and happiness, is rooted in how we let our emotions control our energy. If I outline six paired statements each with a business and sports facet, you can work out the emotion underneath.

- Athlete: 'I am losing to players I should beat.
- Businessman: 'I am losing to competitors we should beat.

- Athlete: 'My seventh (chess) match this month, I am mentally fatigued '
- Businessman: I don't know what to focus on – too many priorities'

- Athlete: 'I'm nervous to go for that last putt.'
- Businessman: I'm nervous on my first shareholder meeting

- Athlete: 'I've lost my confidence in my forehand '
- Businessman 'I've lost my mojo'

- Athlete: 'I can't control my emotions'
- Businessman : The situation is bringing out the worst of my emotions

- Athlete: 'The team dominated us in the second half
- Businessman: 'My peer group is a threat to me'

The negative triggers in each cycle of experience, in running order are: pessimism, fatigue or despair, anxiety, lack of self belief, emotional sabotage and fear of failure.

I am fascinated with sports psychology and its parallels with business. Having grown up with parents who are die-hard sports fans, I had a lukewarm detachment to any ball game – cricket, tennis, golf or football – until recently when I started working with sports therapy in my leadership work. I then realized what I had been missing! So, in my usual 'get my teeth stuck in' approach, I drove my luck in watching the Scottish Football Cup Final, Wimbledon Men's Tennis Final, The Open (British Golf) Championship and India versus England Test Cricket at Lord's, all within an eighteen month period. The parallels between sporting and business emotions are striking.

Even when we are not interested in a sport, we are always curious about top-level sporting athletes. What are the likes of Roger Federer, Lewis Hamilton, Rafa Nadal or Sachin Tendulkar made of? How do they master emotions under pressure? How do they motivate themselves to endure the intensity of training and practice they subject themselves to day in and day out? Why does one football team, with the best players in the world, so often struggle to overcome their competitors? What role does the coach play? That is a book in itself.

Businesspeople are so taken by elite sport that companies pay vast fees to listen to inspirational talks by sporting legends to learn how to pull off that type of balance and grace under pressure which leading athletes possess: Athletes have a *when-then* strategy, for example, 'when I feel anxiety, then I will do...' Sporting athletes are just better prepared in spotting the emotional cycles they fall into and being ready and skilled in managing those better. It is inspiring to see how unruffled they are under pressure and how they display all the ingredients in this book from self belief, focus and resilience to managing their emotions and dark side – they do so with skill, calm, poise and confidence.

What can Roger Federer teach us?

On that note, I couldn't think of a better example of a maestro of managing energy and emotion than Swiss world tennis champion Roger Federer. I admit I am a huge fan! His performing DNA exudes poise, grace and remaining calm under pressure. To me his winning combination comes from the strategic acumen of a chess player who masterminds every move from every spot on the court, only to then execute them with the grace, speed, agility and poise of a skilled ballet dancer. Federer's versatility was summarised by Jimmy Connors as: **'In an era of specialists, you're either a clay court specialist, a grass court specialist, or a hard court specialist... or you're Roger Federer.'** For me Federer's story is about emotional mastery.

However, some of us know, that is not how this Swiss man started. From being an inflammable 16 year old to achieving a childhood dream and setting foot on Wimbledon's Centre Court at 22, what transpired in a period of six years tells us much about the colossal role emotion plays in winning or losing.

As a boy, Federer had lots of tantrums and outbursts when he lost. At first he could not understand his parent's disapproval because he was frustrated only at himself for losing and not at others. As he learned how much these outbursts drained his energy and took his own focus away from his strategic focal point – he realised it was his unchannelled energy, not his skill, that directly contributed to poor performance. He openly admits that it was a sports psychologist who helped him, at the age of 17, to move him from the explosive John McEnroe end of the psychological spectrum towards the poise of Swedish tennis maestro Björn Borg. Although, Federer admits his emotional reaction to success is different from Bjorg's. **'There are people who don't smile when they win, and there are people who smile for weeks afterwards. I'm the kind of guy who lets the tears flow,'** Federer said after winning his first Wimbledon title. This is where we find Federer's ability to show and manage emotion as a real art. While some people see his grace and composure on court as too sophisticated – too controlled or unemotional – the point here is there is a time and place for emotion and he chooses it well.

He didn't, however, start on a winning streak. There were many losses – the seedbed of his learning. Federer's first tournament as a professional was Gstaad in 1998 (12th grade), where he faced Lucas Arnold Ker and lost. Federer's first final came at the Marseille Open in 2000, to fellow Swiss Marc Rosset where again he lost. Roger now holds 16 Grand Slam singles titles, six ATP World Tour Finals and 20 ATP World Tour Masters 1000 tournaments. He also won the Olympic gold medal in doubles in 2008.

With a relentless drive to win, his passion for tennis couples with his enjoyment, emotion and energy for the game. never tries hard to impress anyone which itself makes him even more impressive. His charisma is effortless. This, combined with his genuine humility and self-scrutiny, is inspirational.

From various extracts of Federer's interview with Daniel Huber, 2010, and a recent article with *Sport & Style Magazine*, we see the fire of Federer's emotions:

'**The mark of a leader is the way they deal with a crisis. You certainly need a healthy dose of self-confidence and must face the world head on.' Roger Federer doesn't crack, but others do. Federer does feel every emotion intently but manages them by using the resources to cope with what lies ahead. One can't stop feeling the pressure but learning to harness your emotions is key to succeeding under pressure. Emotions in any given situation are extremely important.**

Roger Federer talked about how the greatest sin on court is to play with an indifferent attitude. He mentioned how he was the typical youth throwing tantrums growing up, always had lofty goals and when he wasn't meeting them he 'spat the dummy'. It wasn't learning to ignore these emotions that made him become arguably the greatest tennis player of all time, but learning to use them properly that made him turn the corner. No wonder he had wanted to become a rock star. For Roger, 'being a lead singer in a rock band has a lot in common with a tennis player, be it the inspiration or the live contact with fans. This is also very direct in tennis and the reaction to a slip-up is immediate and mercilessly slaps you in the face'.

Is he perfect? Nope. The one time I saw Federer lose his cool was in 2009 at the Miami Masters Sony Ericsson Open to opponent Djokovic.

Unrestrained frustration exploded when the world's top-ranked tennis star smashed his racket at the Sony Ericsson Open into a crushed, broken object (spat the dummy) – an outburst characteristic of the 16 year old Federer. Again angry at himself, Federer's meltdown resulted after losing points to opponent Novak. Federer ended up losing the match.

I have seen him time and again using the frustration of a bad shot to drive his inner self to play the next one better, rather than let it play on his psyche. He is just as adept at using the fulfillment of a good shot to inspire him to repeat it again.

In that sprint cycle of finite energy, managing negative emotions is critical. Dr. Jim Taylor says, **'This is where negative emotions and energy collide. Negative emotions can raise your performance at first because they increase your intensity and get you to fight harder'. Let us say a tennis player is losing to an opponent that he believes he should beat but, no matter what he tries, he can't seem to turn the match around. The tennis player is likely to experience frustration and anger initially. These emotions can be helpful at first because they motivate him to fight for control of the match. But if his tactics don't work, he may experience despair and helplessness, accept that he can't win and give up.**

Can you see parallels with the role of a CEO?

After a short time though, your performance will likely decline and it usually spirals downward into a vicious cycle from there. Negative emotions can risk your self-belief. You end up drawing attention to all of the weaker aspects of your performance.

In business and sports, the same is true and many athletes will carry emotional baggage from earlier, less successful events in their career.*

'Consider the best athletes in the world. Sports are very important to them because it is their life and livelihood. How upset do they get when they perform poorly and lose? Some get very upset. Overall, though, considering how important sports are to them, most great athletes handle mistakes and losses pretty well. In fact, one reason why the best athletes in the world are at the top is because they have the ability to control their emotions rather than their emotions controlling them'.

---

* *The cluttered mind uncluttered by Jim Taylor, Ph.D. has tremendous lessons for the business world.*

The next one to watch is the angry, gritty, young Scotsman Andy Murray whose leadership DNA is undergoing a massive morph in 2012. Murray has always been a complex character to analyse – almost winning a title but never quite making it – but the last five months have introduced another factor into his mysterious ups and downs: the presence of his new coach and mentor Ivan Lendl, one of the best tennis players we know but someone who has no coaching experience. There is also what seems to me to be the changing role of his mother on court to whom he always looks to for emotional approval. Based on my strong instincts, something feels right about this Lendl-Murray partnership. No wonder – as I write this Murray has just defeated Frenchman Richard Gasquet, on French soil, at the French Open in June 2012. That's no mean feat especially given he was booed and shooed by a roaring French crowd as he walked onto court. But no emotional interference was stopping Murray. Is Murray turning an emotional corner?

In his words: 'It is almost like playing in a football match – and I like football. I enjoyed myself today. It is the most fun I've had on the court in a while, so I wasn't shying away from the fact that the crowd wanted me to lose.'

Murray has suffered the frustration of losing all three of the major finals he has contested in an era dominated by what many regard as three of the greatest players of all time: Federer, Rafael Nadal and Novak Djokovic. Will I, just will, I hedge a bet on his performance this year as a proof of concept of mastering emotions to strengthen your leadership DNA – an Olympian tribute to London 2012...maybe?

So if you ask me the penultimate question: during critical moments – what makes the difference between success and failure? I would ask, how well can you manage your negative emotion under pressure?

The emotional bestseller – a word from my mentor

As you now know, emotions are not just 'touchy feely' reactions: they are powerful influencers of behaviour, relationships, decisions and actions. A close mentor, Mervyn Gunn, said to me about ten years ago while I was learning the ropes of leadership and the test of emotional courage through crises in tough assignments:

'If you could sell confidence in a bottle you could be a millionaire. But if you could sell emotional mastery in a bottle, you'd be a multi-millionaire. So much in life is ruled by how we feel!'

Your code for Ingredient Four: Emotion

Pause. Ask yourself what you remember from this chapter; list the key takeaways and ideas that had an impact on you – something inspiring, something relevant or something you would like to try.

Now make a note of the following [the term 'things' below can refer to behaviour actions, conversations, skills or even an attitude]:

1. List three things you would like to START doing to strengthen your EMOTION...

2. List three things you would like to STOP doing to strengthen your EMOTION...

3. List three things you would like to CONTINUE doing to strengthen your EMOTION...

On an ascending scale of 1 to 10, how robust is this ingredient in your DNA?

Ingredient Five

INSTINCT

—'I sense'—

Instinct is how we just sense, know and act on things without knowing why. One of the most powerful yet most underused gift we have, the word intuition comes from the Latin word intueri, 'to look inside'.

Imagine.... it's easy if you try (as John Lennon sang to us)

Imagine. Sometimes a single moment of instinct between two people, if pursued, can change the course of the universe forever. A Big Bang moment. Something is instinctively created that impacts everyone and life is never the same again. I would like to dedicate the chapter to one such moment in 1962.

I had the enormous privilege of meeting the legend who is widely considered to be one of the greatest record producers of all time. His own Big Bang moment came from a most unlikely source. On 13 February 1962 he met Brian Epstein, manager of a group of four young primal boys from Liverpool not really known in the music industry. Epstein had already been rejected by several record companies and was nearing the point of desperation.

Yes, I am talking about Sir George Martin and his genius creation of the Beatles. A music maestro who blended the primal, rock instincts of the band. To me, he is the master blender of all ingredients that combine instinct, self belief and focus. I couldn't believe my luck when I was seated at his lovely home in an Oxfordshire village, sharing a couch with this timeless legend, a cushion apart. An unprecedented moment of excitement had just washed over me a minute before, in his guest toilet, seeing all his world famous record labels on display.

I opened with 'You to me are an epitome of instinct, aren't you, Sir George?'

'I guess you could say that. In 1962 an instinctive moment became momentous. I was on the point of turning these four boys down because I didn't think they were very good. [I laughed] Now, you laugh, Rhea, but it's true. And their manager, Brian Epstein, had got an interview with me through the EMI music publishers. I was working for EMI running the Parlophone label and everything on that label was stuff that I produced. So, I was looking for a band of this sort because I was very envious of one of my colleagues who ran Columbia, which was Norrie Paramor, and he had Cliff Richard. And it seemed to me that Cliff could record anything, from the Bible to God Save The Queen and he would still be a hit. I'd been working on comedy records for a long time because I had to find a special niche for my little label. So, I worked with Flanders and Swann and the Beyond The Fringe crowd, which was Peter Cooke, Dudley Moore, Alan Bennett, Jonathan Miller, people like Rolf Harris, Charlie Drake, Bernard

Cribbens, Peter Sellers of course, and Spike Milligan, all these kind of people.

To shape their records I had to be very creative. I had to think of the idea, what we were going to do, and each record that I made was jolly hard work. I couldn't then say, "Oh, we'll make another one in a month's time," and it would come out. It didn't work out like that, you had to start from scratch each time. Whereas with Cliff Richard, as I say, Norrie would select a song for him, take him into the studio, bing bang with the group The Shadows, and he'd have a hit. So, I wanted something like that.

Well, when Brian Epstein played the tape to me first of all, the demo tape, which included some of the stuff they'd done for a test recording at Decca, I said "Look, if I have to judge this act on what I'm hearing, the answer's no." He looked very crestfallen so I thought I'd give him a lifeline. I said, "But if you bring them down from Liverpool I will give them an hour in the studio to find out what they can do." He said, "Thank you, thank you, thank you," and went away.

I remember Sir George Martin saying to me, 'Instinct matters because that's all I went with when I heard The Beatles play for me that first time. Musically, I wasn't sure – that's what my technical, rational brain told me – but they were interesting and I liked them as people. I acted on my instinct and signed them to the label.'

That was a little taster on instinct. We will meet up again with Sir George in the chapter on Creativity.

Meanwhile, bringing it back to every day moments of instinct, have you ever called a friend and they said they were just thinking about you? Or walked into a room and just sensed something unprecedented was about to happen? Or met someone and felt you have known them forever?

If so, you already know that your instinct is powerful but this chapter explores how you can act upon it more consciously. Although we refer to it by words and phrases such as 'gut feeling', 'my heart is telling me', 'it doesn't ring true for me', 'I saw the whole thing in a flash...' in fact, we make decisions intuitively all the time.

Here is an example. I often use first impressions as an energiser in our leadership workshops. On the first day of a programme, twenty or so participants from different cultures and markets, who have never met before, walk in and meet and greet each other. The rule is they have to jot down first impressions about each other and try to read each other's personalities based on instant perceptions. Questions are not allowed. To my surprise every time, these random assessments often turn out to be very accurate. It is almost as though people can read each other without a code, but my point in this book is that there is a code. It is called instinct.

I use instincts all the time. In my own personal experience, nine out of ten major instinctive choices I have made, however avant-garde for some, have been right, and the tenth one, even if wrong, has gone a long way in teaching me about life.

Not only that. **I believe instinct is not just an exclusive gift some are born with. It is a skill that can be developed and strengthened by everyone. In this chapter, we will see how, like a metaphorical muscle, the more you exercise it, the more it can develop. Intuition, another term for instinct, is increasingly recognised as a natural mental faculty, a crucial element in the creative process, a means of discovery, problem-solving and decision-making.**

The gift and the servant

Albert Einstein, who was as much of a philosopher as he was a scientist, said **'The intuitive mind is a sacred gift and the rational mind a faithful servant. We have created a society that honours the servant and has forgotten the gift.'**

Understanding and harnessing the gift of instinct will be an invaluable part of your leadership DNA. As always, reason is at war with unreason, rationality with the irrational, art with science, but scientists and psychologists now support Einstein's assertion and emphasise the importance of instinct in the realisation of human potential. For example, here is the author and management philosopher Daniel Pink:

> **The last few decades have belonged to a certain kind of leader with a certain kind of mind. But the keys to leadership are changing hands. The future belongs to a very different kind of leader with a very different kind of mind – creators and empathizers, pattern recognizers and meaning makers. These people – artists, designers, story tellers, caregivers, big picture thinkers – will play a seismic role as tomorrow's leaders.***

---

* *A Whole New Mind*, Riverhead Books, 2005.

This may sound a challenging proposition, but before describing instinct in the context of this book, let us appreciate its power and simplicity in everyday examples of nature around us. Have you seen a spider spin a beautiful, geometrically flawless structure – its web? Or birds that build a structured round shaped home, a nest for their young ones? All creatures are born with an innate ingredient of how to survive, read the environment and respond to it. The ability to build a web is programmed into a spider as a nest is in a bird, for you never see them attending management training courses. They simply train their instinct! The message animals and humans demonstrate is that instinct is within us and ready to be accessed.

My entrepreneurial career: the art of 'sniffing'.

I grew up with a curious saying in my family: **'If you've strong instincts about people, you are probably cut out to run a business.'**

I had no idea how instincts and business were linked. I didn't really know the full extent of the word entrepreneurial either in any formal sense until I was at least in my mid-twenties. So today when I'm asked to give motivational addresses on my entrepreneurial career it always leaves me a bit bemused. Is it really an achievement? India, where I grew up, is after all a land of entrepreneurial self starters. Entrepreneurship is everywhere, from roadside vendors to the women who run boutiques from home, we see tiny businesses that scale heights with absolutely zero investment at times.

But did any of these people really have a business plan when they started? Did they look for investors/venture capitalists, or did they just follow their instinct and let the rest take shape?

Take this endearing example of instinct. In Calcutta, I still remember an amusing incident. I must have been around nine. Early one spring morning, our local laundry man (Hiralal) turned up unexpectedly at 5 a.m. leading a goat with a bell around its neck, raving with excitement and waking us all up. Having sensed too much competition from mini launderettes, he decided to try a new venture: he decided to outpace his competitors by becoming a milkman with a twist. So he started selling the product (fresh milk) from its direct source (the goat) at the doorstep, creating a totally transparent customer experience. The man was the same but the trade had changed and so had his unique selling proposition. I remember liking Hiralal. An entrepreneurial instinct, pure self belief and courage of conviction, sparked by sniffing out a timely opportunity changed his fate forever. He became a star attraction in our neighbourhood and bought five other goats by the end of the year. Imagine his reaction if we called him an entrepreneur!

Decades later, while working for a large corporation, I thrived on the art of sniffing. I was sniffing and spotting opportunities where none existed, or drawn to those bids and tenders no one else was interested in. It was lonely in a sense as I faced some opposition pursuing these, but my instinct became my mentor. **Sharpening my nose, smelling opportunities and gaps and reading between the lines is not a very logical process but it is full of adventure and the unknown**. With a low boredom threshold, I liked the unknown. Here is the story behind my biggest sales one year. One afternoon, I was walking over to the coffee machine when I saw a fax lying unattended on the floor. I picked it up to see it was a half-smudged tender document from a Middle Eastern government to our firm, but not addressed to anyone in particular by name. I took it to a few peers and the verdict was 'it sounds like something we don't offer'. That to me is always a red rag to a bull. I decided to take a risk and prepare a bid for it anyway. The next thing I knew, it turned into a competitive bid and four other consultancies had been asked to tender. My enthusiasm was dampened but I persevered with putting my best RFP submission forward. One year on, it had become one of our biggest accounts. We won the contract. The winning was based on a simple sniff, just that sense that there might be something in this to go for. So when my then coach asked me if I'd ever considered being an entrepreneur, I'm afraid I laughed off the proposition.

I assure you, when years later I did make the decision to start my own business, leaving a secure directorship was hardly based on reason. Instead, I was guided by a strong hunch that I had reached a stage in my life experiences where taking a big, bold risk would help me discover the next version of myself. That discovery would make me very happy, which in turn could translate into a tangible success for the world to see. Note the link between happiness and success from the Chapter on self. I remember a friend saying to me, 'Rhea, your nose is getting restless in wanting to sniff the entrepreneurial dream.' I also remember bouncing the idea around a group of 20 well-wishers. At least 80% of them said that I had lost my mind. The point is, it can be a lonely undertaking to listen to your instinct in altering your life course. At such cross roads the world, used to the norm, can't make sense of your irrational choices.

Whenever we take a new road in life, we need to feel that going down this route will in some way make us happy and fulfilled. To be an entrepreneur that self-belief becomes your closest ally as not many

others may see or smell your vision. We are often led to believe that entrepreneurship is the domain of a select few. I don't agree. Not everyone can be wildly successful, of course, but we all have that dormant instinct of standing out, starting something and making a difference. The dormant neurons just need activating: DNA!

A Frenchman from British Petroleum

Even if you are not a classic entrepreneur, you can still make entrepreneur-esque choices in your career, like my close acquaintance Jean Baptiste Renard who left the pinnacles of BP based on one crisp, strong hunch. Starting his career as a service manager in a gas station in France, he left as the Head of Europe and Southern Africa for BP, revered as an industry expert across the oil value chain. His exit in 2010 saddened his colleagues no end, as evidenced by this email from Billy: 'I have just heard the unbelievable news that you are retiring from BP. Is it possible to retire before you reach 40? What will you do?'

JBR, as I fondly call him, shared with me: 'I don't know what lies next... while I have tasted success, I realise everything in my life so far has been linear – from a great education to a great career. Some hard work, some stress at times, some choices, but at the end, the system has taken care of me. At some point, I had to break that trajectory.' We then lost touch for two years until LinkedIn brought us back together in 2012. As I opened his email, I paused with bated breath to see what this inquisitive Frenchman has done with his life. He had become a pro bono consultant for social entrepreneurs. An interesting choice, I thought to myself. I read on. 'Well, I am not an entrepreneur although I have a deep admiration for them. They are bold, they put everything they have at risk every day. When kicked out through the doorway come back through the window! All these things I am not good at, after a long career of delivering results through a well-established structure and framework. But here's what I am good at – I spotted a gap. I noticed usually entrepreneurs don't like help. Even truer in the case of social entrepreneurs, as they realise they are great at the social aspect, great at running a small outfit, but struggle when it comes to strategy, replication of a business model, and aggressive but not well organized growth. So that was my niche – a unique opportunity to bring something to the table of people I so admire without becoming one of them.'

Surely, I thought to myself, that can't be an easy connection. Social entrepreneurs don't speak the language one has learned in large organisations. 'Yes, but the complementarity can be a great win-win.' As an example, JBR is working with a man who created the first headhunting firm for the 'banlieues', these deprived areas in France where social unrest turned to riots a few years ago. The firm outplaced 550 (struggling) grads from those areas last year. 'If I can help them replicate their model efficiently in other geographical areas, we could move from 550 to 5,500 per annum, and more. Quite something to be excited about!'

JBR, like me, had broken that linear career trajectory, driven by instinct.

While every entrepreneur follows his/her own formula, we know that entrepreneurship is fundamentally a creative act and involves creating value where previously there was none. In that entrepreneurial vein, instinct is a sort of opportunity-driven action.

Wayne Gretzky, arguably the greatest player in the history of ice hockey, said: 'to be a winner, you don't skate to where the puck is, but you skate to where it will be.'

Gretzky relied heavily on his intuition and was incredibly successful as a result. I am sure he would have agreed with Einstein about the gift (instinct) and the servant (reason).

With examples from Sir George Martin's fleeting hunch which produced The Beatles, to Einstein, to my own humble example and to Jean Baptise Renard, let us pause and unpack how this instinct ingredient manifests itself. We will then journey through more examples.

How instinct manifests itself

Instinct tends to manifest itself in the following ways:

- **As a feeling** – a mood or an emotion.
- **As a physical sensation** – a shift in energy such as changes in our heart rate and in our temperature, a feeling of stress, an exciting flutter, or even as unpleasant physical symptoms such as cold palms and a dry mouth.
- **As a visual** – a picture or image, for example, in a potentially fatal situation, we see our life flash before our eyes, as our brain scans the image to try to find a solution to our predicament.

An instinctive feeling does not last long, sometimes as little as a fraction of a second. It is, by its very nature, elusive, but it is very important to act on that tiny window of opportunity and invest in what our instinct might be telling us.

Sports and Instinct

We hear of people who have a special gift for always being right on the money when it comes to making business decisions. What is true in business is just as true in sports. World-leading golf pros, footballers, tennis players and chess grandmasters have very strong instinctive skills; when they are playing their game, in the heat of a high pressured win/loss, they rarely have the time to get enmeshed in long strategies. They act on instinct.

Take Mahinder Singh Dhoni, the current Indian Cricket Captain, now rated as number one in the World. Defying convention, his gut feeling is his principal tool of trade and is also his master stroke. It is his ability to read the game and the weaknesses of his opponents, which more than compensates for the lack of major strategy. 'He has always flummoxed rivals with his field placements, his use of bowlers or his frequent changes in the batting order, which invariably turned the match in his team's favour. This is because he reads the game very well,' says Ravi Shastri, commentator and former Indian skipper.[*]

Also, instinct more than strategy predominantly drives Dhoni's decision making. It was instinct that prompted him to bring on an inexperienced Joginder Sharma to bowl the last over against Pakistan in the T-20 finals in 2007. Or more recently in IPL 4, when opponents KKR were cruising to victory chasing a modest CSK total of 153 runs, Dhoni overlooked the more experienced Scott Styris and handed the ball to Suresh Raina. In both the matches, the bowlers delivered and Dhoni's team won.

Standing at the crossroads....

Dr Franz Humer, who we met in Chapter One, chairman of major international pharmaceutical organisation Roche and of the global drinks company Diageo, summed it up well for me:

Most of us find that there are three or four crossroads in our lives where we could go one way or the other and the decision we take can quite fundamentally change our lives. When standing at a crossroads, where we find that we're faced with two equally weighted options, what swings us in one direction over the other is neither logic nor experience but that fleeting hunch or instinct.

---

[*] Source: *Business Today*, May 2011, Leader by instinct: The transformation story of Mahendra Singh Dhoni

Can you see the role instinct plays in that all powerful fleeting moment of go/no go, right/left, yes/no and how it drives our happiness and our success? We can never know how many crossroads we'll face in our lives, but I do know that the choices we make instinctively go a long way towards determining who we are, what we are, how we live our life and what we make of it. As indeed the Diageo CEO, Paul Walsh, says: **'Your values originally drive your instincts and your experiences improve your instinct.'**

Are you now wondering if instinct is a mystical super gift? No. It has a strong rational element to it.

It is time now to explore the science behind the art of instinct.

The rational part of instinct

Instinct, at some level, is unconscious reasoning; it has a science to it. What happens with our brains is that as we accumulate knowledge — whether it is through people, information, events, preferences or experiences—we start to recognize patterns. Our brain unconsciously organizes these patterns into blocks of information—a process the late social scientist Herbert Simon, PhD, called 'chunking'. Over time our brain chunks and links more and more patterns and stores these clusters of knowledge in your long-term memory. When you see a tiny detail of a familiar design, you instantly recognize the larger composition and that is what we regard as a flash of intuition.

I would say a decision based on instinct is a function of three conscious steps:

1. **Rational stimulus.** Somewhere an instinctive urge is always anchored or rooted in an original rational stimulus. If you trace it deep and hard enough, you will know the first flicker of any fleeting urge is prompted by a rational need such as survival, winning, nurturing, safety or needing to prove something.

2. **Likelihood.** What are the chances of this instinct being true and leading to success?

3. **Final value judgement.** This is the go/no go decision. Shall I go with it or shall I not? Will I trust it or won't I?

Instinct and the brain

Understanding how our brains process instincts helps us to better understand them and use them to our advantage. **Our brains are divided**

into two hemispheres. As we know, the left hemisphere is sequential, logical and analytical; the right hemisphere is non-linear and intuitive – like, dreams, opportunities and ideas.

While these distinctions have often been caricatured, they offer a powerful metaphor for interpreting two of mankind's greatest resources.

'The two hemispheres of our brain don't operate as on/off switches – one powering down as soon as the other starts lighting up. Both halves play a role in nearly everything we do. For instance, the left hemisphere specialises in text, the hemisphere specialises in context. The left analyses the details, the right synthesises the big picture'. Analysis (left) and synthesis (right) are two most fundamental ways of interpreting information. Instinct is driven by the right hemisphere.[*]

As a child I remember being told 'to be logical – solve a puzzle and to be creative – learn to paint'. I am not sure I agree with the absolute polarization anymore. Art needs logic just as much as puzzles need creative thinking. Both halves of the brain play an integrated role.

Our subconscious mind somehow finds links between our new situation and various patterns of our past experiences. We may not recall most of the details of those experiences and even if we did, it may be very hard to express the lessons we learnt in a form acceptable for analytical reasoning. Yet, our subconscious mind still remembers the patterns learnt. It can rapidly project our new circumstances onto those patterns and send us a message of wisdom. That message comes through our inner voice – or sixth sense – and will most likely be expressed in the language of our feelings. For example, 'that feels right', 'there's just something wrong about that', 'I don't sense a great vibe' and so on.

In leadership work, I will often ask clients to cite a list of their high-risk, high-stake decisions. Regardless of nationalities, gender or age, the list is always the same. Investing money, changing jobs and moving countries are all examples of decisions that carry high risk and high uncertainty with the potential for high reward or high failure. Yet recent brain imaging studies show that the higher the level of uncertainty, the more likely it is that instinct, not logic, will rule.

Here is a fact worth exploring. The root for all instinct is survivor instinct.

---

[*] Dan Pink, A Whole New Mind: Why Right-Brainers Will Rule the Future, 2005

Survival instinct – the basis of vital life decisions

The kind of instinct I want to spotlight here is the instinct that informs and, so to speak, powers most of our major life decisions.

This powerful story from my grandfather's life provides a compelling example of how instinct can drive huge life decisions. When the Partition of India happened in 1947, both sets of my grandparents were living in what is now, East Pakistan. The Partition was the largest mass movement in human history. A deeply traumatic event for the masses, it left my grandfather with nothing. He lost both security and stability – a large family estate and a successful law practice, overnight.

One evening, the riots broke out without any notice. It was a dark night and my grandfather received an alert to leave with my grandmother and their seven children through the forest as quickly and as quietly as they could. My grandmother was also pregnant at the time. They took a path that led to a bluff overlooking a tributary river. There was a slender, deserted bridge. On the other side were the Indian Army fortifications. A line of newspapers flapped in a light breeze above a series of bunkers. He peered through binoculars at men peering through binoculars. He said to me; 'They waved. I waved back.'

As the night wore on, my grandfather had a choice to make – he knew of a familiar road that would lead to a refugee camp about an hour away. Going against every grain of logic and rationality, he chose not to. Instead, he took a narrow, winding road to an unlit and unmarked shelter in a derelict nunnery. I often asked him why he chose to reject the known, familiar route to safety. He said, 'Instinct. We could all have been killed. Every hunch in me said I should avoid the rational choice and that there was a safer, more obscure place in store if I charted this other road, which I never had explored.' It was true. They hid through the night until the early hours of the dawn when they started again. They reached the borders of Calcutta the following morning. Fast forward ten years. After a relentless passage of struggle and resilience, he was settled with his family of nine and a secure legal practice again. The refugee camp he avoided? It was destroyed the week after he decided to avoid it. His instinct was his only guide to surviving an impending tragedy, like an animal's awareness of a predator.

Let us ask if my grandfather's life saving choice was one of leadership or of plain survival instinct? It was certainly in no way different from Dr Humer's cross roads analogy of an instinct driven choice point.

Lead researcher Professor Hodgkinson, from the Centre for Organisational Strategy at Leeds University, supports this: **'People usually experience true intuition when they are under severe time pressure or in a situation of information overload or acute danger, where conscious analysis of the situation may be difficult or impossible.'** Indeed, one diver faced with a shark attack saw in his mind an image of a documentary he had previously watched on this very situation. It showed how to punch the shark in the gills. He applied this memory and IT saved his life.

'Another example is a Formula One driver who braked sharply when nearing a hairpin bend; thereby avoiding an unseen pile-up ahead and saving his life. His instincts saved his life, for if he had rounded the corner at a high speed he would have hit a pile-up of cars on the track ahead'.

Professor Hodgkinson explains: **'The driver couldn't explain why he felt he should stop, but the urge was much stronger than his desire to win the race. The driver underwent forensic analysis by psychologists afterwards where he was shown a video to mentally relive the event. In hindsight he realised that the crowd, which would have normally been cheering him on, wasn't looking at him coming up to the bend but was looking the other way in a static, frozen way. That was the cue. He didn't consciously process this, but he knew something was wrong and stopped in time.'***

Here are a few examples of how that rational stimulus marries up with the likelihood or probability of realisation for a final go/no go decision.

The case for instinct: what cars, Starbucks, FedEx and iPads have in common

Many world-changing inventions have resulted from instinct but note the unconscious reasoning behind Cars and Starbucks or FedEx, a hundred years apart in their invention.

Henry Ford once said, 'If I'd asked my customers what they wanted, they'd have said a faster horse'. He followed his instincts and built a car – something that would give them the effect of a faster horse, but in a different form. His customers couldn't have told them they wanted a car, because the vast majority of them would never have seen one.

---

*   Hodgkinson, G.P., Langan-Fox, J. and Sadler-Smith, E. (2008). Intuition: A fundamental bridging construct in the behavioural sciences. British Journal of Psychology, 99, 1–27.

The instinct factor here is based on trusting that you have gained that deeper insight into your customers' wants and needs, even though they can't express those needs and wants as they exist outside their current frame of reference. Innovators need the courage to believe that their new invention will provide them with that new frame of reference. Instinctive leaders must believe in their chosen route and not look for constant external validation.

A hundred years on from Ford, Apple follows its corporate instincts to great effect. They are less interested in giving the market what it says it wants than they are in giving the market what it doesn't yet know it wants. When the market sees what Apple has created, they lap it up, almost without exception. Apple is always prepared to predict what customers will want.

Many now-famous businessmen claim that their initial idea came from an intuitive moment of just sensing a need. Fred Smith, founder of FedEx, intuitively knew his idea would work, even though his college professor gave him a C on the paper he wrote about an overnight delivery service that would guarantee next-day delivery. Howard Schultz, founder of Starbucks, was relaxing at a cafe in Milan when he suddenly knew that Americans would pay $3 for coffee-and-conversation

The great French scientist Louis Pasteur observed: **'In the fields of observation, chance favours only the prepared mind.'** William Shakespeare expressed the same sentiment 250 years earlier in Henry V: **'All things are ready if our minds be so.'** Or early Greek philosopher Heraclitus of Ephesus: **'a hidden connection is stronger than an obvious one.'**

In all these examples, we can see that for instinct to be turned into something valuable and tangible, there is an unconscious reasoning that underlies its inception. Being ready to act on that reasoning, without ignoring it, which is the easier route, is what I call preparedness.

When I asked John Heaps, the chairman of the large international law firm Eversheds, about his promotion from CFO (left-brain domination), he said, what serves him best in his decisions about people and trust is instinct: '[a] hunch sometimes gives me a validation that no resume or testimonial ever can'. Trust a lawyer to trust his instinct.

I'd go even further. **I would say that instinct is the biggest differentiator in leadership quality. I'd even say that to be able to go beyond what you know (knowledge/logic) and what you see (experience) to what is**

unseen and untaught, yet very strongly present and waiting to be tapped, is to create new possibilities and new realities that didn't exist before.

In 2006, I was sitting with the chief executive of an asset management bank in a succession planning review for his management team and was struggling to see how, despite two candidates (let us call them Tim and Brian) presenting equally strong credentials and a strongly comparable track record, he'd been able to choose one candidate over the other.

In the final selection procedure, he chose Tim over Brian. On hearing my baffled 'Why? How did you decide?' (neither candidate was present at the time), he quietly said 'I can't explain it, I just sense Tim is more ready'. Notice his answer to my question is found not in his logical mind but in sensing his instinct.

Amazing leadership instinct can be found in nature too.

Lessons from nature

Nature is an excellent classroom for the study of leadership and survival. It offers us our own MBA in instinct.

One of the aerial delights of changing seasons is seeing migratory birds fly home in a V-shaped formation. When we see migrating flocks of geese, for example, there is always one lead bird which sets the pace for the others. When the lead bird tires, it will move out of the way and retreat into a position behind the tip of the V. Another bird will rapidly move forward and take the lead position to maintain the formation. Aviary research teaches that the lead bird feels no shame in falling behind in the V and neither does the succeeding bird feel any pride in leading the V. It is simply an innate behavioural pattern. The flock multiplies its strength by sharing the lead among all birds, thus conserving energy and extending their range.

The example also demonstrates an instinctive, team instinct. One bird does not lead the flock all the time. Their shared efforts lead them to safety. Shared leadership, just like in contemporary business, when pooled, gives teams a collective expertise they would not have had individually. In short, it gives them energy and synergy.

This suggests it is instinctive in nature to maximise strengths, overcome weaknesses, capitalise on opportunities and minimise threats. What the animal kingdom knows innately is something that contemporary businesses need to learn more; how to value instinct over data.

From the skies down to the forest, seeing a bear approaching, our ancestors would have had to make an instinctive decision: flee or hide, commonly known as the fight or flight instinct. Sea turtles, newly hatched on a beach, automatically navigate back towards the ocean in a return migration to nest at their natal site after a decade of absence; honey bees communicate to a hive the distance and direction of a food source like nectar through dance. Other examples include animal fighting, animal courtship behaviour and internal escape functions. This concept is also called innate behaviour. It demonstrates a natural tendency to know what to do without any experience or guidance.

A leader, too, regardless whether emerging or experienced, is prone to displaying a similar natural tendency and gravitate towards instinct.

Instinct, trust and risk: a trio partnership

If some of you left brain people want me to prove if instinct works, I will. Let us keep it simple. Just think of God, technology and children. These three entities are a feature of all societies.

- **Belief**. Instinct works because we haven't seen God but most of us believe in God.

- **Advancement**. Instinct works because we didn't know Google or Apple would change our world for certain but their creators were highly intuitive people who went with their instinct, despite any guarantee. They leapfrogged technology.

- **Innocence**. Instinct works because children have a strong sixth sense even before they are formally taught, shown or hard wired into how to make sense of things.

Instinct, no wonder is natural. It is in our nature. If you are up for investing in your instinct, you have got to be able to trust it more, for the link between instinct and trust is inseparable. Then, the crucial issue to consider in relation to our instincts is, of course, knowing when to trust them. When can we be confident enough to act on them? Or when do we sense that the risks are just too high?

From the last decade, I picked the top ten decisions I have made based on strong instinct – about people, places, jobs, location, relocation – including writing this book. I then thought of the ten big decisions my mother has made based on her instinct. I then tried analysing any commonality of process across the two. I realised every time we have acted on a hunch, we have also tested and ran that hunch past a circle of trust – friends, family or networks – who knew us closely and knew what we stood for. Regardless of whether everyone supported us or not, the responses we received from them fed into our subconscious and our brain started chunking and living the patterns in to a final yes or no.

If we think of great hunches that have played out, as in some of the examples mentioned, we owe it to ourselves to, at the very least, invest in it enough to check it out. We can't resist trying to work out what the future will bring. We build internal models of the world based both on our experiences and what others tell us and then use these to guess what will happen next, but now we know throughout all this our (rational) subconscious is working away very hard guiding us behind the scenes.

You could compare it to futures trading which has been with us for longer than most people think, dating back to Aristotle's time. Stuart Gulliver expands on this in the chapter on Expression. Trading is based on brain chunking, linking past patterns, and forms the inseparable link between instinct, trust and risk.

In essence, trust is a function of instinct and risk. The first and most obvious correlation here is the direct relationship between risk and trust. The stronger the instinct, the greater the need to trust it.

Here's an example from one of my passions in life – food! Next to my office is the flagship branch of the Carluccio's restaurant chain. I'm often in there and having enjoyed it so much, I was eager to meet Antonio Carluccio OBE, the man who originally started this very successful business and who expanded and changed the UK perception of Italian food from sloppy lasagna and ketchup-ed pizzas to simple tagliatelli and uncreamed risottos. I love this man's obsession for loyalty to his natural ingredients. For Antonio these include wild mushrooms, stinging nettles and crab apples, truffles, strawberries, samphire and crayfish. For me his wild ingredients from nature resonate with my ten innate ingredients that make this book. After spending nine months trying to get a meeting, I finally sat in his restaurant, this time waiting for the big man himself.

Finally he walked in, wearing an ocean blue casual linen shirt and a big smile emanating through a gruff 'Hello, Rhea, am I late?' Then within the first two minutes of our meeting, he pulled out the label of his shirt to show where it was made. Fab India, a well-known organic textile chain. While I wondered at his need to prove this unrelated and seeming irrelevant Indian connection, he said 'I am proud of the Fab India label because I trust that country's love for food. It is fab! That love for food is in their eyes'. As Antonio accurately observes, you eat with your eyes first. In conversation we realized he moved to London the same year I had moved back to India. 1975.

Antonio's own origins are simple. The son of a railway station master, he followed his instinct for food nurtured by a mother, who always made sure there was delicious food even in tough times. Antonio and his siblings often foraged in the hills of Piedmont to hunt mushrooms and wild rocket.

'My cooking principle is simple: it's MOF MOF – minimum of fuss, maximum of flavour. I am a cook, not a chef, Rhea,' he said. 'A cook loves food, a chef learns a trade. A cook simply does that – he cooks, with passion and instinct.'

Just as he said the last word, while enjoying the last of his summer jelly dessert, he called over the waiter and asked for the head chef. A young, nervous man came scurrying upstairs to our table, no doubt expecting the worst. Antonio smiled and told the chef, 'This is a good summer jelly but it's predictable. There's nothing new. How will we ensure we keep driving the customer's instinct of walking into Carluccio's in that split second when he is faced with ten other good choices of restaurants? Now, let your instinct guide you: take a sprig of fresh mint and rub it against some dark chocolate in the jelly. Sometimes follow the recipe, but at all times follow your instinct. Do something different that makes you unique. The customer will always value that and return to your creation.'

A question just popped out of me, 'Antonio, I can see you value instinct but how do you know when to trust it?'

'The eye is the vehicle for trust. You first see trust, then you feel it. People eat with their eyes first. First, they trust the food they see and smell in front of them, after which they decide to put it in their mouth. Let your eyes and life experiences guide you.'

I loved the clarity in his pronouncement and the reminder to use all our senses – simple.

This chimes with my disposition to let your subconscious cues guide your brain into a yes or no. It can recognise a situation or a response as a familiar pattern worthy of trust and can therefore suggest a response even before you know it. Give your subconscious the freedom to try this and over time experience will improve it. Antonio's childhood instinct of finding fresh ingredients and making simple food had led him from Piedmont in Italy to London's Covent Garden. I trust his story implicitly. Antonio is not only an instinctive businessman; he also exudes an aura that triggers his customers' instinctive potential for enjoying the ambience of a great Italian restaurant. No wonder the chain he founded has been so successful.

That day, that conversation activated one of my dormant neurons! Antonio sparked in me the idea of using a food-related challenge in a leadership bootcamp. The Restaurant Challenge is an experiential leadership simulation, which teaches leaders how to trust their instincts in high-stake situations. In 2012, we used the theme of the Olympics opening ceremony and asked a group of 22 international rising stars to create a three-course meal which was unique, instinctive and representative of all the myriad cultures they represent, but the challenge didn't lie just in the cooking! These included people with no cooking experience – some hadn't entered 'that part of the house which has pans and pots' (as said literally by one person). They were given no recipes, minimal ingredients and certainly no instructions. The only given ground rule was to complete this exercise without the use of the head (logic). The results turned out to be phenomenal. Primed by the innate survivor instinct, their subconscious brain guided them to produce a fantastic five-course meal with no casualties the day after. I mean that.

The aim of the programme is to challenge and extend the capabilities of senior managers and leaders for them to realise how to unleash their instincts and not fall into the recipe trap of tried and tested logic alone.

Thank you, Antonio!

Adding instinct to your DNA

The following five action points are designed to help you understand, manage and make the most of your instinct. **Remember that experience and exposure improves your instinct so if you are a young leader embarking on your career, or a mature experienced leader looking back at your career, the more you use instinct and the more contexts in which you use it will improve your chances of trusting that hunch, nudge or gut better.**

1. **Look back at previous successes.** This way, you will be able to see the sequence of moves that have led you to where you are now. Pick three situations where you trusted your instincts – maybe it

was a key business decision, or an important relationship, or even just that time you ignored your GPS and followed your own direction. Whatever your situations were, write the answers to the following questions for each one:

- What were your intuitive triggers?
- What questions did you ask yourself when you made an important snap judgment?
- How long did it take from initial nudge to make your final decision?
- Most importantly, how did that situation ultimately turn out?
- Finally, can you identify a pattern of where instinct manifests itself in your body – pulse, heartbeat – for our bodies never lie to us. They hold a vast reserve of our experiences and signals. You don't have to climb to the top of a mountain or pay thousands of pounds for some weekend seminar to attain that wisdom. All you have to do is listen to what your body is trying to tell you.

You'll be amazed to see how your instinct may have guided you so often in the past without you even knowing so.

2. **Look back at disappointments**. Next, make a list of three situations in which you ignored your instincts. Simply by making these two lists you will immediately double the sharpness of your intuition by becoming more aware of how you reacted to things and why.

3. **Audit your instinctual skills**. Now that you've brainstormed a series of experiences, you'll need to give yourself an overall intuitive evaluation. This isn't meant to be a science but a self guided score on a scale of one to ten. Are you a hopeless two or an aspiring seven? For example, ask yourself: how do you treat your own intuitive promptings. In what areas of your life are you most intuitive? Under what conditions are you most intuitive?

4. **Commit to enjoying moments of stillness and learning from them**. After a year of practising yoga, I've found my instincts to be sharper than ever before. Here's why. The most challenging part is being calm amidst chaos. In stillness, you have control. Stillness gives us a laser sharp focus we see in the chapter on Focus. Ask anyone who indulges in quieting the mind – yoga, music, floating. The highest benefits are found outside the experience. It may be worth your while making the time. How many people who rush around in a constant buzz of frenetic activity are really likely to connect with

their instinct? As Oprah Winfrey would say, **'be still and your inner genius GPS will always guide you to your north star'.**

You can't train your instincts if you're constantly in a whirlwind.

Personally, my biggest weakness until I was in my mid 30s was this: I was always on 'on' mode. There was no 'off' button for me at any point. As an entrepreneur, I have learnt how to 'press mute' every now and then, only to come back even more charged and with a stronger instinct eager to drive more results. Reflection holds hands with intuition. Sometimes that's all your intuition needs – to be nudged out of hiding and onto centre-stage.

5. **Behind every instinct there's a question trying to ask itself**. To step back from life's situations and figure out what the question of the moment is: every time you want to believe your instinct, ask yourself – Why? What is the reward? What could go right that hasn't been fulfilled yet? What do you fear? What could go wrong? What are you depriving yourself of by sticking to the familiar?

Educating instinct in the new generation

As a child, I can't remember attending a formal class on Instinct, or being graded on a subject called Instinct. Can you?

Gen Y, the millennial generation, boys and girls born since the 80s, are just entering the job market. Since they are a bigger cohort than their predecessors (Gen X), their influence on society, politics and business over the next decades will be significant. I have, over the years, addressed business and management students at London Business School or London School of Economics on topics of ambition, leadership or diversity. This generation does ask bold and difficult questions. Sometimes a question from them is harder than one from a chairman or CEO client. Most of these students are incredibly bright, wise and hungry for inspiration. One post graduate student from Brazil even said to me, **'the educational crisis may be bigger than the economic crises. Any thoughts from your world of business?'**

My best response is to kick start this dialogue:

- *Me: 'OK, I hear you. Where does the crisis start?'*
- *Student: 'Internally, a lack of fulfillment. Sometimes I have an unusual sense, like a feeling I can't prove that tells me what I want but I have no one to help me validate it.'*
- *Me: 'So, what is it you want?'*

I noticed three distinct patterns in their responses, regardless of culture or institution.

(1) Happiness – the need to follow my instinct (2) Originality – the need for self-expression and (3) Inclusion – the need to be with and involve others. Interestingly, going back to the happiness versus success dilemma in the chapter on Self, success did not feature as an obvious response. I somehow think that's because they know happiness is key to success, not because success isn't important.

Now I know that modern students are learners, graduating into a world that is much more ambiguous, complex and maverick minded than the one of the past. Our learners will find themselves in what I call an age of instinct and originality. They will have multiple interests and multiple choice points with no single, right or wrong answer during their lifetimes.

There is an interesting paradox here. Why is it so blatantly wrong then that children who are so instinctive by nature are ripped of all instinct in school and then let loose on a world that needs instinct? The cycle feels wrong as an education critic shows us. The answer may lie in the prevailing arguments against extrinsic rewards such as grades and gold stars.

Grades create a preference for the easiest possible task. Impress upon students that what they are doing will count toward their grade, and their response will likely be to avoid taking any unnecessary risks. They'll choose a shorter book or a project on a familiar topic in order to minimize the chance of doing poorly – not because they're 'unmotivated' but because they're rational.*

In his book "Punished by Rewards" (1995), Alfie Kohn maintains that reliance on factors external to the task and to the individual consistently fails to produce any deep and long-lasting commitment to learning.

They need to be equipped to make their own opportunities. They need less intellect and knowledge but more self-reliance, social and cultural capital, appreciation for lifelong learning, creativity, conflict-resolution, team-building skills and ethics. I wonder how educational institutions are training instinct and creating those conditions so that students are most likely to feel that they can be successful?

A client once shared with me a parent-teacher conversation at his five year old's school meeting, 'Ben is a very skilled painter but has no aptitude for

---

* *Punished by Rewards*, Alfie Kohn (1995)

maths or computing. I am worried about Ben'. The point being that Ben's artistic skills are valued a lot less relative to his reasoning skills.

There are many Bens who are getting lost in the crowd because they are not ticking the 'fit for success' boxes and as a result we are not ticking them in the talent list. I want us, leaders and teachers in the broadest sense, to be coaches and facilitators and to help build instincts in children, people and businesses. **Teams are like children, too. In exploring the linkages between the child and the leader, I know business adults, like children, when made to feel important will do amazing things if they feel their contributions are adding value. It is a myth that incompetence is the only cause of poor performance.** Often leaders don't give instinctive nods and nudges in the moment to direct a dormant performer's energy in a positive way. For leaders, unlocking people's dormant instinct is the most worthwhile job. What title can we give that job – Head of Instinct Incubator?

In my life and work, I fully endorse this philosophy. A leader's responsibility as a coach at work is no different to a parent's responsibility as a coach for his children. The tools one learns at work sometimes have a bigger place at home in developing young minds that can be tomorrow's leaders. All this is not spelt out anywhere but it is all within us, in our very instinct to nurture, survive and succeed.

The Parable of the Eagle

At this point let me offer this parable to you. It appears in many sources but I like this version by a missionary, James Aggrey from 1920.

Once upon a time, while walking through the forest, a certain man found a young eagle. He took it home and put it in his barnyard where it soon learned to eat chicken feed and to behave as chickens behave.

One day, a naturalist who was passing by inquired of the owner why it was that an eagle, the king of all birds, should be confined to live in the barnyard with the chickens.

'Since I have given it chicken feed and trained it to be a chicken, it has never learned to fly.' replied the owner. 'It behaves as chickens behave, so it is no longer an eagle.'

'Still,' insisted the naturalist, 'it has the heart of an eagle and can surely be taught to fly.' After talking it over, the two men agreed to find out whether this was possible. Gently, the naturalist took the eagle in his arms and said,

'You belong to the sky and not to the earth. Stretch forth your wings and fly.'

The eagle, however, was confused; he did not know who he was, and seeing the chickens eating their feed, he jumped down to be with them again.

Undismayed, the naturalist took the eagle, on the following day, up on the roof of the house and urged him again, 'You are an eagle. Stretch forth your wings and fly.' But the eagle was afraid of his unknown self and world and jumped down once more for the chicken feed.

On the third day, the naturalist rose early and took the eagle out of the barnyard to a high mountain. There, he held the king of birds high above him and encouraged him again, saying, 'You are an eagle. You belong to the sky as well as the earth. Stretch forth your wings now and fly.'

The eagle looked around, back toward the barnyard and up to the sky. Still he did not fly.

Then the naturalist lifted him straight toward the sun and it happened that the eagle began to tremble and slowly he stretched his wings. At last, with a triumphant cry, he soared away into the heavens.

It may be that the eagle still remembers the chickens with nostalgia; it may even be that he occasionally revisits the barnyard. But as far as anyone knows, he has never returned to lead the life of a chicken. He was an eagle even though he had been kept and tamed as a chicken. Just like the eagle, people who have learned to think of themselves as something they aren't can re-decide in favor of their real potential. They can become winners.

The single biggest lesson is this: **Don't forget you are an eagle no matter what your circumstances. Every instinct that tells you can soar high is a nudge for you to do something different and strengthen your leadership blend.**

If you could be a genius...

So, readers, my strong plea is let us rethink education, leadership and inspiration through instinct and originality. Try this exercise I do with students. I tell students to suspend judgment for five minutes. Then take a flipchart and write down **'If you could be a rockstar, a healer, genius, athlete, painter, storyteller, hero, entrepreneur and leader, what would you do?'** Before you finish writing the statement, students start scribbling like crazy. I repeat the same exercise with teams, young managers to senior executives. They start scribbling like crazy too. Regardless of age or stage, the inner child never dies and always stays intuitive.

I then tell them, that last five minutes was the right brain activating the innate instinct of the genius within you.

Back to John Lennon, the legendary Beatles.

Imagine – being a genius.

Your code for Ingredient Five: Instinct

Pause. Ask yourself what you remember from this chapter; list the key takeaways and ideas that had an impact on you – something inspiring, something relevant or something you would like to try.

Now, make a note of the following: the term 'things' below can refer to behaviour actions, conversations, skills or even an attitude

1. List three things you would like to START doing to strengthen your INSTINCTS...

2. List three things you would like to STOP doing to strengthen your INSTINCTS...

3. List three things you would like to CONTINUE doing to strengthen your INSTINCTS...

On an ascending scale of 1 to 10, how robust is this ingredient in your DNA?

Ingredient Six

CREATIVITY

——'I imagine'——

Creativity and Instincts are like chopsticks; one is redundant without the other. Together they can feed and nurture our souls.

CH$_6$

Much has been written about creativity, so how about I present an eclectic mix of examples from the Beatles, to Frankenstein, whisky, Eton, Bollywood and the light bulb to tease out the power of this innate raw ingredient we all possess in abundance but are often unaware of?

Creating the future

The future of the world will depend on the activity of entrepreneurs who create opportunity, businesses, jobs, new rules, new behaviours and a new way of leading. The essence of entrepreneurship is 'creative disruption' – tearing up the old to make way for the new.

An ingredient of pure delight

This chapter is about one of the most delightful and exciting ingredients in your DNA. Whatever current use you are making of this ingredient, it is almost certain that you could use it more and that the more you use creativity, the more fulfilled you are likely to be – and probably more successful too.

Yes, this chapter is about creativity, but also creativity's seedbed – the imagination. We will focus on:

- the power of dreams in sparking creativity;
- creative impulse and spontaneity;
- how imagination starts inside the mind but can develop as a muscle;
- the different types of creativity;
- how there is a creative entrepreneur in all of us;
- mental blocks to creativity;
- traits of creative leaders;
- the point where creativity becomes real innovation

'When we use the term "creativity", different images come to our mind. There are bright persons who express unusual thoughts, who are interesting and stimulating. Unless they also contribute something of permanent significance, these people must be called brilliant rather than creative. Then there are people who experience the world in novel and original ways. These are individuals whose perceptions are fresh, whose judgments are insightful, who may make important discoveries. Such people personally are creative. Finally, there are individuals who change our culture in some important respect. They are the creative ones without qualifications.' Mihaly Csikszentmihalyi, Flow.

Creativity is at the heart of most human achievement. Being creative is also thought to be good for us: there is anecdotal evidence that the satisfaction derived from being creative is one of the deepest satisfactions in life and that it gives us a happiness and psychological well-being that can build up our immune systems and even help us live longer. Pablo Picasso, the world-famous painter who could draw before he could talk, was convinced that being creative would stave off death. In the event he lived to be 92, so maybe he was on to something.

Being creative is good for the soul for many reasons; not least because it helps us to recapture, as adults, the delight of play that we first experienced as children. Indeed, in 1946 Picasso, then 75, acknowledged this in a remark he made when he visited an exhibition of children's paintings. He said, 'When I was the age of these children I could draw like Raphael; it took me many years to learn to draw like these children.'

Picasso's feeling that there is an instinctive creativeness about children and how they see the world is something I'm sure we've all noticed. Don't children so often say extraordinarily witty and perceptive things, even given their linguistic limitations? **Evolution has made children so creative that it is difficult not to feel that this creativity is hard-wired into our own biological DNA. Unfortunately, children then confront life which teaches them in many cases that conformity is safer than creativity and this is why – sadly – so many people give up being creative from their teenage years onwards and never recapture it.**

Picasso had no doubt that when he was being creative, he was not only recapturing the inherent childhood creativity within himself, but was also walking hand-in-hand with his own personal perception of who, or what, God might be. He once said, 'God is really only another artist. He invented the giraffe, the elephant and the cat. He has no real style. He just goes on inventing things.' (Source : Life with Picasso)

Certainly, whatever faith we might have, none of us could doubt that we inhabit a world which contains an inherent and profligate creativity that is truly mind-blowing. New species are still being discovered almost every week. The planet itself is wondrously rife with life. As for human artistic genius, it is endless. What about human technical ingenuity? Think about it: everything we have made for our world – cities, cars, aeroplanes, houses, televisions, computers and the millions of different manufactured items we use in our lives – have been created from the rough, unrefined materials we found on the surface of the earth or dug down to discover. What a remarkable species we are, for all our faults! How right Shakespeare was when he gave Hamlet the following observations:

'What a piece of work is a man! How noble in reason! How infinite in faculty! In form, in moving, how express and admirable!'

Admittedly, not many of us will necessarily quite feel like that when we get up first thing on Monday morning, but let us acknowledge the infinite potential we have is unquestioned. Yes, our sense of wonder at ourselves, like our creative instinct, is something we need, as adults, to make an effort to keep in touch with. The daily demands of life can so easily make us lose sight of how unique we are and risk losing an infinitely precious creative part of ourselves.

We frequently imagine that creativity is something one is either born with or not and that if one isn't then there is nothing one can do to acquire it. Even our understanding of the very nature of creativity is weak; we frequently compartmentalise creativity being the forte of only artists or inventors. Now, that's a flawed assumption.

Three social experiments

Try these three simple social experiments that I often use as warm-ups in our leadership programmes to explore creativity:

1. Look up at the night sky and its stars. If we do this for some time, we often start to see patterns or shapes emerging. You may see a giraffe, I may see a reindeer. Or a geometrical shape. Or a number eight. Or something else, utterly random. The point is we will all see different patterns looking at the same sky. We will create our own patterns or realities. **I call this type of creativity 'pattern making' or 'sense making'.**

2. Take a metaphorical dive from that night sky straight into a boat on a stormy sea. Imagine that the boat has capsized and that you, along with a few fellow survivors, have managed to hit a barren island. Obviously you want to survive and be rescued but you can't see anything around you at first glance that could help you build a rescue plan. As you keep thinking harder and harder, your eyes, guided by your brain under crises, spot all sorts of raw material that could help you create a base – like a raft or a floating device – crude as it may be, that will get you back to shore. It is also true that the raft will be stronger and more well thought through than anything you may have created before

following scientifically perfect instructions. Wonder why? Your ability to think outside the box and create and define your own instructions under severe crises is often near flawless as we saw in the third chapter on Instinct I call this type of creativity **crisis-induced lateral thinking.** Our creative juices flow exponentially under crises.

3. Finally, imagine you have a sibling with whom you share similar talent and abilities. Your parents are entrepreneurs who would like you to try your hand at something completely new. You are each given a month to come up with a new business idea. Your sibling chooses to retreat to his room and work on the idea in great depth, with plenty of analysis and research but keeping it a secret and not sharing with anyone. You instead choose to venture out, speak to ten other friends, visit a few other start-ups in the neighbourhood, ask lots of questions, sample the idea and seek feedback before you develop it. Who do you think will have a better idea? We could argue either of you could win, but the one that would have sparked several other dormant neurons into action would be you! That's because collaboration infects others to be creative. I call this **networked creativity or collective intelligence.**

Imagination: from the mind to the muscle

While musing on this chapter in a restaurant, my attention was arrested by a young waiter named Ross who, despite his young age, carried a real energy and confidence about him, connecting with customers. He really 'had the floor', as we say. I struck up a conversation with him and he asked me what I was writing about before commenting, 'At the age of 11, out of the blue, I created a cookbook for my school friends. I was an only child and as an only child I had a lot of time to myself, so my mind was my best friend. I didn't know I would be in the restaurant business but maybe my subconscious was telling me something'.

The message here is simple and not different from what teachers and professors have taught us – if you really climb inside your mind and explore its contents, with curiosity and without judgment, you will find a treasure of creative intelligence that can unlock your path to success.

The more we work the mind, the stronger the muscle of creativity develops – organically.

Given I was in Scotland at the time of writing about this natural ingredient, Phil decided to take to me to the heart of Scottishness – to find out more about that favourite 'water of life' or the 'liquid gold' people across cultures and generations savour. Yes, I'm talking about whisky! Curiosity laden, I visited a distillery in the hills above Pitlochry in the southern Highlands of Scotland. Beautifully situated by the river Tay, Edradour Distillery is the smallest in Scotland. Old Jim was our guide.

Although this book looks at ten raw ingredients being blended to produce your unique leadership blend, whisky needs just two: water and barley. That's all it is and together they create one of the world's golden liquids. I am sure Leonardo da Vinci, whether or not he drank whisky, would endorse this with his saying **'Simplicity is the ultimate sophistication.'**

Whisky's inception was a creative accident too. Originally used as an anaesthetic and antibiotic by pharmacists and monks and since wine was not easily available in Scotland or Ireland between 100–1300, barley beer was distilled into liquor by the monks and became...whisky!

At the distillery, we entered a cold and musty room, dark with a few hundred old beaten brown casks or whisky barrels. Everything was hand-made and reminded me of the machines used in the tanneries my father engaged with to process leather from raw hide to finished goods. The dirt, the smell and the rawness of the material being blended would all come together to produce a beautiful end product. The distillery reminded me of that innate craftsmanship, the expert touch and the watchful eye. There is something magical about handcrafting whisky without any automation, using craftsmans hip handed down through generations. A magical fortune, too, as Jim, our host, slipped in the value of that old, cold store room – in double-digit million pounds! Who would have thought so? But isn't that often the way? Real potential or opportunity can be overlooked under the dark rocks and musty boulders strewn in life's way. These hidden containers do not look inviting but all we need to do is lift the damp, gritty, mossy rocks – or in this case, open the cask – to be pleasantly rewarded in so many ways. Remember the old man's box of gold in the opening chapter?

Who are the people shaping and blending these ingredients into the final product? Well, I learnt, it is still a human process in which the master blender (much like a leadership coach) takes the youngest malt (akin to a rising high potential in a business), once he senses whether or not it is ready or mature enough and then works out which older malt he will need to add to sharpen the young malt further. It is an innately human art that technology will never be able to replace. In this example, whisky has a unique parallel with the leadership blending process in this book.

The blender or coach's skill is in finding the nuances that identify the unique blend that he is looking for to put in a unique cask to mature in 5–12 years' time. As a leadership coach, that in principle is identical to how in businesses my firm and I seek to blend rising stars, managers and directors (e.g. by adding some focus here, reducing the dark side there, sharpening the instinct) in a 'development cask' for 18–36 months to mature as a 'ready-to-be-tasted' (read tested) leader. According to some, professional master blenders need to have an exceptionally good sense of smell (remember the sniff in the Instinct chapter) and exceptional blending skills (coaching skills) in order to correctly assess the readiness and qualities of each single malt and choose the malts that will eventually be used to sharpen the blend. Because every blend, like yours, is unique.

The final creation should bring out the unique taste and character of each single malt within the blend. How does one create that optimal blend? To blend a world-class scotch whisky, master blenders may sometimes have to taste over 100 different samples a day to find the perfect leader composition. Spot the parallel here! Whoever said finding the perfect leader was a quick and easy task is wrong. Sometimes businesses have to experience (taste) hundreds of potential candidates before finding the right leader; sometimes businesses select under-prepared or even the wrong leaders in haste, which costs fortunes in cost, quality and reputation. **A good blend put in the wrong cask, or a rough blend put in a very expensive cask, can leave a bad taste on the palate and a bad return on investment.**

Blenders are extremely secretive about their blending methods. We, too, sometimes have to keep our cards close to our chest at CorporateDNA and while that may hint of elitism, it is more than humbly and adequately balanced by the value, depth and quality of our blending programmes.

To close on whisky, Thomas ('Tommy') Dewar (1864–1930), the famous Scottish distiller behind the internationally famous Dewar's brand, once said, 'The mind is like a parachute: it only functions when it's open.' I think I know what he meant when I did my skydive. I would extend that to say the mind is most creative when it is open to dreams, possibilities and opportunities – without any boundaries.

The mind is a hot house for creativity. Why am I giving you these examples? Simply to show you magical creations get produced through simple raw ingredients and if we are alert to this, it only takes a discerning eye to spot and seize the opportunity. 'The art of blending whisky is like the work of a composer: not only do you need to completely understand the musical characteristics of every instrument, but you must also understand how to combine them to build an unforgettable, spellbinding symphony.'*

Like the master blender of whisky and the master coach in sports and business, our DNA needs mentors and coaches to accelerate many dormant neurons into action.

That entire process all starts with Imagination.

What is imagination?

Ability and education are not important components of creativity. In fact, sometimes too much knowledge can crush creativity by imposing rigid rules. The most important factors are dreaming and imagination (vision), both of which are intuitive rather than learned skills.

Dreaming and imagination give leaders the ability to provide direction to their employees and helps them create a company where people want to work. It allows parents to instill a vision in their children so that they in turn can dream. When we read about human history, we find it presented from a variety of perspectives. We hear about humans as explorers, politicians, warriors, inventors, artists and so on, but we seldom hear about humans as dreamers. Yet so many of the significant advances of civilisation have been inspired by individuals who simply had a dream. I could give you grand examples. Instead I will give you one humbling experience which maybe tiny in significance but grand in its human appeal.

In December 2011, I was visiting Fatehpur Sikri in India, the old capital of the grand Mughal Empire, which had been abandoned in 1597. The beautiful architectures in Fatehpur Sikri reflect the fusion of the religions in its mosques, temples and courtyard palaces. I walked through the deserted but magnificent estate of Emperor Akbar and the fortified palace he built for his three wives – a Hindu, a Muslim and a Christian.

After two hours, I walked out into the narrow side streets to return to the car and saw a disabled young man. He was sitting, humming gently, with the most childlike, blissful smile. I stopped, drawn to his smile, and noticed he was holding small key rings. When I stooped for a closer look, I saw each one was a calendar made of thin, cheap brass no more than an inch

---

* Colin John Scott, a master blender of Chivas Brothers, interview by Shanghai Star, 2000.

in diameter. The calendars were not for the upcoming twelve months, though, but for the next forty years! I was astonished to see each round brass dial told you the date, day, month and leap years by simply rotating a small thimble in the middle. They were so intricate and creative. I was fascinated to know the source. He began by explaining how in a bad road accident, he actually lost his legs and spent two years distraught and gripped with fear only to realise that such a state of mind would lead to nothing.

As a child, clocks had fascinated him and suddenly he had nothing other than time on his hands so he let his imagination run wild until he created these small miracles. He now sells them for fifty rupees – less than £1. Imagination and creativity doesn't always need massive budgets and enabling machinery; sometimes it just needs the mind to be given the freedom to explore possibilities. While it may be unfortunate that the financial value placed on his creative invention is small, that's not the point. The point is our minds breed creativity in abundance if we allow it to take form and be expressed – no matter what the circumstances.

One could say his dire necessity became his trigger for invention. That's partially true. More specifically, I'd say we all have an innate imagination, a seedbed, waiting to be nurtured, explored and developed. If only we believed in that and used that muscle, we'd all be a lot more inventive than we give ourselves credit.

Creativity comes in many forms and types

My point is that creativity is not just about bringing forth an epic invention, creating a masterpiece, writing an immortal novel or poem, composing a symphony or directing a superb movie.

There are other kinds of vitally important creativity that are more everyday and not even physically visible. For example, helping people to make the most of their potential within the corporate environment can be extremely creative. Starting a new business, thinking an out-of-the-box solution, helping someone or even making a latent connection for good benefit .

When I took the giant step of starting my own business, it felt like – still feels like, in fact – the most momentous thing I've ever done. Fear of failure sparked a creative ambition like never before. The creative ambition to plunge into running my own business was massively creative, both by choice and chance. The business relationships I foster today and the new approaches to the work we do, I'd say push and stretch my creative limits everyday. It is like an edge I thrive on. My creative impulse is leading to more spontaneous connections in other fields like art, media and philanthropy and it all seems to come together in a grand way of expanding my universe. I have often wondered why nurturing this kind of spontaneity while juggling risk and restraints is proving so worthwhile? It is maybe that, as an entrepreneur, I instinctively have to think for myself, instinctively appraise and reward myself (there is no boss), instinctively network, instinctively keep several balls in the air at once. See how the creativity and instinct 'chopsticks' work together? You are the founder of the business and you are the business.

Yet in a consulting services business, your offering can sound like someone else's. Words like leadership, talent and succession are used, overused and even abused every day. I would describe my creative instinct as starting with a blank sheet of paper and first throwing out all the known definitions and rules of the game. Along with that, I also relinquished my need for comfort, familiarity and certainty. There is a lot of letting go before you can embrace letting in new ways of being. People tend to find letting go very hard. It is a fear of the unknown. To penetrate the market, I then had to take my creative approach and rewrite the rules and redefine my own mindset to create a proposition that not only looked and sounded fresh but was bold and believable enough to stand out. Only that would create a whole new pie rather than fight for another slice of the old pie. An innovative menu to stimulate a fresh appetite for clients who want something new over old, familiar competitors.

Remember that many entrepreneurs take great pride in their start-up business and some even refer to the business as if it were their baby. It is likely that, just as a parent would want to mask his/her child's shortcomings to strangers, entrepreneurs would be reluctant to admit the deficiencies of their business to third parties. I was no different. I soon learned that making mistakes is a very positive part of the creative engine. The more mistakes you make, the more creative ideas you generate because every trial and error becomes a learning cycle of experimentation and discovery and a new threshold for winning. Every day is now a creative one for me.

'The critical thing is getting off your butt and doing something. It is as simple as that. A lot of people have ideas, but there are few who decide to do something about them now. Not tomorrow. Not next week. But today. The true entrepreneur is a doer, not a dreamer.'*

---

* Nolan Bushnell, founder of Atari and Chuck E. Cheese's.

What would it be like to have the creative genius of Walt Disney?

Today, Disney as a brand generates billions from an experience – from merchandise, movies and theme parks around the world. But did you know that Walt Disney himself had a bit of a rough start? He was fired by a newspaper editor because 'he lacked imagination and had no good ideas'. After that, Disney started a number of businesses that didn't last too long and ended with bankruptcy and failure. He kept plugging away, however, and eventually found a recipe for success . The magic of his success lies in the 'imagineering' (imagination + engineering) process.

What is the imagineering process? Robert Dilts, one of the early developers of NLP, whom I had the great joy of meeting, has modelled the genius of Walt Disney using NLP and developed a process that we can all use whenever we need to create something of value. Whether you are writing a book, solving a business problem or expressing yourself artistically, moving through Dilts' imagineering process allows you to call upon your creative powers and progress from vision to implementation.

At CorporateDNA, we often use the Disney imagineering process in our leadership workshops to help people connect with their own dreams and creativity and with the organisation's creative vision. Dilts pointed out in his book, Strategies of Genius, Volume I, that Walt Disney used a specific strategy to create his movies, amusement parks and business plans and to realise his Disney empire.

As Dilts explained, the genius behind Disney's ability to take an idea and turn it into reality developed as he honed his ability to explore an idea from three different perceptual positions. He had three of them:

1. Dreamer – 'what' new ideas or dreams to generate;
2. Realist – 'how' to make the idea happen;
3. Critic – 'why' would the idea work or not work.

Disney fully associated with each perceptual position and stayed in it until the idea was formed enough to move to the next position in the process. To anchor these perceptual positions, Disney created three rooms, which he and his staff used to work through ideas.

- **In the dreamer room, Disney and his staff came up with ideas and solutions.** These ideas were focused on solving current problems and creating innovative products – nothing was off limits and while the staff were in this room, no one was allowed to critically evaluate the ideas that were being created. By allowing ideas to be dreamed and expressed without challenge, Disney avoided inhibitions and the stunting of ideas. This room was home only to possibility, hope, vision and the future. The focus was on **what** (what to create, what to do, what to have). Disney and his staff looked from top down and saw the whole picture, the thousand foot view. Then they verbalised, outlined and drew out the basic blueprint of their idea.

- **Next, Disney would move into the realist room. Here, Disney was focused on action and felt out the idea.** He became the idea, the story, the character, the solution. It was assumed in the realist position that the idea created in the dreamer room could be done – it was just a matter of working out how to make it happen. If the team was working on a new rollercoaster, like Space Mountain, they imagined what it would feel like to be sitting in the ride as it raced around each winding turn, slowly climbed each steep incline and rapidly dropped down each descent. They noticed how the seat and the straps felt on their bodies. They heard the sounds of the rollercoaster and saw the lights flashing as they coursed through the whole ride in their minds. The realist filled in the blanks of the original idea created by the dreamer by writing the steps to make it happen for real.

- **Finally, Disney would move into the critic room. Here the focus was on why (why do it this way? why do it at all?).** Logic was used to find the holes in the plan. Disney looked at the plan from an external audience perception. He called this his second look. The goal of the critic was to examine the idea or plan (not the person who created the idea or plan). In this room, the idea, plan or project was fine-tuned. If a question arose that required a creative solution, the whole team walked back to the dreamer room to solve the problem with a creative idea. When Disney was in the role of critic, he wanted to determine whether this new idea or plan was better than the current way of achieving the goal. The critic helped work out whether the idea was worth using, or whether more work needed to be done.

Try the imagineering what-how-why process on something new (a dream, a project, a problem) and see if it helps you unlock your creativity, but remember to follow the dreamer–realist–critic process in linear sequence and in true form.

I remember the first time I walked around and went on the rides in the Magic Kingdom and sensing this energy – not in these 'imagineering' words of course. Behind the scenes, I could just feel the creative dreaming that went into making his magic – the dream, the detail, the layout, the context, everything!!

Dreams: creativity is often hidden in the subconscious

There are many who would challenge the implicit assumption that leaders can develop creativity. They would argue that creative people are born, not made. Indeed, much of the anecdotal literature about creativity would suggest that it is some rare gift that only a chosen few possess.

I have often studied the after-the-event trends surrounding well-known examples of great leaps of creative thought including the mental processes that led to them. If you really reconstruct the chain, we can conclude that creativity arises naturally and comprehensively from the everyday abilities of perception, understanding, logic, memory and thinking styles. There is no secret magic, even though it feels as though there is. The beauty of this is it not only feels good but has the added bonus that it is perfectly attainable by any one of us who applies the described principles.

'Scrambled eggs...all my troubles seemed so far away.' No, this is not me lamenting over the wrong choice at breakfast. Scrambled Eggs was the working title for one of the most covered songs in the history of recorded music. Paul McCartney, one of the greatest songwriters and singers of our day, composed Yesterday – performed over 7 million times in the 20th century – in a dream:

> **I woke up with a lovely tune in my head. I thought, 'That's great, I wonder what that is?' There was an upright piano next to me, to the right of the bed by the window. I got out of bed, sat at the piano, found G, found F sharp minor 7th – and that leads you through then to B to E minor and finally back to E. It all leads forward logically. I liked the melody a lot, but because I'd dreamed it, I couldn't believe I'd written it. I thought, 'No, I've never written anything like this before.' But I had the tune, which was the most magic thing!***

---

* Quoted in *Dream Encounters: Seeing Your Destiny from God's Perspectives* – Barbie L Breathitt.

Back to Sir George Martin CBE, the legendary Beatles man, who we met in Instincts and who worked on the score and produced Yesterday. He describes Yesterday beautifully – 'it is the pure simplicity that is the genius of the song. This captures the very essence of the song – if it was more elaborate it would cease to exist as we know it'. This is necessary confirmation for all of us in the form of very, very simple writing, that couldn't be anything else; if it were it would destroy what the point of the song is, which is utter simplicity. **We do sometimes overcook things and I think this is one of the best examples of how less can be more.**

Sir George self-deprecatingly ventured that it was possible that he hadn't been 'over-educated in music' so that he had a kind of naivety as well. There is something appealing about naivety – something of a seasoning quality to my ten leadership ingredients. It takes me back to Picasso's quote about children and what I mean about unlearning to relearn. **Most of us are fortunate enough to look fondly on our childhood. Well, indeed it is true that many of our attributes from those formative years are worth keeping and using in adulthood. Don't always be too keen to grow up! Naivety lets you ask the probing question, seek out the simple solution and appraise an issue with objectivity. Never let a question go unasked.**

In my work I try to be conscious of how an audience will see my messages. Sir George adapts this to the medium of sound as he says, 'recording is not what one hears, but what one must make others hear'. I had always felt this, but had never attempted to put it into words or heard it articulated so well. Rather than creating a perfect professional presentation, I have now learnt to pause and ask myself what does the client really want to see, hear, believe or feel – a presentation? A story? A picture? Maybe, just a conversation. What exactly am I trying to show them? It always pays to start with not what I see but what I want my clients to see. The creative form then automatically starts taking form. Of course, the 'what' is where Walt Disney starts from.

This is also no difference from Michelangelo's maxim, 'Every block of stone has a statue inside it and it is the task of the sculptor to discover it.' Michelangelo was given a block of damaged marble 19 feet tall and three years later he unveiled his 17-foot tall 'The David', which was then transported from his studio behind the cathedral to the Palazzo Vecchio, Florence, a process which took 40 men five days to complete and included tearing down archways and widening streets to make way for the colossal work.

The gemstone of simplicity that George sees in Yesterday struck a similar chord with the simplicity of ingredients and dreaming in making whisky and producing Disney.

Talking about simplicity, there is one such man, from the world of Bollywood, who has been simply following the creative Disney/ Imagineering code, without even knowing so, to revolutionize Indian cinema into a creative and international commercial success. Yash Chopra.

Yash Raj Chopra – the legend of Bollywood

In December 2009, I had the privilege of stepping into the much talked about world of glamour, dreams and sensation – Bollywood, the mega billion dollar Indian film industry. I was keen not to experience it as a star-struck fan but instead pick one protagonist who has blended mainstream Indian sentiment with an evocative international appeal. Someone who combined tradition with innovation.

After Hollywood, the second largest film industry of the world has contributed many talents. Very few of the Bollywood film makers, however, have enjoyed long term consistency in their creative endeavours and even fewer have managed to create an 'organization' or a corporation that has become an integral part of the entertainment business in India. This is where Yash Chopra's leadership story lies.

I met with Yash Chopra (or Yash-ji), one of the first directors who took great creative risk to redefine films and film making. Born in 1932, in a village in Punjab, his life started with humble, middle class roots. The son of an accountant in Northern India, who worked hard to make the longest career span in the film industry and realised great national and international acclaim, winning no fewer than 22 awards and honours worldwide.

He has directed and/or produced over 70 films since 1960 and his creative instinct and risk taking lies at the heart of his success. He was hell bent on making films which were decades ahead of his time because he believed the Indian society, going through radical reforms post-Independence, needed strong unconventional messages. Albeit uncomfortable for viewers to fathom, he sparked many social, economic and cultural revolutions. He wanted to re-shape India's DNA. He fought from the inside to make the Indian psyche – its system and its way of thinking – a better one.

He was also the first to take his camera to countries such as Switzerland, Holland, Germany and the United Kingdom. This has often led to a direct increase in visitors to those countries and governments have not been shy in taking note. The Swiss Government has honoured him for helping rediscover Switzerland. In addition to France's highest civilian honour, the Legion of Honour, he is the first Indian to be honored at BAFTA in 59-year history of the academy.

The only film maker who has created his own multi million USD globalised market, among the overseas Indian/NRI – Non Resident Indian-audience (diasporas). I met Yash(fame); Raj(reign) in his 20 acres sprawling studio – his name itself is a legacy, a league of its own in the Indian entertainment industry for the last five decades.

I walked into Yash-ji's colossal glass office and saw a man behind the desk of unassuming stature, grace and rare warmth as he said, 'Rhea, welcome in'.

Very soon we were locked into a very deep conversation, taking its own course. He emphasised time and again, 'Our generation, we are emotional fools..... We take from life and life takes from us. I am not a logical person, not a business man. I live my life on my emotions and act on my instincts. I don't "do" films, I live, eat and breathe films.'

Something offset the wealth and immaculateness of the office. It was this refreshing paradox. I was struck by the simplicity and creative impulse in Yash-ji's character. He offered to share his lunch with me; a simple stainless steel Tiffin box (resonating in my mind with the dabbawallahs in the Focus chapter) of 'home cooked roti and paneer', in true Indian finger aided style, I listened to his leadership story across the last five decades. The more I heard, the more I gleaned principles and values that could be just as relevant back in the corporate world.

- Don't forget your origins. It adds resolve and humility to you character. It helps you define better where you want to go next. It struck me later how small the world is and how much more closer the human spirit is aligned across cultures than we ever think when I heard almost these exact same words from the lips of Stuart Gulliver, HSBC Group CEO, in the chapter on Expression.
- You are only as good or as bad as your last success or failure. As a leader you can never rest on your laurels.
- Your test as a leader comes not when you are struggling but after you have become very successful. Success is very hard to digest. The second test is when you face conflict. The temptation to go into alleys/diversions and act on lapses of judgement is not only high but

irresistible. Resisting that fatal temptation is what makes a good leader.

- As a leader, if you want to change the system, fight it from the inside. Be in it to make it a different one. Don't drive from the back seat or the outside.

- People these days are 'scared to feel' because of the fear of getting hurt. One should never control the urge to feel. Instead, let these feelings come and express themselves. The key is not to act or to decide on all these feelings. The small decision is more important than the big one.

- You can't know or decide if you are a leader or not. People decide if you are. This is why you must ensure decisions and actions are in your followers' best interest.

- Love is the only evergreen constant after rain, snow and the green grass. So allow yourself to love and be loved. Start with loving the purpose you give to your life.

Even after seven decades, his vitality and creativity remain undiminished and a new Yash Chopra or YRF film continues to remain the most anticipated event in the film calendar of India. To many Indians, a Yash Chopra movie has been their passport to a world outside the one they inhabit.

That is the leader and this is his leadership story.

Lessons from Eton College

The question of how to educate leaders has long exercised the minds of philosophers, educationists and policy-makers, as well as those of some leaders themselves. Both Plato and Aristotle had famous, even if not altogether successful, attempts at educating leaders, notably Dionysus II of Syracuse and Alexander the Great of Macedonia respectively. Machiavelli's attempt to educate the younger Lorenzo de Medici also springs to mind. Today it is no different. We all know how the education of future leaders preoccupies most of the world's governments and business schools. It is the subject of innumerable policies, schools and executive development programmes and sustains armies of advsiors, consultants, executive trainers and coaches

But returning to England at the age of 26, I was someone curious to explore the British institution, *the public school*, in its recent form which evolved in the 18th and 19th centuries as the breeding ground for political and military leaders.

A chance meeting took me to one such iconic public school. Eton College. For all its controversy and attraction, one thing I believe Eton teaches is creativity and imagination. The school was founded in 1440 by King Henry VI, whose dream was to build boys of good character, competent at reading, Latin and music. The scholars were to be housed, clothed, fed and educated for free. Throughout nearly five and a half centuries, the college has never closed, despite wars, floods and fires. There are now over 1,000 fee-paying boys who live in 24 houses in the care of housemasters. The pupils arrive at Eton at the age of thirteen and remain there for five years. If you follow their progress after Eton, many of them take up leadership positions of significance. That sparked in me a curiosity about who is behind, or rather inside this institution: who is Tony Little, the Headmaster who leads it today? Tony was at Eton during the 1960s, but he doesn't look or sound like an Old Etonian. **With his refreshing wit, his Harry Potter specs and sociable, unassuming manner, Tony relishes the point that the students learn as much outside the class as inside and from their peers as much as their teachers. He is clear that nurturing imagination and a creative instinct is key to building leadership instinct in children:**

> **Firstly, imagination helps growing minds solve problems by allowing them to think through different ways to deal with different, or difficult, situations. Secondly, imagination allows the young brain to practise real-life skills for the real world. Thirdly, an imaginative instinct instils a rich vocabulary by expressing yourself, your ideas and existing concepts in new ways.**

Adults who were imaginative children often become problem-solvers, innovators and creative thinkers.

For example, in Eton, concerts will be held at the same time as exams – because it teaches pupils, in later life, how to deal with more than one issue at a time and make choices between two equally attractive options. Furthermore, theatrical plays have no prompters, no safety nets, no chance to start over – you have to jump in and pick up as you go. The college's new Greek theatre places the actor in the middle. Just as in life, we, the actors, are centre stage. There is nowhere to hide and nobody to feed us our lines. Going back to my leadership 'stage and script' theme right from the first chapter, this bodes really well.

As I observed the boys at Eton, I realised imagination and creativity are also essential ingredients in ambiguity. In Tony's words, **'Students are in a class with people they don't naturally all get on with, but they cannot opt out of it. They need to be creative in building pathways in connecting with these people who are different from us. "Different-ness" and "Difference" are treasured at Eton for stretching the boundaries of one's mind. "Learning to get on with people you don't like" brings children back to earth. It helps them create, invent, stretch new ways of forging connections. Again, this groundwork for life prepares children for the fact that they will not always be able to work with the people they naturally prefer.'**

The lessons and examples in Eton come fast and furious. It is something I have always felt that education and learning are not exclusively classroom based or confined to childhood, but a 24/7, life-long process that is integral to our very being. Again it reminded me of what my grandfather said about how we never stop going to school. The more we understand that we can learn with almost every breath we take and from everything and everyone around us, the more open and fertile we can become. This is yet another of the many reasons I decided to leave the golden key ring on the cover open, because our learning is never complete and open minds open more possibilities. This reaches beyond the usual concept of a time and place for education and in turn reaches out to other aspects of our development.

Which brings us back to leadership. The UK as a media or nation can sometimes be obsessed by 'bad leadership'. What you focus on is what you get. My question is, what stops us from developing our equally strong positive obsession about 'good leadership'?

Finally, for creativity to be nurtured, Tony shared with me how the mindset of assessment versus achievement is a discerning difference – a very necessary one. 'In schools and universities, most of us are trained to develop an assessment mindset (getting the answers right, getting all of them right and getting them before anyone else gets them) which further instills an ethos of fear of making mistakes, risk aversion and lack of lateral thinking'. This resonates with Alife Kohn's point on adverse effects of test scores and grades, as we saw in the Instinct chapter.

Achievement, on the other hand, is about accomplishment. The quality, depth and a sense of uniqueness in how you achieve what you achieve is part of an organic cycle which nurtures curiosity which, in turn, instills creativity. It helps us be different while being integrated to the world, as we read in the chapter on Self.

You can be highly assessed on your knowledge, but it is what you do with what you know. How you integrate and how you perfect the blend of your ingredients.

The power of dreams

Let me share three examples of creative inventions to prove how important dreams can be:

1. In the summer of 1816, 19-year-old Mary Wollstonecraft Godwin and her lover, the poet Percy Shelley (whom she married later that year), visited the poet Lord Byron at his villa beside Lake Geneva in Switzerland. Stormy weather frequently forced them indoors, where they and Byron's other guests sometimes read from a volume of ghost stories. One evening, Byron challenged his guests to each write one themselves.

   Mary Shelley's story, inspired by a dream, became Frankenstein.

2. Jack Nicklaus nicknamed 'The Golden Bear', is the American professional golfer who, winning a total of 18 career major championships, is widely regarded as the most accomplished golf player of all time. But Jack found a new way to hold his golf club in a dream, which he credits to improving his golf game. In 1964, Nicklaus was having a bad slump and routinely shooting in the high 70s. After suddenly regaining top scores, he reported: 'Wednesday night I had a dream and it was about my golf swing. I was hitting them pretty good in the dream and all at once I realised I wasn't holding the club the way I've actually been holding it lately. I've been having trouble collapsing my right arm, taking the club head away from the ball, but I was doing it perfectly in my sleep. So when I came to the course yesterday morning, I tried it the way I did in my dream and it worked. I shot a 68 yesterday and a 65 today.'*

3. Elias Howe invented an advanced form of the sewing machine in 1845. He had the idea of a machine with a needle which would pierce a piece of cloth, but he couldn't figure out exactly how it would work. He first tried using a needle that was pointed at both ends, with an eye in the middle, but it was a failure. Then, it seems,

---

* Jack Nicklaus, as told to a San Francisco Chronicle reporter, 27 June 1964

one night he dreamed he was taken prisoner by a primitive tribe. They were dancing around him with spears. As he saw them move around him, he noticed that their spears all had holes near their tips.

When he woke up, he realised that the dream had brought the solution to his problem. By locating a hole at the tip of the needle, the thread could be caught after it went through cloth thus making his machine operable. He changed his design to incorporate the dream idea and found it worked!*

Here we see creative impulse is a gift. These famous dreams are just a small sample of those that have been recorded. There are hundreds of examples of famous creativity, ideas and discoveries that have been induced by, or materialised from, dreams and the dreaming subconscious. Untold numbers of great writers, poets, musicians, scientists, philosophers and entrepreneurs have had amazing dreams of this type throughout history.

Most of these dreamers follow a common theme: while dreaming, their mind continues to expand or work on a problem or thought through dreams, very often in a much more creative and inspirational manner than they could have achieved while awake.

Spontaneous and emotional creativity comes from the amygdala (which we covered in the Emotion chapter). The amygdala is the region of the brain where basic emotions are processed. When the conscious brain and the pre-frontal cortex are resting, it is possible for spontaneous ideas and creations to emerge. This is the kind of creativity that you think of when you recall great artists and musicians. Often these kind of spontaneous and emotional creative moments are powerful and can be compared to an epiphany, or a life changing experience. There is no specific knowledge necessary (it is not cognitive) for this type of creativity, but there is often skill (writing, artistic, musical) needed to create something from the spontaneous and emotional creative idea.

When you sleep your mind does not turn off. Quite the contrary, your mind continues to work out solutions to real-world life and work problems, tapping into your innate creativity and problem solving skills to do so.

The old adage 'to sleep on it' when faced with a problem is very true. Your sub-conscious is often a very powerful problem-solving and inspirational tool.

---

* A Popular History of American Invention, (Waldemar Kaempffert, ed.) Vol II, New York, Scribner's Sons, 1924

Enough about dreams. What about translating dreams to reality?

The creative process

At CorporateDNA, we often train people on what we call the 'moving from idea to implementation cycle' because I see a trend where ideas freely occur but rarely get implemented. Why? They can be generated in abundance because when you ask someone if they have an idea, the answer is most often, yes. People love being asked and to contribute. It gives them a sense of purpose and self-worth. I believe, especially after watching some of the more inspiring communicators in the last decade of leaders, our ability to express is at the core of the importance of creativity. As humans, we have a very strong need to express ourselves and we are happiest when other people understand what we are trying to get across to them. Indeed, the first stage is our ability to express, which is at the core of the importance of creativity – an idea that is not meaningfully communicated soon passes its expiry date. The second stage is a period of incubation, during which ideas dance around at a sub-conscious level. This is when unconventional connections are likely to be made. The third stage is insight, when the pieces of the puzzle fall together.

The fourth stage is evaluation, in this case, deciding whether the insight is valuable and worth pursuing. This is often the most emotionally trying part of the process, when one feels most uncertain and insecure. This is where, as previously seen, instinct is invaluable. Is this idea really new, or has it surfaced in another guise? Is this an innovation worthy of implementation?

Three types of creative thinking

For me, there are simply three kinds of innovation:

1. **Invention** – this is about creating something new from scratch, something from nothing: this is rarer than you might imagine.

   For example, Thomas Edison, the inventor of the electric light bulb, was a deliberate and cognitive creator. He ran experiment after experiment before he would come up with an invention. In addition to the light bulb, Thomas Edison also invented the phonograph and the motion picture camera. One of his famous quotes is: 'I have not failed. I've just found 10,000 ways that won't work.'

   Deliberate and cognitive creativity comes from the pre-frontal cortex (PFC) in your brain. The PFC allows you to do two things: pay focused attention; make connections among information that you have stored in other parts of your brain.

In order for deliberate, cognitive creativity to occur, you need to already have a fair amount of knowledge, appetite or curiosity about a topic.

2. **Adaptation and/or reapplication** – taking something that already exists and modifying or reapplying it in a new light with new meaning. For example, let us take the ever-popular concept of going to the cinema. In 2011, amidst a voice-and-colour world, the Oscar for best film went to the black and white, silent movie The Artist, the first such winner since 1929.

'I am the happiest director in the world,' Michael Hazanavicius, the film's director said, thanking the crew and cast, including the film's canine star, Uggie. 'I also want to thank the financier, the crazy person who put money in the movie.' So why did this film win? In this age of high-tech digital, special sound effects and superstar actors, why did the Academy pick this simple story told in a seemingly bare-bones fashion by a director and crew we had never heard of? The film reminds us of the power of the moving image and the depth of human emotions. In an age of cynicism, confusion and doubt, it is a fresh, sweet and heartfelt film, beautifully acted, that gives us something to believe in. In a time of incessant chatter, The Artist forces us into silence and reflection. Is it a brand new invention? No. But it is a creative adaptation from a bygone era to the modern world inspiring a whole new way of thinking and believing in today's motion picture medium.

3. **Synthesis** – taking two different items or concepts and combining them.

A synthesizer creates a new object by restructuring the known. This type finds useful combinations and congruencies to produce reconstructions. People often create new ideas by combining two existing ideas and synthesising them into a third.

Connections occur when you consider a number of ideas together, recognise what is common (or not) and bring them together. The internet is a great example of synthesis: it evolved by bringing together computers and telephone networks.

Adaptation and synthesis are especially important types of creativity in organisational life where complex power and group, dynamics are at constant play. In particular, being able to take commonly used and understood ideas and recombine them in elegant new ways is particularly valuable. Revitalising a stagnant team to a new direction is another example.

So when does creativity become innovation?

Trust me there is a difference! **Creativity is thinking up new things; innovation is doing new things.** In other words, it is no use sitting around dreaming up fantastic ideas unless you're prepared to do the hard work and make things happen, or least, see that others follow through the implementation!

Theodore Levitt expands on this theme in an entertaining tirade in the Harvard Business Review*:

> **'Creativity' is not the miraculous road to business growth and affluence that is so abundantly claimed these days ... we tend to confuse the getting of ideas with their implementation – that is, confuse creativity in the abstract with practical innovation.**

So for Levitt:

Creativity = Ideas

but

Innovation = Ideas + Action

Levitt highlights another important distinction between creativity and innovation:

> **the ideas are often judged more by their novelty than by their potential usefulness, either to consumers or to the company.**

So:

Creativity = Novelty

but

Innovation = Novelty + Value

---

* 'Creativity Is Not Enough', *Harvard Business Review*, 1963.

Levitt's article was written almost 50 years ago, but we still distinguish between creativity and innovation on the grounds of ideas and action, novelty and value:

> **Often, in common parlance, the words creativity and innovation are used interchangeably. They shouldn't be, because while creativity implies coming up with ideas, 'it is the bringing ideas to life' . . . that makes innovation the distinct undertaking it is.***

Let me take a moment to recreate your probable perception of a certain creative company, so to speak. One that, at face value, we think we know very well, what its main purpose and function is. Let us see.

What an iconic British fashion brand teaches us

What enters your mind when I say Burberry? The iconic trench coats? The live-streamed runway shows? Well, it has been rated the 4th fastest growing brand and 13th most innovative company in the world. Angela Ahrendts, the CEO, who we met when talking with Stacey Cartwright on the focus ingredient, epitomises fashion, but has innovation at her core. As Stacey says she is 'her alter ego' and it is not hard to see how they and Christopher Bailey, CCO (Chief Creative Officer) have made Burberry what it is today.

There is as much pride and emphasis placed on the back office as on the front office. Seamless connectivity and efficiency are to the fore. The creative concepts are stunning and the innovation brings them to life. Holographic models appear on screen with their live counterparts, then evaporate in the staged shows. In a sense they are proactively reactive in what one might call an organic digital ethos. Communication is all and its speed and reach is breathtakingly exponential. The external LED screens on the side of the new store in Beijing's Sparkle Row Plaza, opened in 2011, are the biggest in the world after those at the Yankee Stadium in New York. One of the many destinations for the live streaming of their events. As impressive as the technology and, of course, the fashion design is, Angela and Christopher constantly seek the perfect balance between the creative and the commercial. They seem to have the hang of it as this perfect poise and equilibrium between the two seems to pervade the whole company.

---

* Tony Davilla, Marc J. Epstein and Robert Shelton. *Making Innovation Work: How to Manage It, Measure It and Profit from It*. Prentice Hall: 2005.

An endearing quality to Angela is her inclusiveness. It is all about the team, not her, as she often expresses. She has, however, led a truly remarkable rejuvenation at the 156 year old company founded by Thomas Burberry in Basingstoke, England in 1856 and the smile on her face and the twinkle in her eye tells you there is much more to come. Innovation truly is a creed at Burberry that touches everything it does. No question is left unasked.

Interestingly, corporate events have come full circle in Burberry's relative recent history. It was independent up until 1955 when it was acquired by Great Universal Stores. GUS, as it became known, divested Burberry in 2005 and Sir John Peace, its last CEO, became chairman of a once again, independent Burberry. Sir John, now also chairman of Standard Chartered Bank, is a consummate board director and leader in his own right.

Creativity is a mindset

While writing this book, a rare opportunity came up which took me back to India in unusual circumstances. In 2008, I was a finalist for the Women of the Future Awards pioneered by Pinky Lilani OBE, a social activist in the UK. Pinky's own story is truly inspiring. When she moved to Britain from India 30 years ago, her husband was disappointed that his new bride could not cook. Today, she is a pioneer and the founder of several Women of Achievement awards – as well as a self-taught culinary guru.

In 2009, the British High Commission, along with Cherie Blair and guided by Pinky, invited 19 of us from various ward categories in the UK to experience the highs and lows of human existence in a country which is the epitome of scale, contradiction and entrepreneurialism. The country, of course, was India. The city was Mumbai.

Mumbai has the single largest concentration of dollar millionaires outside the US, living alongside slums where people survive on less than $1 a day. This is against the backdrop of the nation's whopping 1.2 billion population, of which 70% is under 30. Every year, Mumbai receives 500,000 migrants over and above its indigenous population. We drove to meet India's largest private bank led by star CEO Chanda Kocchar. Joined in 1984 as a management trainee, today Chanda is an exemplary executor in my opinion. She loves keeping things simple while pursuing radical ideas to help her bank succeed. Her simplicity and grace sat comfortably with her success. She has consistently figured in Fortune's list of Most Powerful Women in Business since 2005. In 2009, she debuted at number 20 in the

Forbes 'World's 100 Most Powerful Women list' and climbed to the 10th spot in 2010. In 2011, she featured in Business Today's list of the Most Powerful Women – Hall of Fame. In 2011, she also featured in the The 50 Most Influential People in Global Finance List of Bloomberg Markets. Inspiration was in abundance.

As we took the hydraulic glass lifts to the boardroom, through the pristine glass façade I could see we were towering above a vast expanse of land – Dharavi. If I looked down, I could see the dust and clutter of this shanty town; if I looked up, I could see a mahogany boardroom replete with state-of-the-art facilities symbolic of ICICI's success. It was the most amazing symbolic juxtaposition of people with hope-and-hard-work, looking up to people they aspire to become. Contrary to many, I saw the positive message of inspiration as most of ICICI's catering and cleaning network comes from Dharavi.

Day 2 took us to Dharavi itself. Walking into the slum from Mahim Link Road, the dreadful poverty almost slapped you in the face. Ramshackle buildings, made of a mélange of found materials and corrugated tin, line unpaved passageways. Sewage runs through the alleys, collecting in puddles alongside playing children. There is only one public toilet per approximately 1,500 residents and most families have neither the means nor the space to have a private bathroom.

But at second glance, the slum is more intriguing and much more inspiring in ways that could spark our own creative DNA. Despite the low education levels, substandard housing and intense overcrowding, Dharavi is an entrepreneurial hotspot. Valued at $720 million in 2009, it has its own tannery, pottery, markets and a recycling industry called the 'green lung' of Mumbai. But the biggest revelation was yet to come. Most of this transformation has been taken on by the women and the 300 slum dwellers which again is 30% of the overall 1.2m population. A woman bathing her toddler son in water she's pumped herself while shouting orders to her neighbouring female colleague on the packaging shipment due for delivery is a natural way of fitting it all in and the work–life balance women in some other countries find so hard to strike. One million people drive a one billion USD production industry which offers 85% employment with everything being produced cheaply but in seriously high volumes. Dharavi, without any planning, resourcing or organising is doing in two years what some may say, it took England 200 years to produce in financial and production worth. Yet there is virtually zero crime and women walk back home at midnight – safely.

Dharavi is a mecca for recycling. If a product can be reused, someone is probably recycling it there. The Guardian reports that in all, Dharavi has an estimated 5,000 businesses and 15,000 single-room factories that produce somewhere between $700 million and $1 billion a year in revenue. As these businesses continue to expand, Dharavi has become a community linked and supported by entrepreneurship. The local businesses are providing small but significant income improvements to tens of thousands of families. As I ventured through its many lanes and into the houses with my peer group, electricity, running water and televisions are now available to an increasing number of households.

But where do the majority of the increased incomes go? According to our tour guide, most families use the money to pay for private school education for their kids. Often illiterate parents are making an investment in the future and local entrepreneurs are developing schools that far surpass the quality of local public education.

Dharavi is already a symbol of change in this generation and the power of entrepreneurship offers great hope for the next.

Ten traits of creative leaders: creativity has to become a habit first

Given the chapter itself, I have a creative need to spell out the traits of creativity in a creative form! How about:

Curiosity is the starting point, then by

Removing self limiting blocks

Entrepreneurs being restless people, always

Ask questions like – Why? Why not? or, How?

Tenacity to persevere, making

Instinct your best friend to help

Visualise a 'what – if'

Imagine then the idea becoming a reality and by

Taking the risks to think it through, soon.....

Your creativity becomes a habit

Closing inspiration from our ancestors

Remember that creativity comes in many guises. It is not a gift for the privileged few. From big, world-changing inventions to a new dance step, adding a new ingredient to an old recipe or even rewriting a story to give it new meaning, we can all do it and help others be creative.

Creativity helped our forebears build civilisations, discover language and create everything that makes the modern world such an amazing place to be. And as I always say, our forebears didn't need consultants and business schools to teach them how to be creative. They simply tapped into the power of this potent raw ingredient within and made the most of it.

How close are you now to Creativity – do you feel an irresistible nudge to set free that instinct within and let your creative habit form?

Your code for Ingredient Six: Creativity

Pause. Ask yourself what do you remember from this chapter; list the key takeaways and ideas that had an impact on you – something inspiring, something relevant or something you would like to try.

Now, make a note of the following: the term 'things' below can refer to behaviour actions, conversations, skills or even an attitude

1. List three things you would like to START doing to strengthen your CREATIVITY...

2. List three things you would like to STOP doing to strengthen your CREATIVITY...

3. List three things you would like to CONTINUE doing to strengthen your CREATIVITY...

On an ascending scale of 1 to 10, how robust is this ingredient in your DNA?

Ingredient Seven

DARK SIDE

—'I slip'—

*Darkness always leads to light. A weakness
can most often be traced back to a strength.*

What is the dark side? Two definitions

Let us be clear about what we mean by the dark side in this book. In everyday life, it usually refers to extreme types of human behaviour. Most people see the dark side in all of us as a form of sinister extremity – something selfish, sociably unacceptable, potentially destructive. For the purpose of this book, however, **I see the dark side as an overdone strength which tips over to become a weakness.**

The Dark Side of the Moon

The year I was born, 1973, saw the release of one of the greatest albums of the 20th century. *The Dark Side of the Moon* is the eighth studio album by English progressive rock band Pink Floyd and became the third best-selling album of all time. The Dark Side of the Moon's themes include human weaknesses through conflict, greed and mental deterioration.

What does that have to do with leadership? For me, it is about moving between two sides: light and dark, between strengths and weaknesses. We move from one side to the other all the time and it is this constant journey, this passage between the two, that is the central factor of this ingredient. Think of the moon. We think we see the moon in its entirety, but it keeps its darker side away from us. It shines so brightly, yet the far side of the moon is referred to as the dark side of the moon, simply because we never see it. Yet there is actually no permanently dark side of the moon. Literally half of the moon is in light and in continuous rotation. This fits with our definition in this chapter. **We all highlight the parts of our personalities that we want others to see and hide the parts we feel are less attractive.**

To continue the lunar metaphor, the dark side is always perceived as cold, evil and strange, yet it is always on a rotation. These very inadequacies can rotate back into strong attributes when exposed to light. Take self-belief, for example, which can swing between bright shades of confidence to dark shades of arrogance or inflated self worth as we explore further in the chapter on Fear. Emotions are another example which can rotate between bright shades of positive energy and dark ones of manipulation and sabotage. **Like the moon, we have both sides that we rotate between, so the opportunity and challenge lies in our awareness of these two sides, the connection we make between them and in controlling the speed and intensity of the rotation, from one side to the other.**

The album cover itself is also worth a moment's reflection. It shows a black backdrop with a prism emanating a spectrum of light. It is unique. It shows neither the band's name nor the album's title and yet it is one of the most effective artworks ever created, but which way is the direction of travel? Are we looking from the outside in or the inside out?

In my view, the symbol could be a metaphor for life and leadership itself. We travel from darkness to light when we are born. Plunging into adulthood, we can be blinded by our own ambitions or other people's expectations and sooner or later our dark side emerges. Another interpretation, simply, is, that dark is not all bad. Passing through it is essential to discover light.

The questions I want to address in this chapter are:

- what the dark side is;
- how strengths, overdone or badly done, tip over to a weakness;
- how to recognise and manage your own dark side;
- how you can best manage other people's dark sides.

Leadership and the dark side

For the vast majority of the time, leadership is a bright, shining concept in management. It is laden with hope, belief, excitement and energy and is constructive by nature – it makes great things happen, but now and again, it slips a bit and its dark side shows. That dark side involves fear, doubt, anger, hatred, insecurity, anxiety and mistrust. The dark is usually what we run or hide from, but this chapter will hopefully illuminate how the dark side can be an asset, once we understand its nature in practice.

You may have heard of the phrase, 'too much of a good thing...' or 'the brightest light casts the darkest shadow'. Well, intriguingly, sometimes the sun is too strong and can blind us into darkness. To be a leader, excessive strength can be too strong and blind into a weakness. This is the main point in this chapter – within a strength can lie a weakness, but equally through weakness we may be able to discover a hidden strength.

One executive – we'll call him Pierre – had recently joined his company's sponsorship committee for the Olympics in 2012 when I met him. He had been the head of events for a large conglomerate before this role. With a great track record, he soon became a role model for many others in the business. Full of ideas he was also a great executor and was soon put on several other committees with top executive visibility. Soon we heard people saying, 'Pierre is a bit too forceful'. While he was recruited for his experience, he never stopped vocally projecting this experience. On one occasion, for example, this dynamic played out in his very loud opinions over the company's proposed marketing budgets for other charity sponsorships, which in effect was beyond his remit. In one meeting with the main board, the CEO expressed his disagreement for Pierre's views and Pierre took this as a lack of appreciation for his track record and left the meeting, in a storm, before it finished. By taking his forcefulness to an extreme (in staunch defence of his position), he flipped over to negative. This is an example of the cost of overdoing a strength. **His assertiveness, valued at the start, then became an entrenched defence of his position – in other words his bright assertiveness tipped over to dark aggression.**

Once you overplay a strength, you're at risk of reduced capacity on the opposite end of that scale. Let us imagine a leader's ability to get things done on a continuum with two end points; one being engaging others in decisions while the other is timely decisiveness. For example, a leader who is good at getting people involved in decisions and has been encouraged to build on that strength, may not realise that sometimes engaging too much or too many others prevents traction and getting things done. Among the senior managers we work with, those who overdo engaging, consensus-building leadership in some respects also under-do timeliness and decisiveness. **Unfortunately, few leaders recognise when they are overdoing a strength, thus causing it to swing to the polar opposite – the weakness end of the scale. Any extremity is bad.** One, being too consensual and never reaching a conclusion, the other being too hasty and assertive thereby alienating colleagues. **It is about finding that balance which we later introduce as the golden point, or just the right amount.**

It is not hard to see why overdoing a strength can get you into trouble and that to find some balance you also have to come to terms with the roots of your behaviour. Pierre, for instance, had always viewed his strength in a positive light; he was making himself heard, being direct. What's not to like? To be fair, such qualities are strengths – to a point. Pierre was shocked to discover that people found him overly aggressive because he wasn't catching himself overplaying that strength.

However, stepping back to normality was reassuringly easy for Pierre. Through feedback from his peers and targeted coaching he discovered that despite the negative feedback, the business still held his contributions in high esteem. Understanding that he already had their respect helped him recalibrate the degree of forcefulness as he no longer felt he had to keep proving and projecting himself.

Eclipse

Eclipse is the final track of Pink Floyd's *Dark Side of the Moon*. The final words sung by Roger Walters on the song and, indeed the album, tells the listener that '…everything under the sun is in tune, but the sun is eclipsed by the moon'. This term *eclipse* is a relevant concept for the dark side in this book. Walters explained the meaning of these words as well as the entire song by asserting:

> **I don't see it as a riddle. The album uses the sun and the moon as symbols; the light and the dark; the good and the bad; the life force as opposed to the death force. I think it is a very simple statement saying that all the good things life can offer are there for us to grasp, but that the influence of some dark force in our natures prevents us from seizing them. The song addresses the listener and says that if you, the listener, are affected by that force and if that force is a worry to you, well I feel exactly the same too. The line 'I'll see you on the dark side of the moon' is me speaking to the listener, saying, 'I know you have these bad feelings and impulses because I do too and one of the ways I can make direct contact with you is to share with you the fact that I feel bad sometimes.**

The point is well made. We all have dark sides. We hide or suppress them so as not to feel exposed or isolated. Sometimes we don't even know what our dark side is. Sometimes the term *shadow* replaces dark side. According to Carl Jung, the shadow is that part of the personality one chooses not to see or show. Not even acknowledged by the conscious mind, the shadow can run wild when we are under pressure or threat. It is as if an unidentified dark side within us is eclipsing our bright side throwing off a rogue shadow that, unknown to us, adversely affects our personality and actions. This is why finding and neutralising our dark side can be so transformative.

As people climb the management or leadership ladder and become exposed to pressures, rising expectations and growing responsibilities, the strengths they've relied on thus far could eclipse into liabilities. When we listen to the daily news or read the exposés of leaders who rose to the heights only to subsequently slip from success, that's often

what has happened – their dark side has eclipsed an original strength, exaggerating it into a weakness.

As with Pierre's over-egged passion, which had to be recalibrated to ensure it didn't tip over into forcefulness. Let us explore this in detail.

Recognising your dark side

Less is more.

According to recent management wisdom, you should maximise on your strengths rather than focus solely on your weaknesses. The chances are that you'll be more successful playing to your strengths than you will be at trying to fix every weakness. It is a realistic approach that emerged as a response to a previous unhealthy fixation on weaknesses in human nature. However, my point is this: while maximising your strengths, watch you don't go too far. In other words, excessive maximising of strengths is dangerous.

In February 2009, Robert Kaplan cited in a short *Harvard Business Review* article, the value of understanding your strengths – and not just because it is hard to overcome weaknesses.

The article referenced a brilliant media executive who considered himself unexceptional. Although he grasped complex concepts more quickly than most people, he didn't realise his tendency to outpace and outsmart others – so he was impatient with colleagues who, in his view, couldn't keep up. Only with some pointed feedback did he see that he was sidelining his colleagues. In other words, he had unknowingly compromised his quick-wittedness by taking it to excess thereby losing the opportunity to bring his colleagues with him and leverage the power of the many good ideas in the room.

This is a common problem. Most managers can point to a leader who is slightly out of kilter—the supportive boss who cuts people a little too much slack, for instance, or the gifted finance director whose relentless focus on results leads to hyper control. But it is extremely difficult to see the triggering of the dark side in your own self.

That's where, with recent leadership programmes, I realised tools such as personality assessments or pure strengths-based profiles are incomplete unless there's a mix of the bright and dark sides. **Polarising qualities simply into strengths and weaknesses implicitly ignores those halfway scary strengths which are overdone. An assessment based on strengths alone overlooks a key lesson from decades of research on derailment: more is not always better.**

The poet John Keats had a perspective on the dark side and one way of understanding this was his view that there are many shades of darkness. There is much benefit to be gained in knowing which shade to go for in the middle – neither too light nor too dark. Let us refer to this as the 'golden point' we mentioned earlier.

Pairings of bright and dark sides

The simplest way to understand this ingredient is to take a strength and scale it to a positive and negative extreme. For example, the positive attribute of confidence has a dark side attribute, arrogance. There are a vast number of such pairs. To take just a few examples:

- artistic/eccentric
- loving/obsessive
- ambitious/ruthless
- enthusiastic/overwhelming
- introverted/shy
- extroverted/loud

and so on.

Clearly, the difference between the two attributes that form part of the pair lies not in their essential nature but rather in where they lie on the linear diagram of the dark side – my point around the golden spot.

We are comfortable with someone being artistic; we are less so with someone being eccentric. We are moved by seeing and knowing love, but obsessiveness makes us uneasy and wary and so on. In fact, the way the human psyche works, changes from the positive side of the pairing to the dark side can happen almost instantaneously: an ambitious manager, for example, can become ruthless in his quest to scale the corporate ladder. In each case, we are less comfortable with the 'dark side' attribute because we recognise its potential to attract criticism and for upsetting social balance. In addition, there is no preset timeline to gauge when we are entering the dark side. Being aware of it and alert to its remedies is everything. So let us see how we can achieve this.

The golden point

The golden point, as I have already alluded to and as you might expect, is all about just the right amount of strength – but not necessarily bang in the middle. It all depends on context. There was a time when a colleague of mine in the UK was posted to Japan. He had a good sense of his own worth, but within six months, he was being perceived as arrogant in his new cultural context. On investigation, we realised it wasn't that he *became* arrogant but in a culture of reserve, the way he demonstrated confidence needed to change – in other words, he needed to turn down the projected self esteem a notch or two. When I went to Japan myself a year later on an assignment, remembering my colleague's lesson, I turned it down too much to avoid being misjudged and ended up hesitating to make any major decision for fear of upsetting the Japanese team. The lesson is simple. **It is just as harmful to under-do a leadership strength as it is to over do it. The advice is to recalibrate the golden point based on context. It is often either the midpoint, or just near midpoint.**

I say, acknowledge when you overuse your strengths. It is not always easy to do this of course and most of us have a blind spot in this regard. It is almost as if your dark side doesn't want you to find it, because once uncovered, it will be identified and removed. Every CEO I engaged with acknowledged, as leaders, we have a choice to hide behind the shiny façade,or peel off our layers for longer term good.

My own dark side ... over the last three decades.

Let us say recognising my dark side took me longer to grasp.

As a child growing up in India, my dark side was trapped in an apparent strength. I was driven by a passion for doing things independently. As a single child around thirty-one first cousins, this desire to compete and prove myself was strong. I was told by teachers and family to watch this tendency; little did I realise this would be a useful lesson for later.

A decade later, in fact. In my twenties, in PricewaterhouseCoopers, my primary role and motivation came from generating sales, building relations and delivering client work. As I had an international client portfolio, this meant I travelled a lot. One year I overshot my sales target by 40%. I did that fairly independently and in an area which was fairly new to the firm. At the end of the year, I was in for both a surprise and a bit of a shock. The former was being put on the fast track to directorship while the latter came in the guise of a 360 feedback session, where I learned that others saw me as being too independent and that I ran the risk of being detached. It was a wake-up call for me.

Another decade on. Now in my late thirties and running my own business, I have built a great team of talented individuals. It seems my dark side now is to find the golden middle between leading the team and being led by them. As a natural creative-extrovert, I love leading our vision for CorporateDNA and sparking new ideas, but after six years, I seem to equally enjoy sitting on the sidelines watching the team run the show. I have a real introverted colleague in my team. Initially his long pauses between answers made me impatient but I am now drawn to how his mind works in coming up with the quality ideas rich in reflection.

With the world's dominant mode being extroverted, I am turning my attention to stop polarizing the world into these two camps. Instead, with my personal example and those of many others, I have evidence that we all of combine a bit of both, the continuum of which can differ vastly. For example, what can we learn from the likes of Bill Gates, Mark Zuckerberg, Abraham Lincoln, Michael Jackson, Gandhi or Steven Spielberg? They are not introverts entirely. They have a bit of both with perhaps a stronger touch of introvertism in their DNA. Knowing how and when best to channel your energy outwards or inwards is key.

I have realised my dominant personality trait is creative and extroverted and my golden spot will be to find that optimum balance between leading and being led. Mihaly Csikszentmihalyi, based on his book *The Creative Personality* (1996): **'Creative people tend to be both extroverted and introverted. We're usually one or the other, either preferring to be in the thick of crowds or sitting on the sidelines and observing the passing show.'**

He adds, **'In fact, in current psychological research, extroversion and introversion are considered the most stable personality traits that differentiate people from each other and that can be reliably measured. Creative individuals, on the other hand, seem to exhibit both traits simultaneously.'**

Managing your dark side

Redirect your strengths

It is often true that the stronger your preference for one leadership style, the stronger your distaste for its opposite.

Most leaders lean one way or another. If you are ready to embrace a new mind-set and reset your golden spot, you merely need to stop overdoing a given attribute and underdoing its opposite number. That is, of course, a lot harder than it sounds. The good news is that leaders can sometimes reapply their strengths to recover their balance. That's what we saw with

Pierre: his innate resolve eclipsed from virtue to vice (light to dark) and back to virtue (light). Once he accepted that others saw him as overly aggressive, he changed his behaviour through sheer will, boosted by the awareness he had his colleagues' respect.

Let us take Jenny, another executive I've worked with, as an example. She was a general manager at an insurance company. One of the few women at senior management level, she had a great track record of success and was known to be a caring people person. While being consensus-driven, Jenny almost had too strong a preference for securing buy-in and going around endless rounds of discussions which eventually tested her team's patience. Beyond a certain point, people sometimes just wanted her to step in and decide.

While striving for harmony and alignment, Jenny was lopsided on the consensuses/decisiveness duality. She was a star when it came to strategy and engagement, but that was undermined by her inability to make quick decisions and start executing. However with feedback, she curbed her urge to always target 100% consensus and settled for 75%. Immediately, her meetings became much more productive – and the 25% who didn't agree didn't mind because at least their views had been considered. As she said herself, 'I feel relieved with this new balance. It feels like less effort'.

Although it was uncomfortable, she also made herself become tougher on people who were falling short in their delivery of performance.

The Dark Side is not evil *per se* – it leads to light

As noted above, light can emerge from darkness. One of the first things I ask my new clients to do is write down three of their key strengths and three of their flaws in a table. Typically, what I get back often resembles this:

Strengths	Flaws
attention to detail	lack of delegation
analytical focus	lack of creativity
drive for results	poor people management skills

I then ask clients to look carefully at what they have written. Often, they look at the paper and then at me, asking me to explain. Rarely do they see the connection at first glance. The fact, as you may now have gathered, is that our flaws are often the mirror image of our strengths and we now know and see that over-developing our strengths can turn them into flaws.

Excessive attention to detail means one doesn't then have the capacity to delegate enough. Too much analytic focus means the right brain creativity is being curbed. Finally, an exaggerated drive for results means you may compromise interpersonal relationships for the task.

The golden spot is about the optimal point in any scale, for example, you need to be sure that confidence doesn't border on arrogance, humorous wit doesn't slide into sarcasm and diligence doesn't become perfectionism. We all know of leaders who have fallen into the strengths/weaknesses trap. Having been praised and rewarded for demonstrating particular strengths throughout their careers, they become blind to the shadow sides of these strengths. Often, research shows blindspots can derail a career in senior leadership roles by 33%.

It is important to note that a dark side is not irredeemable. My advice to all my coaches is to pause before attaching a stigma to a dark side and labelling it as a weakness in its own right. Instead, what is powerful is to look at the dark side and trace back the original strength hidden somewhere therein. Thus you can start to resolve your dark side from a position of strength, rather than feel that you have to recover from a weakness.

I have noticed this trait in a reduced degree in exceptionally bright children. For example, in a family with thirty-one first cousins, I can now think of many in their teens who had a strong positive self belief, yet suffered from social detachment and became too independent. It is because they can expect a lot more quality and content from their social relationships and often get disappointed. With appropriate guidance, though, they can regain a balanced poise quite quickly and realise not everyone has to be bright to be good or be liked.

To the reader, I present a Gen Y emerging leader with whom I have enjoyed many 'dark side' conversations with. An avid fan of getting the balance right, his name is Supratik Baralay and he is the only son of a long-term client of mine who came to the UK at the age of six. An impressive student at school, with the ability to excel in anything he turns his mind to, he is currently reading Classics at Oxford. Let us listen in.

'Coming to Oxford, an individual's personal history can be either of enormous help or of hindrance. Knowing how a personality trait colours your reputation to the bright side or tips you to the dark, is key. Two dark sides I have learnt to manage better are controlling opinion and controlling emotion. Let us take each label in turn.

At school, lots of students wonder whether it is better to be an extrovert or an introvert in the big bad world. I'd answer this by saying (note, Supratik is an introvert) that I always want to have an opinion because I don't want to be a bystander who is seen to be neutral. But what I have learnt is to stick to my opinion when I am on "solid ground"' but equally I am happy to let go if someone else has a different but better-informed view. The opinions of others are arguably just as important as your own; your own opinion is important to give yourself an identity in the crowd but understanding and learning to become compatible with the opinions of others is perhaps just as crucial: your entire life is lived in relation to others, not in a bubble. If you can't understand and learn to deal with the opinions of others efficiently and quickly, it will only lead to alienation. For example, in a social situation, when one is trying to meet or get to know many new people for the first time and quickly, I have found that people are far more welcoming or receptive if you give their views/stories some credence and appreciation. That way you are accepting and open, yet still retain a personality.'

He then reflected on the recent artificiality of 'needing to show extroversion'.

'As a student about to step into the big world, I see there's a rising popularity about showing emotion in public – leaders who even cry in public, but somewhere, tears manipulate too. I'd say, absolutely show your emotions to a point where it adds value, but not to a point where it is a mere distraction or you risk being labelled too emotional for the sake of it. Show what needs showing as long as it's authentic and guard what needs guarding.'

This young man is all about balancing the excessive ends of any spectrum.

Tipping points

So when does strength tip over to a dark side? There are some common triggers:

- Being under pressure – deadlines, impression/reputation, responsibility;
- Undergoing crisis or significant life-events – health, death, wealth, career, success;
- Coping with fame/spotlight – too much attention;

- Loneliness – too little attention;
- When the person lets down their guard or lets their 'social mask' slip.

11 Common Causes of Derailment

David L. Dolitch and Peter C. Cairo describe eleven derailers that lead to failure in their book *Why CEOs Fail* (2003). They are part of the dark side of leadership characteristics—there is even some strength in each of these under normal conditions. Under stress, these characteristics lead to errors in judgment that can be fatal to a career and often to an organisation. The key is to recognise their existence and to manage them before they become damaging:

- Arrogance: You're right and everybody else is wrong.
- Melodrama: You always grab the centre of attention.
- Volatility: Your mood swings drive business swings.
- Excessive Caution: The next decision you make may be your first.
- Habitual Distrust: You focus on the negatives.
- Aloofness: You disengage and disconnect.
- Mischievousness: Rules are made to be broken.
- Eccentricity: It is fun to be different just for the sake of it.
- Passive Resistance: Your silence is misinterpreted as agreement.
- Perfectionism: Get the little things right even if the big things go wrong.
- Eagerness to Please: Winning the popularity contest matters most.

On average, we have two or three derailers and some can be both strengths and weaknesses. Some CEOs are more vulnerable than others to derailment.

The constant interplay of yin and yang

In relation to the dark side, I use a Chinese concept to determine the tipping points of the strength versus weakness continuum. In *The Art of War by Sun Tzu*, an ancient, revered Chinese book of strategy, the author talks about how winning a war is all about *positioning* tactics. One of the most widely studied works in human history, learning this book's powerful principles is like mastering leadership simply by reading. Historically, the conceptual base for Sun Tzu's views is the ancient Chinese concept of yin and yang.

Yin and yang represent the ancient Chinese understanding of how things work. The outer circle represents the universe while the black and white shapes within the circle represent the interaction of two opposite energies.

- The black shape: yin – dark, passive, downward, cold, contracting and weak.
- The white shape: yang – bright, active, upward, hot, expanding and strong.

The yin and yang shape indicates the continuous flow of yin to yang and yang to yin.

We refer to this concept as complementary opposites to avoid the many conflicting cultural meanings of yin and yang and because Sun Tzu didn't use that terminology himself.

In today's world, we can express this idea of complementary opposites in a variety of ways. In physics, we talk about positive and negative charges. In statistics, we talk about digression and regression to the mean. In economics, we talk about supply and demand. In leadership I talk about the bright and dark sides.

Two dark side stories from my coaching world

Gary

I coached Gary, a stressed senior vice president of a financial services company. In his mid 40s, it was odd at first to note he had moved between three organisations in five years. The coaching process started with Gary apportioning his stress levels to the economic crises and cost cutting measures, which necessitated his frequent moves. In his own words:

'I was a top student all the way through and my triumph in school was related to my flawless preparation so it was natural for me to use this same approach at work. I have been recognised as a manager who can spot mistakes and my impeccable attention to detail has meant that projects run smoothly. This really helped me advance in my career. In the first seven years, as you can see, I have had three fast tracked promotions.'

By now, I could see his blind spot. As Gary's sphere of responsibility and influence increased, there was a corresponding increase in pressure and stakes. He started fretting over every little detail across several large-scale projects. He worried about how one mistake could cost the company millions. Sometimes it perturbed him immensely that he couldn't oversee every aspect of every decision. He became uptight. He also fell into a trap of over-preparation and would rehearse management summaries for days to be sure they came off without a glitch or he would endlessly review reports and plan figures in a budget to make sure they were achievable.

Certainly the worst trap he fell into was not delegating. He stopped giving his directs due responsibility as he was convinced that none of them could or would pay as much attention to all aspects of a task as he did. He was spending undue time on jobs his team could have handled which meant he was causing delays and slipping deliverables.

In dark side parlance, his diligence tipped over into perfectionism which was seen by others as controlling and micromanaging. While it is tough to unlearn a previous strength, through feedback and his own self awareness, Gary realised that it is possible to start recalibrating how much of the strength, in his case diligence, you do, while trusting others to do the rest. Pure perfectionism can be a real negative for leaders, as we will cover in the chapter on Resilience.

Catherine

By the age of 28, Catherine was a senior programme manager managing one of the largest IT transformation projects with a global energy giant. Of Austrian nationality, she was spotted by the CEO as a rising star and invited to move to a group position at the London Headquarters. With an enviable pedigree – a first degree from Oxford and a MBA from the London Business School – she had fast tracked her climb up the corporate ladder. It wasn't just pure ability. She had a real energy, passion and an infectious enthusiasm and if you asked anyone for feedback on her, the response was unanimously fantastic. Her passion to make a difference increased with the power and influence she gained within the organisation and she invested every ounce of energy in delivering to that expectation. People found her fervour and zeal made a real difference to increasing morale in the culture.

Soon she was given a young team of six managers. At first she enjoyed the challenge of leading them, but soon there came a time where Catherine started receiving feedback about having endless expectations, about pushing her team to breaking point and so on. Her seeming enthusiasm and excitement was unmanageable and causing unrest and confusion. She stopped listening to her team's ideas. Slowly but surely, Catherine started losing trust and respect among her peers. She turned others off. Some even said Catherine's reputation was like a volcano: 'if you came too close to her, you could get burnt.' Each piece of feedback ended with 'she needs to calm down and turn down the volume' but Catherine couldn't see it; all she *could* do was put in her own enthusiasm for projects.

It was not until she received some very consistent feedback at the year end appraisal that she realised all the signals and cues given to her throughout the year meant that while projecting her passion and energy, she was also letting off some very negative and frustrating vibes. She was indeed getting easily annoyed with her team, which manifested through explosive mood swings and clear disappointment with people and their ideas.

Catherine's enthusiasm had become too large to contain – it had turned to volatility. Such is the price paid for an overdone strength. Although tough, with gritty feedback, Catherine found her 'golden point' of how much enthusiasm was optimal.

Derailing, or tipping over

Previously successful leaders can suddenly tip and 'fall off the track'. Research on executive effectiveness has found that 33% of executives selected for senior positions fail. Some estimates run as high as 50%. So is there a way we can signal if a rising star is headed for a crash?

Drawing from several sources (executive leadership literature reviews, my professional experience as an executive coach, working with CEOs and so on) one startling fact emerges: there are amazing similarities between the careers of successful individuals and those who derailed, so although it is often hard to see a derailment coming before it is too late it should be possible to trace a pattern and devise an early warning sign.

All leaders, including you, could be vulnerable to the following eleven derailers. They are based on the work of someone I admire, Dr. Robert Hogan, an industrial psychologist and professor on personality assessment, leadership and organisational effectiveness. He designed the Hogan Development Survey (HDS) to make the dark side easily accessible to us. I use the eleven Hogan scales extensively and have summarised the polar bright and darks ides styles of extreme behaviour below:

- **Enthusiastic – Volatile**

Bright side: Tends to invest a great deal in projects and relationships with accompanying high energy and expectations. Feels passionately about new projects and relationships.

Dark side: Concerns seeming moody and hard to please, being enthusiastic about new people or projects and then becoming disappointed with them. Has high expectations that can lead to disappointment if not fulfilled. Easily annoyed, looks for faults/failure in others. Disenchantment can be visibly obvious when interest wanes.

- **Shrewd – Mistrustful**

Bright Side: Astute, alert (especially to signs of deception), not fooled easily, aware of people who may have a hidden agenda.

Dark side: May seem cynical, mistrustful and doubtful of the true intentions of others. Suspicious, may feel that people have ulterior motives.

- **Careful – Cautious**

Bright side: Prefers to play it safe, may be innovative within his/her comfort zone. Likely to be well prepared before contributing. Restrained.

Dark side: Seems reluctant to change. Overly concerned about making mistakes for fear of rejection or negative evaluation by others. More prone to feelings of social anxiety. May miss opportunities to contribute valuable opinions

- **Independent – Detached**

Bright side: Self sufficient, not easily distracted. Takes little notice of office politics.

Dark side: May seem aloof, uncommunicative and lacking interest in, or awareness of, the feelings of others. Unconcerned with social feedback, displays a lack of sympathy for other's feelings or moods.

- **Focused – Passive /Aggressive**

Bright side: Good at working to their own timetable and own standards, seems obliging, has a pleasant façade. Likes control over own work.

Dark side: Too independent, refuses to be hurried, ignores other people's requests and becomes irritable if they persist. Can be stubborn when asked to change track. May be less inclined to be part of the team.

- **Confident – Arrogant**

Bright side: Happy to take on responsibility. Gives strong first impression. Happy to take the lead, socially confident.

Dark side: May seem unusually self-confident. Has strong feelings of entitlement, is unwilling to admit mistakes, listen to advice or attend to feedback. Over-estimates talents. Emphasises his/her own accomplishments while playing down shortcomings.

- **Charming – Manipulative**

Bright side: Knows how to work a crowd. Can sell a vision. Is exciting to be with and can use their social skills to win people over.

Dark Side: Concerns seeming to enjoy taking risks and testing the limits. Can make uncalculated or reckless risks. May embellish/exaggerate to make a point. Mischievous. May not learn from mistakes, easily bored and seeks excitement.

- **Vivacious – Dramatic**

Bright side: Strong first impression, seeming lively, expressive, dramatic, Performs well in public, knows how to create an aura, entertaining.

Dark side: Can be over the top. Superficial, strong need for attention. Hard to reach and wanting to be noticed.

- **Imaginative – Eccentric**

Bright side: Creative, original, source of good ideas. Thinks outside the box, comes up with off-the-wall ideas.

Dark side: May be so unique that ideas are extreme and thus irrelevant. Unpractical, obscure.

- **Diligent – Perfectionist**

Bright side: Meticulous, precise and organised. Structured, careful and conscientious.

Dark side: Fussy and critical of others' work. Slow productivity, struggles with priorities. Controlling and critical of the performance of others.

• **Dutiful – Dependent**

Bright side: Obedient, attentive, maintains trust. Pleasant.

Dark side: Concerns seeming eager to please and reluctant to take independent action. Eager to please. Needs second opinion/consensus to make a decision. Will not 'rock the boat'.

So, yes, you can have too much of a good thing! However, I believe the above shows that the very strengths that can help people become effective and successful can, in certain circumstances, spark dysfunctional behaviours into action.

Wisdom from my homeless friend

I was once volunteering on Christmas Day for the charity Crisis, in their temporary drug and rehabilitation centre. No drugs or alcohol were allowed on the premises. While I have come into contact with homeless people before – from *Big Issue* sellers to those waiting by underground stations – this was my first direct volunteering experience with addicts. On a cold, dark winter morning in London's Battersea area, my first responsibility was to welcome our homeless guests at the gate. A stream of men and women in various states of intoxication flowed through. I was part of a team who served breakfast and chatted to the guests. For some, we washed their hair, helped them to find warm clothes, a bed to sleep in and some hot food. Some people shared their life stories with me, others just sat and played cards. In the afternoon, I ran an arts class which, much to my surprise, became very vibrant. Here's where I came across an astonishing dark side story.

Some of the artistic talent was mindblowing. One man was doodling lots of numbers in bright colours quickly on a piece of paper. On closer inspection, they looked like colourful financial projections. He then explained these were related to derivatives on mutual bonds. I was intrigued to find out more. This guest explained he was a former banker who took a big risk and started his own trading company operating across the Far East in 2000. It went bust after all his investments and savings dried up. Combined with high levels of enthusiasm – which generated risk-taking behaviours including alcohol consumption – he neglected early signs of financial and emotional threats. His misplaced excitement tipped him over to the dark side and sadly, his life spiralled down. He just couldn't recover.

Here we discover a well meaning, ambitious and high achieving individual who underestimated obstacles. Optimism in this case was the underlying trait that helped his motivation, but carried to an extreme, obliterated adequate risk evaluation and reality checks. I was genuinely sad to see the consequences. That Christmas day taught me another powerful leadership lesson.

Chief executives and dark sides

Why is there so much focus on senior leaders and their dark sides? I would say that chief executives are more vulnerable and more exposed at risk than other leaders because of the visibility they have. The greater the exposure and the greater the risk, the stronger the derailment tendency.

Failures can take many forms: delivery shortages, relationship failures, personal blind spots or adjustment crises and many others. If you also factor in workload, time pressures, constant change, media and shareholder spotlight, work/life balance, navigating uncertainty while proving one's worth; the stakes are very high indeed.

Dark sides can be flagged up through warning signs like the following. Notice they all start with the word too, or excess:

- **Too hungry for immediate gratification:** fatal mistakes occur because these leaders can't wait or be patient; they must have it right here and now, leading to blunders and disappointments **(warning sign: the I want it now leader)**

- **Too quick to lose their temper:** these are leaders whose views and opinions are so loud in their own head, they just cannot hold them in. They react in haste, using language or actions they later regret. People around them are very aware of their tendency to outbursts. (warning sign: the hot headed leader)

- **Too quick to feel hurt:** some people are over-sensitive and are scared of being judged or humiliated. They are relatively fragile emotionally and easily provoked. Being thin-skinned means they absorb other people's vibes. They have no 'insulation' and are easy to crack. **(warning sign: the thin skinned leader)**

- **Too caring:** paternal or maternal, with a need to be liked or always be popular. These leaders prefer nurturing over being tough in driving results. **(warning sign: the daddy or mummy)**

- **Too much reliance on what worked for them in the past:** these leaders are always saying 'but what we did in my previous organisation was...'. It is human nature to draw on past successes, but applying yesterday's solutions to tomorrow's problems doesn't necessarily work.
  (warning sign: the in the past leader)
- **Too much ego:** They think all the answers reside in them. They forget to consult others and ask for input or adequate information before making and acting on a decision.
  (warning sign: the I know it all leader)

My bright-dark lesson from Dubai

Dark sides can affect teams, communities and entire nations. One of the toughest yet most valuable learning experiences in my career came during the early days of the economic crisis. It had been simmering for some time, but when it struck, it knocked me sideways.

One September evening in 2008, I had just stepped into Victoria Station in London to go home. My phone rang. That one conversation changed my views on business risk forever. It was our largest Dubai-based client and his voice was shaking gently. 'Rhea, we need to put our work on hold'.

Shaken to the core with this abruptness, I griped '...but we have four programmes starting next week, all flights and accommodation for the team has been booked and paid for already.'

'I'm sorry,' he said, 'I can't help it.'

The world stopped. I had no idea what to do. We had spent two years building eighteen high-performing teams by taking one of Dubai's leading's international business from a start-up with three people to a thriving company with 800 people across multiple sectors and functions. Each team had a mix of more than twenty nationalities and dealt with different challenges and soaring targets.

I tried calling my client back but got no response. More than the significant amount of fees involved, the greatest of all investments was actually the emotional one of hope and fulfilment in helping this business grow from baby steps! It felt utterly surreal. I decided to sleep on it and not react immediately.

No one answered any calls or emails the next day. I read the papers. What had transpired, of course, was the 2008 global financial crash. Virtually overnight, property values halved and markets collapsed. Billions of dollars worth of building contracts were paused – or simply vanished. That wasn't the only thing. For me, a large portion of my annual revenue and a rewarding long-term business relationship also disappeared. Here was my naivety; now exposed bare. For the first two years of my consulting business, most of our revenue was generated from the Middle East and that became a pattern I didn't question or reflect enough on. I took this golden success at face value and continued to pour in effort, energy and commitment into this client account. My confidence in the 'many eggs in one basket' approach, without even realising, had made me complacent and left me open to this profound risk during an ugly financial crisis.

There's a bit of history to this story. I first met the creator of modern Dubai, the Crown Prince of UAE, Mohammed bin Rashid Al Maktoum, in 2004 while leading an extremely challenging assignment of structuring and executing a holding company, thereafter called Dubai Holding, to help consolidate over twenty business operations of his empire. Expecting to meet a bold, vivacious leader, I was surprised by his kind, gentle demeanour – he had an almost understated charisma and a deep humility. Many others have been drawn to his magnetic presence. Every building, from the large glass façades of shimmering hotels to small shops, as well as magazines and food packets displayed his picture. I realised that Sheikh Mohammed was a cross-generational ruler of Dubai; on the one hand a champion of the heritage and legacy of the Middle East and on the other, he was modern and progressive in his outlook to take Dubai to the pinnacle of modern civilisation.

As we were embarking on a big project for him, I wanted to hear first-hand his dreams for the nation. He said, 'my dream is to reach a point where Dubai's vision and endurance meets global recognition while retaining its individuality through great execution.' I still remember the impact his words had on me.

The Dubai skyline, with its jaw dropping spectacles such as the Dancing Towers and The Cloud, is indeed a world of dreams. Size really matters here – the biggest, largest, tallest – equally the promises made to the world seemed to me at the time, bold, big and tall fantasies. Myth has it that the World project, the indomitably constructed archipelago of islands shaped like the countries of the globe, which spans 36,661 square miles, is said to be sinking back into the sea.

People do have varied takes on the Dubai Dream, though. An expat client of ours said of it in 2007, 'Life is fantastic. You live in movie-style apartments overlooking the best skyline in the world, you have a whole team of cleaners, cooks, drivers and gardeners, the best golf, restaurants and malls ...and if that's not enough, you pay no taxes at all! It's one big party all the time'. 18 months later, however, the newspapers reported quotes such as, 'I realised – things in Dubai are fake. The trees ... the workers' contracts ... the islands.. even people's promises are unreal!'

So how does one analyse the leadership story here? What lessons of dark side can we draw from Dubai? One could say the ruler is a leader and in this sense I'd even say he is a dreamer in the positive sense but maybe whose optimism proved too large to contain. Or did he fail to instil a governance in the team below him? His big dream still remains Middle East's hope. I too still remain a follower of his ambitions, but the real lesson for me is realistic optimism, something that Stuart Gulliver, CEO of HSBC bank alludes to always. Enthusiasm without realism can be misplaced.

We have lived in and continue to live in a heroic culture where leaders, including CEOs, are put on a pedestal but we owe it to us and them to see and call out their tipping points before they become flaws. So we may contribute to the heroic myth and enable leaders to steam roll ahead, even when their exaggerated strengths can bring everyone— shareholders, customers and employees—down. Great leaders can be fallible – why not have the courage to call out the *blemishes* before they become dark spots?

It would be unfair to attribute the nation's despair to one leader and indeed unwise to write off Dubai for that matter. Nevertheless the leadership lesson of an uncontrolled dark side is profound. The Sheikh is a hereditary leader whose ruling tribal lines date back to 1833. There is a profound depth to the man and despite Dubai's recent failings, his accomplishments are also countless. Thirty years ago, almost all of contemporary Dubai was desert land. He brought wise leadership, sharp vision and an open mind. His immense appetite for work is matched by a passion for play. These traits have helped him shape Dubai's identity and global footprint. A man of many talents, he is accomplished in tennis football and horse racing.

While the dark side of Dubai hit Dubai itself and me very hard, both the nation and I are richer and stronger for the developmental journey it set us off on. I have every hope that this ambitious country will soar to ever greater heights, having learned through its dark side that it needs to be more realistic and sustainable in its leadership footprint.

As Robert Schuller, a clergyman and prolific author, wrote, 'Tough Times Never Last, But Tough People Do!'. The Dubai crisis shed light on my dark side where I confidently assumed this client would become a mainstay of my business. It made me tougher and became the biggest rung in the ladder of my development at that time. My business soon diversified into a global and more balanced sector mix and today I feel humbled to have an enviable team and a list of clients from across the world. Was it a blessing in disguise? This is my case in point about the dark side – it is all about knowing how to leverage the learning it offers and unleash greater untapped potential within us.

In a strange way, from chaos comes clarity. It has helped me over the years remember an analogy we use in India to prove the learning potential from chaos. Now, what's a small pleasure that unites everyone across the world? Well, you could say – a cup of tea! If you make it the right way, I'd say that of course, using eastern methods. Consider, for example, the chaos we choose to trigger by pouring tea leaves in a boiling pot of water – the leaves colliding, racing and unfurling while becoming bigger, the hot water getting to boiling – there is utter mayhem in a pot for a short while. But let us not forget the decision to turn on the fire was ours because we are sure of the good outcome at the other end. From that chaos, comes clarity and beauty of a great end product often resulting in an 'hmmm' of joy from the drinker. The lessons from the dark side are similar. The recession struck Dubai episode threw me in that boiling chaos only to learn and come out from it richer and stronger. **A seeming crisis or heightened pressure can lead to clarity, so use it as an enabler to learn from wherever you encounter it.**

Dark side and failures are key to success

Everyone wants to be a success. I have never met anyone who purposely set out to be a failure. We all know that bookshelves heave with a raft of manuals on how to be successful. Theodore Roosevelt said that 'the only man who never makes a mistake is the man who never does anything'. Failure is one of those inevitable realities of life. The manner in which leaders meet their own failures will have a significant knock-on effect on their followers and indeed their own organisation as well as others. On the leadership stage, where we are all watching, learning and judging. Our bright and dark sides are all on display, no matter how hard we try to underplay them – others are being affected by its impact.

As a result, people whose dark sides are not managed have a fear of failure which makes them play the game of 'cover-up'. We consciously or subconsciously ignore mistakes because to admit them is to admit failure. We fear the world judges us where they think failure means you are a bad person and you are a failure. This is a fundamental principle which we will explore more in the Chapter on Fear. Sometimes life must engineer failure in us before it can bring about success in us. Our failures are often rungs on the ladder of growth – we should learn from each rung of our mistakes and step up on them rather than shy away from them.

Courageous leaders will act on two principles: (a) knowing that failures remind them of the consequences of our choices and decisions (b) knowing failures can become lessons in equipping them for bigger and better growth.

So let me conclude in a similar vein to where I started, savouring this ingredient. The dark side is not simply black and white. It is neither bad nor foreboding, as its name might imply. It simply exists. It is as much a part of our human psyche as our more familiar emotions and character traits. In this chapter, I have aimed to lift the lid on this phenomenon. By releasing it out of the shadows, we do at least know it exists and can evolve personal solutions to adapt it to our benefit.

To help connect with our dark side, sometimes we need to initiate (or invite) pressure rather than wait for it to happen. We spend our lives running away, avoiding and minimising chaos. I would like you to turn that safety net on its head and say the sooner you show courage to embrace chaos, sometimes even throwing yourself into it, the stronger you will emerge on the other side. Protected shells only make us weaker and smaller versions of our real selves.

Facing the elements of nature helps us grow stronger as I explored in a conversation with Professor Stephen Hopper, a plant conservation biologist, contributing to the conservation of endangered species and ecosystems. Stephen joined Kew Gardens, a World Heritage Site and global plant science powerhouse, and we realised in conversation how the 'conservation principle' in plants, which is all about life protection and facing the elements, has a direct read across to the resilience principle in leadership, also about protecting us from failure and the dark side.

Facing the elements gives us a greater bandwidth of resilience and creativity to manage around our dark sides and one of the ways we can lead ourselves from dark to light.

The Art of War

One of my favourite quotes goes back to what Sun Tzu said in *The Art of War*, **'Of the five elements (water, fire, wood, metal and earth), none is always predominant; of the four seasons, none always stand still, of the days, some are long and some short and the moon wanes and waxes'. I am sure he would have added the bright and dark side to that mix of elements.**

Your code for Ingredient Seven: Dark Side

Pause. Ask yourself what do you remember from this chapter; list the key takeaways and ideas that had an impact on you – something inspiring, something relevant or something you would like to try.

Now, make a note of the following: the term 'things' below can refer to behaviour actions, conversations, skills or even an attitude

1. List three things you would like to START doing to protect yourself from your DARK SIDE...

2. List three things you would like to STOP doing to protect yourself from your DARK SIDE...

3. List three things you would like to CONTINUE doing to protect yourself from your DARK SIDE...

On an ascending scale of 1 to 10, how robust is this ingredient in your DNA?

Ingredient Eight

FEAR

—'I worry'—

Fear, conditioned by emotion is an anxious energy or restricting emotion we invite in. Who invites it in? We do. Often it is imaginary and perceived, but we label it as reality. Fear stands between our dreams and us. Fear can be of many types – of the unknown, of failure, of rejection, of change or of loneliness. Mastered well, however, fear can be good in helping us touch the edge of our discomfort and activate many dormant neurons in us, cementing our self-belief.

My aim with this chapter is to help you understand and break down this ingredient through altering your interpretation of fear and controlling how you use it to strengthen your leadership DNA.

The Cave

To understand fear, let us go right back to our cavemen ancestors. Ever since human beings sat around fire in caves, they used to tell stories to help deal with the dread of danger, the struggle to survive and the biggest challenge of them all – to cope with the fear of the unknown.

The Greek philosopher Plato wrote the Allegory of the Cave to show how humans are afraid of change and of the unknown. He claims we can confuse what we perceive, see and hear with actual reality. In the allegory, Plato describes a situation in which men are living in an underground cave with one entrance located near the top, where a fire casts its shadow. The men in the cave are chained; they can only see the wall and cannot turn around. When objects pass by, they create shadows on the wall. The shadows are the only thing they can see and therefore the only things they know to exist. Somehow, one of the prisoners breaks loose from his chains and wanders outside the cave. He is astonished at what he finds and comes back in to describe the outside world to his friends. The other men think he is mad, however and plot to kill him. This is a simplified illustration of how fear, inherent in the nature of man, is a primitive perception; an abstract, often absurd, imagination of perceived danger.

Human evolution is key to understanding fear. In the beginning, our ancestors needed to survive and safety came from belonging to groups. I call this the 'moving towards' driver, something that propels us towards group belonging and identity. The drive for survival and safety then evolved into a drive to be significant and powerful and our ancestors' fear of danger gave way to a fear of losing status. That's when man started to look for differentiation and individuation, the 'moving away' driver, which seeks to create a separate identity. Read this in conjunction with the opening Chapter on self, on differentiation and integration. Note while our ancestors principally feared nature and its many forms, the modern human fears not bears and tigers, but other fellow humans. It is ironic.

For us today, fear can also be a motivator for action. Let us take a common example. All of us, in some shape or form, present our thoughts, ideas or products to a large group at some point. Let us call this act of presenting a performance, for this discussion. Now think this through. On days when we have an important performance on stage e.g. a public presentation, most people tend to wake up with a strong consciousness 'I have to perform today... I have to prove myself today'. Let us ask, why might that be so?

However, this is simply a feeling that we create because nothing in our physical environment relating to the performance has changed, but we have changed our emotional environment by inviting in imagined threats and dangers about the performance. It may lead us to over-prepare or over-worry, which isn't a bad thing per se but can be draining. Here we are avoiding something that we don't want to happen, but this very fearful energy essentially moves us further towards something else we don't want – exhaustion and negativity. While it thrusts us forward into action, it risks our chances of success.

Now we can also channel this feeling into a different kind of motivation. While you can't just turn the fear switch off, you can channel it to positive effect. If we can turn down the volume of fear so that it becomes useful and manageable rather than destructive, we can then invite in Focus, our third ingredient, to redirect this energy from bad to good e.g. focusing on something that you desire (success, credibility, recognition and so on). By redirecting that energy, we move closer to something we want. In other words, it thrusts you forward and towards success.

After working with a range of left-brain and right brain leaders, I believe that fear, unless it is controlled carefully, can compromise or even corrupt our leadership DNA.

A short story – the modern man's cave

Many years ago, I was coaching a senior manager in his early 40s. He worked in the oil and gas industry and had been earmarked for a big promotion. The business environment was a tough one for him – he had joined from the pharmaceutical trade and was learning the ropes in his new industry – so the stakes for his promotion were very high.

One afternoon, I was helping him rehearse for his first big external stakeholder presentation scheduled for the following day. He knew the subject. He knew the audience. We practised, several times, how to make a winning first impression and get off to a great start. Nothing could go wrong, surely. I was fairly confident and his boss was convinced it would be a breeze, but late that evening I received an e-mail from him – he was losing his confidence! He was beginning to feel anxious and indeed at 7.00 the next morning fear had gripped him. By 9.30, he was having an anxiety attack and his boss was about to step in.

Luckily, fate intervened and the meeting was postponed to the afternoon because of the main shareholder being held up in a press conference. Through coaching, he realised there were two choices. Did he want to let fear get between him and his promotion? Or, could he overcome his nerves and give this opportunity his best shot? I spent an hour walking him through the consequences of his two choices till he finally said **'I realise I am inviting in this negative energy from nowhere and my mind is playing a bad game with me. I don't want to give in to it'. I said to him, 'Don, you can't blame your mind... You are your mind. While you can't just turn the fear switch off, you can channel it to positive effect'.**

In other words you can turn down the level of fear so that it becomes useful and not destructive. Just like too much seasoning can destroy a dish, so just the right amount can energise its flavour and stimulate your taste buds. So a certain dose of fear – not panic – generates a positive anxiety which is a great catalyst for change. To those of you who ask 'how can any amount of fear, however small, be helpful – I don't want to be anxious at all, positively or negatively?' – do read on.

We spent the next few hours in a room thinking of all the reasons he should do well in the presentation, why he was best placed to perform strongly and why he deserved to take the meeting by storm. He then played back all the past presentations that had gone well and how much people had enjoyed listening to him. This helped replace the memories of one recent presentation that hadn't gone well with several other good ones. In human nature, the impact of bad is stronger than good. The power of one bad can override many goods. Hence our tendency to hold on to the bad is so damaging.

In effect, we were using the human mind as a television – to play back good films of previous positive experiences, then bad and then changing the channel when fear crept in to bring back the good ones again; it made him feel different. **In so doing, we changed his negative fear channel to a positive celebration channel. We were using the plasticity of his brain to mould his conscious memory into a 'remote control' for him to maintain a lock on viewing positive channels.** Try it. It is not complex, it just needs practice.

I still remember the round of applause from the chairman that afternoon after Don's session. They signed the contract the following week.

Don's experience taught me an invaluable lesson. **Fear, once identified, can be neutralised. Fear often is not real and when understood, can be managed to our advantage and yes, the human mind really can be like a television i.e. when feeling 'trapped' in a channel, you can change the channel and watch a different show.**

For example, many times in my life this adrenaline-laden amygdala (the almond-shaped structures of the brain, linked with the processing of emotional reactions which we discovered in Chapter on Emotion, has done a terrific job of pushing me beyond my limits to find new opportunities. They love alerting me of potential challenges, but all the while thrusting me to new possibilities. Unless we explore at the edge of our insecurities and fears and channel that adrenaline-laden energy to start a new journey, we would always operate at a lower version of our potential and our dormant neurons would never spark into action.

For me, pushing limits and exploring my own edge, meant giving up a financially rewarding directorship to start my own company against most people's good advice. Was I fearful? Yes and so were my friends and family. It was hard for all of us to neutralise our fear around this, but it was worth it. **Problems begin only when we give in to fear and let it start calling the shots. So the trick is to use fear and not let fear use you.**

Let me show you how and why.

Fear is an energy

At its basic, fear is a type of energy. It is an energy that we empower, we invite in and generate. Now, the only exception to that is when we wake up to find a real, salivating tiger waiting by our bedside. That fear is justified but how often does that happen? Yet, we 'sense' metaphorical tigers around us. Fear originates from inside us, or that part of self that is of the world, the instinct, the intellect that says, I am alone and under threat or in competition to survive – whether in the open wilderness of caves long ago, or in the open forum of presentations of today.

The trigger for fear is always a stimulus, for example something we see, hear, smell, taste, feel, or, even, say to ourselves – like fearing you will lose an audience's attention, or the fear you may forget your first notes on the piano in front of a large group.

We can break this causal stimulus down into two different types:

- **The internal stimuli** – i.e. an inner desire to succeed, excel and come across well – can electrify your senses with nervous energy, but do you internally interpret this as fear or exhilaration? In other words, are they steps to stumble over or ones to climb up to a higher level? You have a choice.

- **The external stimuli** – someone looking at their watch, another yawning or writing notes – can throw you off course too. A lot of it is perception. Should you interpret these signs as people wishing they were somewhere else? That they're bored and making negative memos to themselves? Or are they hoping to be in time to catch you and say how good you are, embarrassed at fighting jet-lag and noting the excellent points you have made? The choice is yours.

Remember I said to Don 'you are your mind'. Taking this approach puts the dial in your hand: you can not only turn down the volume of fear, but also tune it to a positive frequency. Thinking of it like this, why would you choose to internally interpret something negatively rather than positively? This puts you in charge, by corralling what you fear into a controlled setting where you pre-empt what could go wrong and develop appropriate counter-measures. What is left is an acceptable degree of fear – or what we might call adrenaline. It will keep you on your toes and being alert and nimble in your performance will, in turn, stimulate and enthuse your audience.

Our subconscious mind uses filters that distort, generalise and delete information. They consist of memories of past experiences, unresolved emotions, values and beliefs. So, depending on your personalised filters, we are more (or less) likely to interpret reality as something dangerous (or safe). So here is the next clue as to why we see or sense metaphorical tigers, which means understanding how our self, our subconscious mind, is predisposed to see things. For example, the more fear and anxiety we have stored in our subconscious mind, the easier these emotions will be triggered in a self-perpetuating negative syndrome.

In addition, if any of our core beliefs tell us we are not safe, we will subconsciously look for evidence that confirms this belief. Therefore, our starting point, to manage our fear and anxiety from the bad to the good, is to know our subconscious mind and work with it to prevent accumulation of fear and anxiety in the first place. Left to its own

devices, the subconscious mind rushes in to define a drama, create conflict and take us off course.

The effect of fear on the individual

So what are we fearful of? In my experience of watching corporate employees, leaders, students, performers, artists and politicians, fears can be a range of emotions:

- Fear of making a mistake?
- Fear of being found out?
- Fear of upsetting the other person?
- Fear of conflict?
- Fear of success?
- Fear of risk taking?
- Fear of change?
- Fear of the other person's anger?
- Fear of one's own anger?
- Fear of retribution, punishment or rejection?
- Fear of not being liked?
- Fear of failing?
- Fear of compromise?
- Fear of loss?

I believe the concept of a fearless leader is mostly myth and, worse, miselading. Many leaders, at all levels, struggle with fear. Some develop self-confidence to counter it, while others resort to various coping strategies, including over-compensating with either extreme aggression or timidity. Learning to deal with fear positively and productively, then, is an important part of developing as a leader.

Think of it this way. Fear is part of our natural make up. So, the key is to adapt it, not to expend energy eliminating it or pretending you are unique and not affected by it.

Two responses to fear

Science shows our response or reaction to fear is twofold: biochemical and emotional. The biochemical response is universal, while the emotional response is highly personal.

Physical (biochemical) reaction

Faced with (perceived) danger, our bodies respond through sweating, increased heart and pulse rates. This physical response is sometimes known as the fight or flight response, in which the body prepares itself to either enter combat (face the fear) or run away (give in to the fear).

Emotional response

The emotional response to fear is highly individual. Remember the one-inch almonds again – the amygdala conditions fear. Fear and anxiety can make us feel confused and scared and the degree to which this happens influences whether we can or cannot cope with a threatening situation. Once we pass the tipping point and tell ourselves we can't cope or are going to fail, we give in to fear. This manifests itself in behaviours such as avoiding things, fidgeting, shouting, stuttering, withdrawal, aggression or denial. So how do we recognise the tipping point, stop and redirect ourselves towards a positive outcome? Identifying the source, or enemy, that can give fear the upper hand allows you to negate its influences and regain control.

The Enemy Within

This title and exchange from the famous and widely viewed TV series Star Trek outlines the nature of fear beautifully.*

Spock: We have here an unusual opportunity to appraise the human mind, or to examine, in Earth terms, the roles of good and evil in a man – his negative side, which you call hostility, lust, violence and his positive side, which Earth people express as compassion, love, tenderness.

McCoy: Are you aware it's the captain's guts you're analysing?

Spock: Yes and what makes one man an exceptional leader? We see indications that it's his negative side which makes him strong, that his evil side, controlled and disciplined, is vital to his strength. Your negative side removed from you, the power of command begins to elude you.

McCoy: Don't risk your life on a theory!

Spock: Being split in two halves is no theory with me, Doctor. I have a human half and an alien half at war with each other. Personal experience, Doctor. I survive because my intelligence wins, makes them live together. Your intelligence would enable you to survive, as well.

* Source: The fifth episode of the first season – Star Trek, 1966

Spock: [to Captain Kirk] You're the captain of this ship. You haven't the right to be vulnerable in the eyes of the crew. You can't afford the luxury of being anything less than perfect. If you do, they lose faith and you lose command.

Kirk: [about Evil Kirk] I have to take him back inside myself. I can't survive without him. I don't want to take him back. He's like an animal. A thoughtless, brutal animal. And yet it's me. Me!

McCoy: We all have our darker side. We need it; it's half of what we are. It's not really ugly, it's human.

'Good' fear through Creative Tension

'Where you stumble, there your treasure lies.'
Joseph Campbell, American mythologist, 1924

Fear can have some positive dimensions. For me as an entrepreneur and an amateur artist – I do large oil canvases, which are largely unfinished driven by a fear of 'I'm not great at it'. Fear holds **creative tension**. Pause – resist the urge of letting these seemingly polarised words cancel each other. The concept of creative tension is talked about by Peter Senge, author of The Fifth Discipline.* It is also brought to life by someone else I admire. Robert Fritz, the composer and film-maker, who illustrates creative tension in his book, The Path of Least Resistance.**

Someone once said to me 'but how can creative tension work? Isn't tension the very thing we don't want to create'? Well. Fritz shows us, tension can be a positive, stretching energy. Take a rubber band. If you stretch a rubber band, the tension will seek resolution. It will seek to relax and, as it relaxes it creates a momentum that propels it forward. Aim the rubber band at a specific destination and it will have a focused forward momentum. What might happen in your life if you had the same kind of focused forward momentum a rubber band has when it is aimed at and then released at a target?

Tension is so much more than the use of stress or strain or deadlines to push yourself forward.

---

* Senge, Peter. *The Fifth Discipline*. Rev ed. London: Random House Business Books, 2006.

** Fritz. Robert.Path of Least Resistance: Learning to Become the Creative Force in Your Own Life. 1989

If you read the following extracts from Fritz, you will note the point he makes about creative tension.

'A basic principle found throughout nature is this: Tension seeks resolution. From the spiderweb to the human body, from the formation of the galaxies to the shifts of continents, from the swing of pendulums to the movement of wind-up toys, tension-resolution systems are in play.

I call the relationship between the vision and current reality structural tension. During the creative process, you have an eye on where you want to go and you also have an eye on where you currently are.

There will always be structural tension in the beginning of the creative process, for there will always be a discrepancy between what you want and what you have. Why? Because creators bring into being creations that do not yet exist. Structural tension is a fundamental principle in the creative process. In fact, part of your job as a creator is to form this tension.'*

'You can create your life in the same way an artist develops a work of art. Expressed another way, you can be the playwright and also the lead actor and also the audience for your own life play. You can be your work and you can be its author. And, like the artist, writer, playwright, filmmaker and composer, the creative process can be your operational practice.'**

Think of a time when you really wanted something and then realised you can't have it. We have all felt a gap open up between where we are and where we want to be, when we have an unresolved problem or an unrealised desire. It is as though a sweep of tension fills this gap and the bigger the gap, the greater the tension and level of instability and the more likely we are to feel fear. But, lo and behold – as we seek stability and resolutions, our unconscious mind continuously searches and this gives rise to a 'ping' moment, in other words those wonderful moments when, in the middle of something else, or when you wake up first thing in the morning, you find the answer you are looking for. So, allow the creative tension to drive yourself – it works wonders.

---

*   From Creating: A practical guide to the creative process and how to use it to create anything – a work of art, a relationship, a career or a better life. by Robert Fritz (1993)

** From 'Your Life as Art' by Robert Fritz, 2002

Understanding 'Bad' fear through the frog experiment

In the corporate world, this gremlin manifests itself in those fearing a loss of face, being ridiculed and sometimes rejection. For top sports players, it is the fear of slipping down the rankings. For musicians, it is the fear of losing the impact on their audience. For investment bankers, it is the fear of the market turning against them. For consultants, it is the fear of losing their clients. This fear leads us to freeze or give up.

A good example to demonstrate this point comes from an experiment done with jumping frogs. Several frogs were each placed in separate glass jars and then covered with a lid to prevent them from escaping. Food, air and water were provided for them.

At first, the frogs kept jumping trying to escape, but each time they jumped they would hit their head on the lid. After 30 days, the lids were removed but the frogs no longer even attempted to jump. They had learned that escape from the jar was not possible and so formed a belief that the top of the jar was as high as they could go. Even when the lid was removed, this limiting belief kept them where they were. Pavlov's dogs from the Chapter on Emotions and the frogs here are teaching us much about our mental patterns.

This simple experiment shows the power of our belief system and of our conditioning. We have all formed certain beliefs as a result of our past experience and many of us still hold onto those beliefs even though they may no longer be true and are limiting our true potential.

To realise your true potential, even with seeming obstacles, realise that the seeming lid on your jar is not permanent and that you can jump out. The 2008 recession and its adverse impact on my consulting business taught me freezing is a definite sign of inviting defeat.

My fear could have lasted longer than the recession. It is important therefore to break the response habit, by avoiding patterns of recurring behaviour brought on by fear. When, for example, people fear they will fail, certain responses can become habitual, as they did with the frogs. These, in turn, through familiarity, lower our defences and can lead us to give into fear. Recognising these response habits and confronting your fear head-on in this way will break the response cycle and allow you to dissolve or redirect your fear instead of being led by it.

'Bad' fear plays the role of antagonist in the story of your life.

Dealing with your fears

Here are two stories from my personal experience to show you how fear and the nine other ingredients can be blended to a positive outcome. I call this the ledge factor and let me illustrate why.

Story one: Skydiving in the Eiger

Somewhere I had heard 'Skydiving is not just falling; it is flying – the closest we have been able to come to be free and to fly'. In the summer of 2011, Phil and I both, after a long draining work spell, agreed to 'drop from the sky' (we did use those exact words!) In a strange and simplistic sense, skydiving is literally a real bird's eye view. The helicopter becomes your wings and you fly, not only above the clouds, but above your life – you see the panorama of everything and, as you dive, you feel as you have never done before. The physicality of the 11,000m altitude, in the Eiger, the intensity of the experience with a roller coaster of emotions where stakes are high, but so are the risks and rewards ...extremely high! It was only afterwards that I realised I had run the whole gamut of this book's ten ingredients in the experience.

Wanting to sky dive had to start with self-belief – believing that I really did want to do the jump and that everything would work. I needed to focus and concentrate on the instructions despite being caught up in the excitement of the moment. My instinct would tell me when to tune into the parachute. I had to manage the intensity of my own emotions and keep in check my dark side, which could mean that I was too confident or too independent. I needed resilience to stick to my guns and do the jump, even though doubts and others had tried to put me off. I stuck to my creative tension in wanting to do it and being able to imagine the end outcome of achievement in a stunning setting after the moment of the jump... Expression plays a vital role in the words you are telling yourself – you become the voice that guides your thoughts, your behaviours and action (and, of course, the communication with your instructor). The whole experience couldn't have happened without the luck, which came out of the research in choosing the place (that improved my chances of the perfect weather) and the hard work and commitment during the preparation. But here's the real learning that came just before the jump.... I will never forget the penultimate 30 seconds of standing on the helicopter ledge, as the helicopter door opened, with gusts of wind buffeting me and my toes burrowing into it. I saw Phil drop and disappear out of sight in a flash. **Fear gripped me. It seemed as though the only thing that existed in my universe at that moment was this four inch ledge – it was my only contact with the safe world I knew. The thirty seconds wait on this tiny ledge felt like thirty years of my life till date. My big realisation was this : the 'fear of the fear' is far worse than the fear itself.** I felt the fear until the roar of the open door thrust me into the wide, open blue. The ensuing 45 seconds was one of the best moments of my life! All the ingredients had blended to give me the experience of a lifetime. As I landed, the only feeling I had was one of gratitude of being a human on this beautiful earth. Feet on ground, my self-belief was soaring sky high!

Story two: Skydiving in the boardroom

Skydiving resembles leading in a crises in the sense that both require belief, courage and creativity, although clearly in very different contexts. There is a transcendence of self involved in both activities and just as skydivers rely on their ability to pursue a dream while assessing risk, so must leaders pursue a vision while accepting the inherent risk in decision-making and in influencing others.

With one jump under my belt, most skydivers would view me as a novice. In comparison, as a seasoned entrepreneur who has made many risky business decisions, I still remember the one boardroom incident where I drew on all ten ingredients as if my life depended on it. The similarities between the two experiences are uncanny. **It was then that I realised for sure the 'ledge factor' doesn't just exist in helicopters: it can also take the form of the threshold you step over as you enter a boardroom.** A decade ago, as I made a big presentation on a crucial matter to a tough board, I knew the audience before me was a challenging one: the mix of opinions, egos and agendas in the room gave me the same sense of foreboding that the jump had done.

The client was a tricky customer, let us say: in the previous two years, he had hired two different consultants with the same result – no result. Indeed, the only result was that the client became cynical of consultants.

In this case, the 'jump' needed me to have faith in my self and in my ability to focus and deliver my message. I needed instinct to read the room and sense what was not being said. I had to work with the collective surge of emotion and keep it positive by acknowledging other people's fears, hopes and visions. And in a corporate boardroom the egos tend to be massive. I had to keep my dark side in check and not let confidence through preparation tip over into complacency in presentation. I needed the resilience to deal with conflicting opinions while seeking and accepting board feedback and persevering through other people's doubts and critical questions. Cynical of the expressions used, they had come to perceive 'talent', 'succession' or 'leadership' as hollow and meaningless words. That was when I had to lean on creativity and explain the key concept using fresh, unhackneyed language. At the same time, I had to conquer the fear of failure – would the board reject my proposed solution? Two thirds of the presentation through, the CEO checked his phone and gathered he had to leave the room in ten minutes due to an emergency. 'Hang on! I thought I had another thirty minutes but now I only have ten before the big player left'. So I harnessed all my ingredients, fought my gremlins to focus on the salient points, recalibrated my brain and replayed my rehearsal, all the while thinking of a plan B and, of course, looking calm and in control.

That's where luck comes in: I have learned to embrace the fleeting moments where preparation meets chance and becomes luck. The CEO left without a word and then after a second, which felt like a year, turned back and nodded: 'Agreed.'

The hero's journey – fear as a good catalyst

Let me share with you the thinking behind Joseph Campbell's 'The Hero with a Thousand Faces' which holds that many myths and narratives throughout human history, skydives to boardroom bravado, follow a basic pattern and are centred around a hero's adventure that includes dealing with fear on his journey to victory.

This concept can apply to us all, from chairmen to dabbawallahs, entrepreneurs to my mother's local grocer. Campbell presents a composite picture of the heroic quest, which is an archetype of the change process that humans and organisations alike can go through. Try putting yourself in the hero's shoes, whether you are making the step up to CEO or leaving school to embrace the big bad world. This journey is due to pass through both known and unknown passages and is full of revelations unfolding and new quests beginning. I paraphrase his concept below:

His starting point is a wasteland, where old concepts, ideals and emotional patterns no longer fit; a time for passing the threshold is at hand. The call to adventure comes in many ways both subtle and explicit over the years.

Some who are called to the adventure choose to go. Others may wrestle for years with fearfulness and denial before they are able to transcend that fear and embark on their journey. Because we initially pass through unknown territory and feel exposed, the tendency is to deny our destiny because of our insecurity, our dread of ostracism, our anxiety and our lack of courage to risk what we have – in other words, fear is all around. Yet, he believes that we know that to co-operate with fate brings great personal power and responsibility. However, in the face of refusal, we continue our restlessness and then, as if from nowhere, there comes a guide: something or someone to help us toward the threshold of adventure. This may take the form of voices within or people who guide us to see the way – mentors, coaches, allies, friends and family.

We pass through the gates from our known world into a void, a domain without maps. The perilous journey begins and we encounter a series of tests, trials and orders. It is a place of both terror and opportunity.

If we have truly committed to follow our dream, there exists beyond ourselves and our conscious will, a powerful force that helps us along the way and nurture our growth and transformation.

On the journey, inevitably, we will meet with one or more supreme ordeals. These are the tests of our commitment to the direction we have taken and they provide opportunities to learn from failure. In the later stages of our journey, we cross threshold after threshold, enduring the agony of spiritual growth and breaking through personal limitations.

Finally, the quest accomplished, we return with the elixir for the restoration of society. It is difficult to leave the bliss of the final stages of the journey, a state of high adventure, to return to the long forgotten place from which we first came and we are returning only to prepare to journey forth once more. But, we have returned as a potent new being, prepared to go forth again in service of the community.

I believe Campbell demonstrates how we prevail by using good fear. Yes we find that we first have to listen either to our voices within or find guidance from others, or a combination of the two, but it is instructive that when we commit to our dream it empowers us to draw on our inner strength and use all our resources, including staying in control of the fear that swirls around the unknown and the ordeals we have to pass through. It is as though confronting the fear element invigorates us to move towards our destination.

Of course, **no two adventures are ever the same and no one can ever seek to replicate another's journey.** Nevertheless, the overall cycle and the individual stages that Campbell presents were relevant to me. Given the breadth of human history he has studied and the recurring behavioural patterns in our folklore, which continue to play out today, we see that **fear has and always will exist in our lives. Engaging it, rather than avoiding it, frees us to move forward to realise our dreams and enjoy the rewards of both our own achievements and that of helping others individually and society in general.**

What is courage?

Throughout history, all great human achievement has been accomplished by people who have faced their fears, acted in the face of uncertainty and still dared to move forward. In other words, they have practised courage.

These people were no different to you or I. They were not super human, they too had a fear, but mastered how to control and overcome it so that they could move their dreams forward rather than allowing those fears to hold them back.

Winston Churchill is an obvious example, but to the present day let us take a lady who is a living embodiment of these.

A story of courage and conquering fear

Dr Kiran Bedi's story is remarkable. The first woman IPS (Indian Police Service), officer in India, she went on to become the first female head of Tihar Jail, the largest prison in the Asia-Pacific region. She introduced Vipassana – one of India's oldest forms of mind training – inside Tihar and turned the conventional attitude towards fear and crime on its head.

Winner of the 1994 Ramon Magsaysay award (created in 1957 in memory of the President of the Philippines), Kiran Bedi's eventful life has been chronicled in her biography *I Dare – It's Always Possible*, which focuses on the now-famous Tihar experiment.

I was knocked out by Kiran's aura when I met her in December 2009 at a conference hosted by Cherie Blair in Mumbai. My mother, an avid admirer of Dr Bedi, pushed through the thousand delegates to shake hands with this inspiring modern day Joan of Arc! I followed behind, fervently wishing that Ma would succeed in making contact with her. She did and luckily we bumped into her again at the airport on our way back to Delhi. I just had to talk to her. In 1993, aged just 44, she was appointed Inspector General of Tihar. Sprawling over 200 acres and packed with 11,000 inmates, it was in an appalling bad state. Behind the tough and stern looks on their faces, Kiran could see the vulnerability of inmates. She felt that being in the Tihar itself was enough punishment for their crimes.

Listening to her story of the amazing transformation of the corrupt, drug-ridden, overcrowded, under-resourced prison, I was genuinely moved. The (then) Indian government, agitated by Kiran's zeal and success as a policewoman, decided to 'promote' her to the role at Tihar as a way of dumping her in the garbage so ' ... I would soil away in it'. (In the Indian Police Force, a prison assignment is a 'dump' posting.) For Kiran, it was a double punishment, for both being successful where others hadn't and, being a woman. There was no other place left for her and this was her fated punishment. Little did they anticipate that she would create history and bequeath an invaluable legacy for prison systems both within India and internationally and the principle engines behind her transformation? Vipassana is a form of meditation and yoga to help free the mind of past baggage. Remember this is in a notorious prison! In addition, she used other ways to liberate the inmates' trapped minds in the form of sports, music and foreign language courses. By encouraging meditative silence for the inmates, the path was created for complete emancipation from suffering, an overhaul of negative emotions towards a complete change of self-belief, resilience and focusing on life with a new attitude.

She described how, while talking to the inmates later, she was left totally amazed at the miraculous effect the meditation had on them. A case in point was T.P. Singh, who had spent over nine and a half years of his term on the charge of murdering his brother in law. He claimed he was framed by his own parents with whom he had a lot of differences. 'For nine years, I kept the fire of revenge smouldering within me. My parents did not come to visit me once during this period, but now I have written to them requesting them to come and see me just once. I want to thank them for sending me here because that was the way fated for me to meet my guru.'

Or the young Bashir, a Muslim Kashmiri who was allegedly framed by an influential Kashmiri trader from whom Bashir had sought payment of monies owed to him. During his incarceration, his young daughter died and he was refused permission to attend her funeral. That filled him with bitterness and anxiety and he could not sleep anymore. At first he thought the Vipassana course was some form of Buddhist indoctrination, but soon he realised it has nothing to do with religion; it was a life principle of human existence.

Years later I have come across IT and Finance directors for leading banks (note all the left brain references), who surprised me with their familiarity and use of Vipassana. Described as a form of 'brain surgery', it can train the mind to break the cycle of action and reaction. The mind, said Buddha, consists of four processes: **consciousness** (vinnana), **perception** (sanna), **sensation** (vedana) and **reaction** (sankhara). Consciousness is non-judgmental awareness, until *perception* interprets the stimuli either negatively or positively. This interpretation produces a sensation within us, which is either pleasant or unpleasant, depending upon our perception. Finally comes reaction, which is the action the sensation provokes. **The key to self-awareness is breaking this cycle of action and reaction. When things are going our way and we have what we want, we are happy and content. As soon as something negative occurs, our mood and behaviour changes. We become stressed, sad, or angry and these negative reactions perpetuate negativity, contributing to the general misery that characterises all of humanity.**

It is like a cycle without an end. There is no way to ensure nothing we don't like will ever happen in life. Sooner or later, something comes up. It could be illness, bad weather, a spiteful colleague that disrupts our happiness. We react with negativity and so the cycle starts once again. Vipassana is a way to alleviate this type of endless suffering in your life

This incredible transformation can only be attributed to charismatic and responsible leadership of Kiran and the lessons and ethics are the same whether they're used in a business, boardroom, government or prison.

I asked Kiran if she could name the qualities essential to her kind of leadership. She said, while fear is inevitable, controlling it is key by means of:

- an ability to take decisions under threat;
- willingness to shoulder responsibility in danger;
- ability to create an open and honest environment where staff and inmates feel included and as though they are participants in the system, rather than victims or products of it;
- total dedication to making realistic commitments and fulfilling them within a time frame (not just grand, feel good talks);
- courage to stand up for what is right.

I was struck by what she then said. **'Being able to act as a shock absorber between staff and the system, irrespective of the toll it takes on you, ensures genuine followership and a deep leadership loyalty.'**

Now for cynics, meditation is not just an old technique any more than visualisation can be called just a modern fad. Let me add some more science to the technique Kiran used by showing what happens scientifically in how the brain works with fear.

How the brain channels fear

Mental visualisation is simply a method for deciding to direct and act in your own 'film' by imagining incidents or events that occurred in the past, or may occur in the future. Widely used in the field of neuro linguistic programming (NLP) for reprogramming the mind, it works because (as shown by MRI scans) the brain cannot differentiate between an event that is real and one that is imagined. Evidently the same regions of the brain become activated when a person is doing a task in real life or if they are imagining doing that task in their imagination. This is incredibly exciting, because it means that you can use mental visualisation to prepare yourself for future events in a dress rehearsal.

For those unfamiliar with neurology, let me explain that last sentence as it was expressed to me in conversation by my friend Jenny, who gifted me a visualisation workshop as a Christmas present in 2009. Broadly speaking, the more you do something, the stronger the neural pathways related to that experience become in the brain; the stronger those pathways become, the better you become at something. The session run by Headspace founder Andy Puddicombe was powerful. I met monk Andy, by the door, in jeans and a casual jumper with a standard British bloke feel to him, waiting to help us access inside our heads. I liked the fact that Andy is an ordinary guy who set off to become a monk at the age of 22 and after a decade of living with monks, he was ordained at a Tibetan Monastery in the Indian Himalayas. I walked in to the session as a sceptic and walked out as a convert to the powers of 'head space'!

Bringing this back to fear, let us think of the implications of this process. **If you have a strongly entrenched fear in your mind, then you are likely to react very strongly to the thing that you fear because your brain has been wired, or conditioned, to fear it. So no matter how hard you try, unless you are able to change those fear connections in your brain, you will always react automatically to the stimulus that triggers fear.** Recently someone from my team was a live example of how this works. Otherwise brave as anything, she conquered her severe fear of heights, by doing a thousand feet high canopy walk on the Ghanaian rainforests over seven hanging (and very wobbly) bridges!

The Fear - Trap - Loss cycle

Understanding this cycle is a critical part of getting our heads around fear.

Firstly, traps are the basis of most fears. Traps refer to anything that causes a regression to old ways of thinking and acting and that stops us growing, but when we fall into one of those traps, the consequences are immediate and debilitating.

We fall into traps principally when the stakes are really high, things are in extremes (highs or lows) and a lot of 'something' (money, love, fame, risk etc) is involved. When we fall into a trap, a vicious circle can begin to operate and our situation can go from bad to worse very quickly, but if we are aware of traps and remain alert to their danger, we can largely avoid them.

We now know fear is always related to a loss of something. So, how do we combat the perception that we are losing something? Here are my views in an accessible summary:

Fear of -	Loss of (or Trap):	Ask yourself, if you worry about...
– making a mistake?	perfectionism	... being found out? or, not being perfect?
– upsetting the other person?	social dependency	... being challenged? or, unable to rectify an upset?
– conflict?	conflict avoidance	... being insecure?
– the other person's anger?	weakness	... disrupting harmony? or, unable to deflect/neutralise anger?
– making a decision?	responsibility	... not having all your facts and the confidence in them?
– not looking/ coming across good?	narcissism	... ego?
– failing?	being 'found out'	... your sense of comfort in your strengths and weaknesses?
– retribution, punishment or rejection?	fear of the Fear	... your comfort with risk or reward?
– not being liked?	self esteem, inadequacy and unworthiness.	... ego?

Let us try an exercise. The purpose of it is to clearly identify any fears that you may currently have, with the ultimate aim of eliminating them one by one. Next to each fear, write down exactly what the worst is that could happen. For example, you might be fearful of looking foolish, being embarrassed, not being perfect or even feeling unsafe. Whatever it is that you feel fearful of, write it down so that you can clearly see the factors that are contributing towards your fear.

Now, this is where the psychology comes in.

Each fear factor that you have written down is a driver because they are responsible for making you feel anxious, apprehensive or terrified about something. The more drivers you have, the stronger your feeling of fear will be. For each of your drivers, think about whether they are a real threat to you. For example, if you were made to look stupid in a particular situation, what's the worst that could happen? Would you be able to recover and get on with the rest of your life?

What you will most likely discover is that a large majority of the fear drivers that you have identified aren't really a threat to your life at all or count for less than a fraction of your entire life's worth. So if you were to eliminate each of those drivers one by one, you would greatly reduce the amount of fear that you feel towards something or even be able to eliminate that fear completely. As Susan Jeffers inspires us through the title of her book, 'Feel the Fear and Do It Anyway'.

Stardom and its fearful side

Let us take one of the most commonly cited traps in leadership stories – narcissism. In the ego filled corporate world, I often hear, 'He is a bully. He is aggressive. He doesn't listen. He is the centre of attention. It is his way or the highway.' **Narcissism is sometimes the grandiose aspect of the individual, the part that needs attention, the part that brags and always needs to be in the centre.**

CEOs are not the worse culprits. Pop stars, actors and athletes can suffer plenty from this syndrome. A famous filmmaker once said to me: leaders fall in love with their self-inflated, make-believe versions. The scale and speed with which a common man becomes a star gives them a sense of infallibility and somehow the star starts believing in their own specialness and sense of entitlement.

Hollywood superstar Marlon Brando in one of his later interviews admitted, 'An actor's a guy who, if you ain't talking about him, he ain't listening.'

Narcissism is often the part that puts on a show, the part that appears to have no fears, no hesitation and no weaknesses. It is the part that doesn't believe it needs anybody or anything else to succeed, to excel. Unlike the Narcissus of Greek legend, who was enchanted by his own reflection in a pool of water, researchers say that beneath narcissism lies a fear of insecurity and self-loathing, not confidence or self-acceptance.

Here we have false arrogance masking a real fear. Fear comes in many guises and this one is as real as any other. In this example, the enthralling reflection conceals the weaknesses. Strip it away and you see the fear exposed as those shortcomings in your DNA that need attention.

Coping with the 'ledge' factor

Back to my ledge from the skydive. However you came by your current role – whether you've been toiling away for years or have rocketed to the top very quickly, someone has spotted your talent for you to be where you are. **While we are born with various attributes that might help or hinder our leadership skills, in my opinion, most leaders are made extraordinary by courage and belief. The only way to learn the ropes, alongside developing, nurturing and adapting is, by making a bold quantum leap forward without waiting for the right safety net to come about. So step off, or over, that 'ledge' (by all means with my book under your arm) and enjoy.**

In summary:

Acknowledge your fears

To become a fearless leader you must first of all acknowledge your fears. This is all about accepting them without prejudice, not denying them or hiding them under excuses. By all means, use the Fear-Loss-Traps exercise to be honest with yourself.

Deal with ambiguity

Accept the reality that one of the key challenges and opportunities of leading comes from dealing with ambiguity as we saw in the first chapter on the self. That is all about not 'freezing' by fearing to make a decision when you feel you do not know the full answer. Learning to make decisions with limited information and unlimited good instinct is a powerful leadership skill. It is not failproof and if you make a mistake or the wrong decision, acknowledge it early, be candid (a cover up, as they say, is worse than the deed) and find a solution.

Keep making decisions

You are going to get things wrong. Probably more often than you can bear to think about. So it is best to use the 'now get over it' maxim and move on. The only thing worse than making a bad decision is holding your followers hostage by not making a decision at all. Think of it like this: unless and until you make that decision, you will never know whether it is right or wrong. If you're right, fine; if you're wrong, it is fine too as long as you spot the problems early on and act promptly to rectify them.

Stand on and touch the 'ledge'

The ledge, from my skydive example, is the very edge of fear, but don't step back from it, allow, what is in effect, the creative tension from it help you to grow taller. Make your jump. You will gain confidence through the knowledge that that which scares you can be turned around to help you improve; that beyond what you think you can do is what you will be happy you have done; that if you can manage and survive this big thing you have reduced to a small thing, you will surely be able to manage and defeat the next big thing.

We are all skydiving now.

One final story

The year before I met Kiran Bedi in Mumbai, the city suffered a brutal terrorist attack on the Taj Mahal Palace, one of the world's top hotels. Paul Polman, the Dutch boss of Unilever, was trapped inside as the attack took place. His office resides in one of London's most impressive neoclassical buildings, but I have never met a more down to earth man. He is an eclectic Dutchman and when we met he greeted me with a classical Namaste (the Indian greeting) it took me pleasantly by surprise. Behind him I could see samples of Ben & Jerry's cartons and Persil bottles, along with boxes of Lipton Tea, Domestos, Dove soap and Marmite – products that form the Unilever empire – one of the biggest consumer goods giants in the world, the third largest in fact.

Speaking with Paul in the relative calm of his London office and hearing his personal experience of this trauma couldn't provide a more vivid contrast. This was a real life example of being there at the inception of a crisis, surviving it and emerging from it with new focus.

Paul has always believed in 'never wasting a good crisis'. So he has used the recent financial crisis to drive the changes needed at Unilever for it to be more agile and adapt to today's markets than it otherwise would have done.

He has always sought to engage. Early ambitions to be a priest gave way to thoughts of being a doctor, then to studying economics before spending twenty six years at Procter & Gamble, where he mastered four other languages before moving to Nestlé and rising to vice president within two years. Junior managers would be invited to join him on his early morning runs in this early part of his career.

Paul also takes his current CEO role at Unilever in his stride and he is attuned to the environment he operates in, including an awareness of fear, complacency and motivation. He says that 'good fear' helps him to stay ahead of the competition: **'you have to have a certain level of paranoia that someone out there is trying to make you obsolete'.** Complacency is kept at bay by remembering that 'in fast-moving consumer goods, if you think you are winning you are probably already losing'. Motivation is on each day's agenda as he says: **'you can't really bank on past achievements for future successes. So I tell myself every morning, without forgetting what I've learnt hopefully, that today's my first day.'**

Which brings us back to the Taj Mumbai and what that day held in store. I summarise some of the reports at the time to give you a flavour of the event. Paul was then CEO-elect, attending a farewell dinner for his predecessor, Patrick Cescau. As they served the main course, they heard what they thought were fireworks at a nearby wedding. These, in fact, were the first gunshots from the terrorists who were storming the hotel. The staff quickly realised what was wrong and led by a twenty four-year-old banquet manager, Mallika Jagad, took steps to protect the guests. They stayed there all night, listening to the terrorists rampaging through the Taj, hurling grenades, firing automatic weapons and tearing the place apart. The staff kept calm, tending to the guests needs during this maelstrom. Early the next morning, a fire started in the hallway outside, forcing the group to try to climb out the windows. A fire crew spotted them and, with its ladders, helped the trapped people escape quickly.

During the onslaught, thirty one people died (including eleven staff) and twenty eight were hurt, while between 1,200 and 1,500 guests escaped. Studies show that the Taj employees' actions of handling the crises weren't prescribed in manuals; no official policies or procedures existed for an event such as on that day. It was instinct, resilience and fearlessness – natural ingredients in our DNA.

Paul recalls that **'it wasn't a pleasant situation, but at the same time I think we came out stronger as a team – I became a little bit of an Indian, if I may say, coming out of that (with a quick witted Indian head tilt) – but above all, my character changed, as did my understanding of what being a team and leading a team really meant.'**

We remained silent for a minute or so before he said, **'Facing up to fear as a leader is an important part of growing up and succeeding. In today's 'new normal' where all the rules are being rewritten, to succeed, you'll need to develop the right balance of self-confidence, fearlessness and humility and that will come with time or experience or both.'**

Provided leaders can make the right choices on how best to respond to them, fear-factors are weaknesses that can be turned into strengths.

> **To the degree you face and name and deal with your failures as a leader, to that same extent you will create an environment conducive to growing and retaining productive and committed colleagues...To the degree you attempt to hide or dissemble your weaknesses, the more you will need to control those you lead, the more insecure you will become and the more rigidity you will impose prompting the ultimate departure of your best people.***

Don't fear, fear. Controlled fear can be a good stimulant with a positive energy to unleash our creative tension and push us to grow.

Having stood on the ledge of this chapter, are you ready to explore the edge – maybe even jump off – of this powerful ledge?

---

* Dan B. Allender Leading with a Limp, Random House, 2008

Your code for Ingredient Eight: Fear

Pause. Ask yourself what do you remember from this chapter; list the key takeaways and ideas that had an impact on you – something inspiring, something relevant or something you would like to try.

Now, make a note of the following: the term 'things' below can refer to behaviour actions, conversations, skills or even an attitude

1. List three things you would like to START doing to protect yourself from your FEAR...

2. List three things you would like to STOP doing to protect yourself from your FEAR...

3. List three things you would like to CONTINUE doing to protect yourself from your FEAR...

On an ascending scale of 1 to 10, how robust is this ingredient in your DNA?

Ingredient Nine

RESILIENCE

—'I don't give up'—

Success can teach us a lot, but I believe, failure can teach us more. Resistance and failure are inevitable facts of life. They make us stronger. Resilience is the ability to face resistance; deal with it head on and not let it deflate our intent, energy or self-belief. Interlocked with self, focus and instinct, resilience helps us renew ourselves.

CH$_9$

Do you know people who have an indefinable element in them, whereby they:

- bounce back from setbacks with renewed focus
- turn problems and challenges into opportunities
- don't let rejection or resistance deflate their energy
- use mistakes and failures to learn from
- do not let anxiety and doubts overwhelm them
- maintain a sense of humour and realistic optimism under stress
- do not feel shame or depression in the face of failure
- reject the word 'victim' and celebrate being a survivor
- are always open to taking risks

Or, just don't give up?

That element is resilience. We can all tap into it, whoever we are and wherever we are. Let me open with my memory of a nameless, resilient young hero – from the streets of Hong Kong.

In 2002, I was in Hong Kong on business crossing a very busy road, streams of people, business folk in pinstriped suits rushing about in their lunch hour, the vast majority of them on their mobile phones. The street was frenetic. Car horns blazing; people and traffic galore. Amidst all the din and bustle, I saw a young boy of around nine or ten years of age in a pair of torn shorts, trying to cross the road, both hands occupied with holding two younger children and with a baby tugged in his arms. He looked poor, hungry and tired, yet the glint in his eye was one of firm resolve, stoic responsibility and determination to see his younger siblings safely through to the other side of the road. It brought a tear to my eye. The young man's steely inner strength affected me profoundly. Resilience is a natural life skill, one that is untaught, but enables us to do whatever it takes to see something, or someone, through 'to the other side'. That sheer resolve in his eye, makes me hope fervently that wherever he is now, that young man is a leader and leading something, in some shape or form.

I learnt a lesson that day. Somewhere, vulnerability, crises and adversity become great teachers of resilient leadership; showing us how to cope and thrive against resistance. Have you noticed resilient children tend to have low dependency and high self-esteem. They are caring but firm and compassionate but detached enough to be strong.

If that's my nameless hero, how about some named and known heroes, who have shaped our world in so many ways and yet overcome so many setbacks and disappointments en route:

- Akio Morita, founder of giant electronics company SONY, first made an electric rice cooker. It burned the rice and only 100 units were sold. Today, SONY is valued at US$66 billion.
- Albert Einstein, the father of modern physics, had such low marks at school that his parents feared he had learning difficulties.
- Bill Gates, Microsoft founder and one of the richest men in the world, was a Harvard university drop-out.
- Soichoro Honda, founder of the world's largest motorcycle manufacturer, failed to get an engineering job at Toyota and was unemployed until one of his neighbours took a chance on him.
- J K Rowling, the author of the Harry Potter books, was rejected numerous times by publishers before being accepted by Bloomsbury.
- Walt Disney's first cartoon production, launched in his garage, went bankrupt.
- Churchill failed 6th grade but eventually became an MP and then British Prime Minister, steering the country through World War II.

The common thread above is of overcoming resistance. **We all know that often, breakthrough moments of success and discovery do not happen in linear, sequential plots; they come about as a result of trial and error, strife, setbacks and persistence. The path to victory usually runs in zigzags, so what we need to do is train our minds to pursue our goals relentlessly. There's no room for 'it is too hard' or 'I quit'.**

Just like athletes undergo resistance training – a form of strength training in which each effort is performed against a specific and opposing force generated by resistance (i.e. being pushed, squeezed, stretched or bent) – leadership potential can also be exercised in a similar way. When we truly test our mental and emotional limits and boundaries, we realise we can in fact go a bit further than we thought – another step, another inch – and soon we set a new, more stretching limit to reach. In other words, our potential has an infinite capacity and it takes a lot before we reach peak resistance.

Success can teach us a lot, but learning from a setback or failure is more deeply felt and leaves a more lasting impact.

An aikido student asked his master, 'Master – how is it that you never lose your balance?'. The master replied, 'I continuously lose my balance. I just regain it faster.'

Back at school, I can't remember attending a class on resilience or resistance. Can you? Some of us experience it in the playground, but nonetheless we see it around us every day in our leaders. Think of what our grandparents went through during wars and conflicts. Or sports stars who win championships after years of trying and endurance. Or CEOs going through everyday crises?

I'm sure you are familiar with a lot of the above, but often it is pausing and looking at the familiar and asking ourselves what is behind it. Is there a pattern or trend? Are there new aspects to what I think I already know? Also, of course, what do others do that I can learn from? So to look at the power of resilience, through someone else's eyes, I would like you to hear what five CEOs, an ex-minster and two social activists have to say through their endurance journeys.

Peter Clarke – CEO of Man Group

Take Peter Clarke, CEO of Man Group's, the world's largest listed hedge fund in a trillion dollar industry, managing funds worth some US$60 billion. I smiled when he told me 'life is a marathon, not a sprint'. Preserving energy is key to coping with the challenges that life throws at us. Stepping up from CFO, Peter succeeded Stanley (now Lord) Fink, who has been described as the godfather of the UK hedge fund industry. In short then, Peter has been following in the footsteps of a pioneer and his own marathon has been non-stop since he took office in March 2007. He's had to steer his company through the credit crunch, the ensuing global financial meltdown, the Bernard Madoff hedge fund fraud and the sovereign debt and euro crises. He then led the US$1.6 billion acquisition of GLG Partners, a US global investment manager, in 2010.

Resilience, Renewal, Recovery and facing Resistance is Peter's trademark. Dealing with an array of international crises, battling against the strongest market headwinds we have known for nearly a century and integrating a material acquisition. All the while, he has been fostering innovation and nurturing organic and geographical growth. It is a measure of his resolve and intense tenacity that he has been resilient enough to stay focused on the medium and long term plans.

Let us peek into Peter's childhood. He says, 'As an Army child, the upside to moving around a lot was exposure and adaptability and learning to get on with people. That makes you adapt to different kinds of resistance'.

This wiring of his DNA, set against the Mangroup's backdrop of inception in 1783, demonstrates a remorseless ability to reinvent itself, overcoming resistance to change both internally and externally in adapting itself to the changing business world.

So I asked how Peter manages this: 'we let people stretch, create and innovate and even make mistakes. But as the leadership team, we try to provide the frameworks within which people can succeed or fail and create enough observational checks and balances to work out when someone may reach break through or go off the rail.' I also discover this cohesion starts on day one for each new employee, as Peter makes a point of personally meeting all new recruits soon after they walk through the door. This introduction, it would seem, sets the tone that looks beyond the individual to instil resilience across the whole team.

Could it be, I wonder, that there are two sides to his approach that mirror and motivate his leadership? The relentless pursuit of innovation and adaptability in tandem with the drive for permanence and resilience?

I have no doubt that, for Peter, resilience is the key to turning resistance to success, underpinned with a strong tap root to his dogged ability to focus. No wonder, he shared how he often starts his business day by doing long divisions (1/17386!) in his head while doing his morning runs .... you sense from the twinkle in his eye how adept he is at bringing his own mental acuity to bear on such calculations.

That's one man. There are many others. Sometimes, even entire nations are resilient. Let us take an example from West Africa.

Ghana

In May 2012, a last-minute assignment took me to Africa for the first time. Ghana is becoming a leader on the African continent, the first nation south of the Sahara to gain independence so 'resilience along the way' has a DNA resonance for Ghanaians.

As I prepared for my trip, I didn't know what to expect and decided to put any preconceptions on hold. I knew that my project involved working with the executive top team of a global company but the rest was uncharted territory. So, suitably punctured with vaccinations and dosed up with malaria tablets, I felt quite intrepid as I touched down on my first sub-Saharan 'expedition'. As the aircraft taxied on the runway in Accra, I switched on my phone. There was a text message; 'Welcome to Ghana, Rhea. I'm on the tarmac waiting in an orange VVIP jacket.' That was our wonderful host was indeed waiting on the tarmac, beaming and radiating true hospitality. I spotted the letters VVIP in his jacket and my colleague, Peter and I were soon ushered into the VVIP lounge.

The next two days were like taking part in a fascinating documentary – the social and business scene in Accra proved colourful and enigmatic. The emergence of a strong, aspiring middle class was defining Accra's cityscape: pastel-coloured houses reminiscent of the Italian Cinque Terre were underscoring the dreams and ambitions of a new professional class. Accra is an eclectic mix – from business goers in designer outfits, with MBAs from INSEAD and Wharton on the one hand – while on the other, mobile recharge sellers from poor families, in bright red jackets, are selling talk time in fluent English.

The programme we designed was a novel experiment. One morning I found myself on a big bus leading an international group of 37 people. It was a business immersion of getting under the skin of how people in the streets of Ghana make decisions. Aptly called a 'happy feet experience' we had to strike up conversations with strangers, walk into banks, police stations, hospitals and shops to interview people on what drove their decisions. To do it the Ghanaian way, we soon found ourselves taking part in what Ghanaians love most – dancing Azonto! A soft form of a happy rebellion and breaking away from tradition, the street was filled with rhythm, laughter, sunshine and an open welcome. Under the amusement of it all was a deep learning experience and not the least, observing which of the twenty nationalities gave themselves the permission to jump in and embrace an unfamiliar environment... which chose to hold back and use reserve... who took a risk... who liberated themselves to be free without any fear of judgment. **In leadership, like life, the environment matters. Environment can be referred to as context, setting or climate. Exposing ourselves to new and unknown settings activates strands in our DNA we would have never known in the familiar world of comfort and predictability.**

I was advised by a local guide to interview a local seller of phones and sim cards. I agreed and was then taken to a little shack. I walked in with a tiny sliver of hesitation but walked out immensely inspired by this guy in his early 20s. In his ramshackle office I got a thorough run-down of competitors, economy and the impact of the industry crises. He could be an economist, an informant and industry analyst all in one – and he was only 22!

Things had changed so much from West Africa's past image of crime, epidemics and poverty. Towards the end of my fortnight, I regretted it had taken me so long to set foot in this amazing country.

Ghana had a metaphorical 'bag of inspiration' waiting for me. One that topped the charts was seeing women in business. Take Patricia Obo-Nai, the telecommunications industry's only female and youngest Chief Technology Officer (CTO), who at thirty eight, is at the vanguard of Africa's imminent – economic revolution and its social renaissance. Research shows less than 24% of CIO or CTOs are women. That immediately attracted me to Patricia. I worked with her for two days in a room and was fascinated to uncover her real assets as a leader in business. With enviable double degrees in law and engineering plus an MBA, I realised her strongest skill was in her ability to stay grounded, cut through noise and clutter and drive her point across and read the room without playing any games. She has spearheaded the expansion of Vodafone's fixed and mobile network and currently manages a team of about 600 people, approximately 50% of the entire organisation.

She has a no nonsense work ethos rooted in self-reliance, independence and 'doing the right thing', I love what she refers to as her Power Principle. 'As an individual, I believe that your power lies in how you value your own self-worth and self-esteem. As a CTO, I believe that whatever you lay your hands on, do it with all your heart and do it well.'

She puts resilience at the heart of her identity. Mother of two, a wife, a daughter, a sister, a boss, a leader her ability to adapt to roles and lead across the various identities, according to her was rooted in her middle-class, grounded upbringing. Inspiring, I thought to myself.

Investors from countries such as India, China, Russia and Brazil are looking to inject their money into Ghana. Last year, foreign direct investment rose by $70 million in the second quarter, despite the financial crisis. But, why Ghana? Why all the interest and excitement in this country? 'Ghana is the gateway to West Africa,' says John Dramani Mahama, the country's vice president.

'Even though Ghana has had its very unsavoury times in the past, what may be different is that we Ghanaians have a level of tolerance, a level of give and take. What is different with us is that we have made democracy work;

we have respect for the rule of law. In 2007, more than 600 million barrels of light oil and natural gas were discovered off Ghana's shores, which could earn it as much as $20 billion by 2030. Signalling hope for a country in which nearly 80% of the inhabitants live on less than two dollars a day. The excitement has spread to other countries as well, creating a number of new potential business partners for Ghana and the first technology park is to be established as part of the commitment to development'.*

The message of resilience and renewal are a key part of the collective Ghanaian DNA. Indeed, on a visit to the hub of Ghanian life, from Nima market to fishing villages, people who have nothing are so emotionally rich. The people of Ghana are all survivors and warriors, fighting daily resistance. Gifted with an amazing resilient spirit, on the streets, everyone is an entrepreneur, up at dawn and relentlessly trying to make ends meet, with a smile. Everyone here wants to help; the care they show is pure. During the immersion, part of my team lost their way. On being reunited we were touched to hear about a local lady, who in her 50s, helped them out, not just by showing the way but by walking with them for a mile until they reached the bus. In the West, a cab driver may refuse to drive you to your destination even if you pay them to do so.

Developing resilience

The belief that leaders have an endless pot of stamina to deliver success year after year is a fallacy. Resilience is an organic ingredient, like instinct, the more you practice it, the stronger it gets. Today, resilience – the ability to bounce back, cope, renew and revitalise – has become a must-have for smart leaders.

Reculer pour mieux sauter

The French have an expression, reculer pour mieux sauter, which means to retreat so that you can subsequently advance more effectively. This idea also seems to me central to the notion of what resilience is: the act of absorbing, the stress of a blow. It may mean that we fall back momentarily but it also means that we can jump forward more successfully subsequently.

Nietzsche's assertion of *'that which does not kill us makes us stronger'* seems to me to be profoundly true as far as resilience is concerned. A definition of resilience for this book, is:

---

* Mr. George Aboagye, CEO of Ghana Investment Promotion Centre 'the ability to recover from, or adjust to, any change, setback or disappointment, while ideally being made stronger by the experience.'

As Charles Darwin wrote: **'It is not the strongest of the species that survive, nor the most intelligent, but the most responsive to change.'**

One thing is for sure: resilience is a kind of catalyst – or perhaps a better analogy would be a vitamin or essential protein in this book. Without resilience, none of these other ingredients are likely to deliver their full value to your leadership DNA.

The locus of control

Do you perceive yourself as having control over your own life? Or do you blame outside sources for failures and problems? It is usually the case that resilient people have what is known as an 'internal locus of control'. Its study dates back to the 1960s, with Julian Rotter's investigation into how people's behaviours and attitudes affect the outcomes of their lives.

The 'locus of control' describes the degree to which individuals perceive that outcomes result from their own behaviours, or from forces that are external to themselves. Dr Kiran Bedi (remember who you met in the Fear chapter) has this powerful principle learnt from her mother: **'100 things happen in life; 90 are your creations, 10 are outside your control. The point being made is to take control of the 90.** While we may be able to put some blame on external causes, it is important to feel as if we have the power to make choices that will affect our situation, our ability to cope and our future.

Problem-solving skills are essential. When a problem or crisis emerges, resilient people are able to stay calm and brace themselves in a way that often means they can spot important details and take advantage of opportunities the problem presents. That strong internal locus of control is key to any kind of leadership.

The seven-year cycle
Resilience and renewal are two sides of the same coin. We, therefore, need to understand the concept of renewal, to fully appreciate resilience.

You may have all heard of the saying, we change every seven years, or that we live life in seven year cycles. These cycles are real building blocks for growth, renewal and resilience only if we are more aware of them as they happen. This is not just a feel good mantra. The origins of this scientific claim roots back to the philosopher Rudolph Steiner. There is a natural release of energy every seven years which encourages us to evolve – should we choose to harness the power it offers us.

Link this to the heart of the book – our DNA analogy. Most cells in our bodies renew over time, otherwise we couldn't sustain our existence. At a biological level, cells are made of proteins and everything that goes on in a creature involves proteins interacting with each other. Proteins are generally 50 to 2,000 amino acids long; making and folding proteins are changes that go on continuously throughout the body. I was honoured to hear a lecture in 2011 by Sir Paul Nurse, a British geneticist and cell biologist. Paul is a Nobel Prize Winner whose passion lies in how the basic unit of human life – 'cells', copy and divide. This added scientific rigour to my already strong instinct on the role of renewal through the seven year cycles.

At a physical/social level, these long, complex folding and unfolding means our personalities change too and key emotional, physical and mental changes seem to occur in similar cycles too.

You and I are not the same person now we were 20 years ago. In fact, what would the 20 year old you make of you now? How different were you just seven years ago? We come into the world with infinite poetntial, open to everything, packed with the ten raw ingredients. The seven-year cycles morph and mould us continuously. Wouldn't it be amazing to make the most of these changes rather than be a passive recipient?

Going Through The Seven Cycles

For our first seven years, in the main we are compliant and in 'accept' mode. Gradually, a growing awareness creeps in, and we feel the need to assert ourselves. From the age of two, we feel a need to say 'no!'. By the age of seven, we begin to support that assertive claim with reason: 'No, because...'

At the age of 14, comes the second series of defiances. We need our own space as we prepare for adulthood, like teenagers, defiant on the surface, are ultimately trying to discover 'who they really are' .

Then at 21, people are usually ready to cut ties and try something new. Often this is when the itch to 'backpack around India' or tour 'South America on a bike' kicks in. This is how we prepare emotionally and mentally for independence. The greatest realisation of adulthood probably occurs at 28, just before the 'crossroads at 30'.

In Step with the Cycles

The cycles of seven, 14 and 21 all deal with internal changes, while the cycle of 28 is the first step in external integration with the rest of the world. Very often the thought is, 'Okay, world, what have you got to give me?'

The thirty-fifth year is the starting of true emotional adulthood. At 35 comes a half-way mark, a wake-up call that gives you the opportunity to say, 'it is getting late – I need to fulfil my dreams, soon'. It is the 'what's next?' factor.

The forty-second year brings a major change because here, the integration of the whole self occurs. The view here is 'World, what have I got to give you?' It is the realisation of all the growth that has occurred and the ability to use it in its most productive way.

At 42, you may begin to have healthy doubts about your life. They are based on the growth gained in the interim years between 35 and 42. Do you want to maintain your life as it is, or are changes imminent?

49 continues to be a period of doubt and sometimes it can become unsettling. There are rumblings of 'Where am I headed? Is this all?' There can be the sense of 'What have I done with my life so far?' There is a tendency to view this cycle as the last chance to be productive, prove ability, or make a name.

At 56, there is very often a tendency to let go of everything that has been and to renew new hopes and dreams. And so it continues.

Each energy cycle is a cycle of growth. As I interviewed people and enquired about how they would define their cycle of growth, the examples varied from 'tweaks' to 'transformation'. For some it is about a house extension; for many others it was about adding a life skill to the list; for others, it involved bigger major life decisions, such as moving from corporate sector to philanthropy, or moving from central London to a village in Asia.

Note the trend: at the end of each cycle and start of another, we either review, repair or renew.

Its not always exact. Cycle reactions will vary according to individual responsibilities of the time. At 49, some people may still be seriously involved in raising children and don't feel free to let go and take on something new. They can use the next cycle to accomplish this as long as they don't take the attitude that it is too late. The point is that there is a natural release of energy every seven years which encourages you to move forward and make changes. It helps to keep you from getting stuck. We have a choice to flow with or resist these natural cycles.

Let us look at a few real-life examples.

Maggy Barankitse – the survivor who teaches resilience through self-belief

'Life is a feast. God won't knock on the door and give you a cue to act on. The sign can come to you through someone you meet or some crises that knocks your door instead. You have got to be ready to read the cue and take action.'

Marguerite (Maggy) Barankitse is a Burundian humanitarian with a big heart. An exceptional lady, she reminds me of Nelson Mandela. Our paths crossed through ActionAid, the global charity I support. We then reconvened at London's King's Cross station, as her train pulled in from Paris. Everything she said has this vibe about her as someone who is giving her every breath to ensure a future for her country.

Burundi, a landlocked region in East Africa, has two conflicting ethnic tribes of *Hutus* and *Tutsis* living in proximity. Marguerite Barankitse was born a *Tutsi*. An interesting connection as years ago, somewhere, I had read a fascinating historical highlight about Tutsis. Apparently when the European colonists conducted censuses, they wanted to identify the people throughout Rwanda-Burundi according to a simple classification scheme. They defined 'Tutsi' as anyone owning more than ten cows (a sign of wealth) or with the physical feature of a longer nose, or longer neck, commonly associated with the Tutsi.

Anyway, Maggy lost her father when she was six years old and her mother at 26. She became a teacher but had to battle with discrimination, which reigned in the establishment between the two ethnic tribes. One day, a young girl who had been raped, thrown out of her home by her family and excluded from her school, came to see her. Maggy took in the girl and her baby and helped her get back to school. However this gesture caused Maggy, in turn, to be rejected by the school and she lost her job.

In 1993, Burundi was caught up in a terrible civil war. After the assassination of the Republic's first democratically elected President, Melchior N'Dadaye, Hutus and Tutsis went to war and over 300,000 people were killed. Maggy, then 36, was threatened and beaten by a genocidal mob. Despite this, she managed to rescue 32 children and, with help from ActionAid, kept them safe throughout the civil war. Since that fateful day in 1993, she has brought her message of peace to more than 10,000 orphans.

As Maggy puts it, 'I am a Tutsi woman. Before the war began, I already had seven adopted children, four Hutu and three Tutsi. When the killing began, no one would protect us, so we went to the Bishop's house, thinking we would be safe. There were many other people already there.

'On 24 October 1993, the Tutsis came and demanded that we handed over the Hutus to them. I refused, but they beat me and tied me up and then covered the building with fuel. I was so frightened, but I remembered I had a little money and I offered them that to spare the children. They did and allowed 25 of the children to live. Then they set fire to the building with everyone else inside and killed 72 people in front of my eyes. The whole thing went on for six hours, from 9 in the morning to 3 in the afternoon. They let me go because I was Tutsi. I was so frightened and distraught but I could not see any of the children, so I went to the chapel to pray. I said to God, 'show me how, show me how I can continue to live after this'. Then I heard my eldest child say 'we are here' and there they were, all seven of them, hiding in the chapel with the other children. I saw then, I decided I needed to help create a new generation. It was my absolute conviction.

'So I took my own seven children and the other 25 to the cemetery to try and find a safe place, I knew that if people saw the children they would try and kill them. We were very, very hungry. I thought 'where can we go to be safe?'. We went to the home of a German man (who was working for ActionAid at the time) and that is where Maison Shalom (House of Peace) began.

'The ActionAid support touched me, because it was not like a project. Our philosophy is the same – it is not to assist but to give people a chance to hold their lives in their own hands. Once a journalist asked some children who had been traumatised – now children of Maison Shalom – what ethnicity they were and they said 'Hu-tutsi'. She then knew her mission was fulfilled. Boundaries had been blurred. Her resilient spirit of leading in crises, is really amazing. Maggy has a big heart and even bigger hands which takes her humanitarian sprit and translates it into direct action.

'We now have over 10,000 children in Maison Shalom. Ownership papers often go to the children, unless there is a good reason that they cannot take responsibility. If they cannot own their own house, then they can never be truly independent. The houses we build are normal, we do not make them any different from other people's, except that we make sure they all have water and electricity. ... Ultimately, however, my dream is to close Shalom House – then I will know that everyone has a house, a job, everything they need to live their own lives.'

Children taking ownership of their lives, reminded me of what Tony Little, from Eton College, always says. The beauty of two polar opposite institutions imparting the same message got me excited.

Identifying As a Survivor, Not a Victim

A great coach of mine, years ago, once told me how important it is to manage negative self-talk during moments of danger and crisis. For me, the first lesson is when you are dealing with any potential crisis, it is essential to view yourself as a survivor, not a victim. Surviving is not just about physically continuing to exist – it is about being able to leap forward and persevere with your attempts to reach your goal, even if resistance hits and solutions are absent or hard to come by. Your core tenacity and self-belief will tell you the solution will come. But giving up will mean failure. Clients often ask, so how do we do that?

I say manage the 'self talk' in your head. There are four types of self-talk to be aware of that are common in people who are prone to low resilience.

1. **The worrier.** The worrier's dominant tendencies include anticipating the worst, overestimating the odds of something bad or embarrassing happening and creating disproportionate images of failure. Typical of the worrier's self-talk is *'but, what if...?'*. **Worriers promote anxiety.**

2. **The critic.** The critic is that part of you that is constantly judging and evaluating your behaviour. It points out your flaws and limitations and jumps on any mistake you make to remind you that you are flawed. The critic may be personified in your own dialogue as the voice of your parents, or anyone in the past that has inflicted you with their criticism. Typical of the critic's self-talk is *'you stupid...'*

and 'can't you ever get it right?' **Critics promote low self belief and cynicism.**

3. **The victim.** The victim is that part of you that feels helpless or hopeless and believes that you are in some way deprived, defective or unworthy. The victim always sees insurmountable problems between you and your goals and complains about your situation. Typical self-talk engaged in by the victim include *'I'll never be able to do that so what's the point in trying?'* and *'nothing ever goes right'.* **Victims promote depression.**

4. There is a fourth. **The Perfectionist**. These people strive for absolute flawlessness and being perfect. 'Almost perfect' or '99% accurate' is seen as a failure by perfectionists. **Perfectionists promote burnout and self defeat.**

Can you imagine a team with victims, perfectionist and critics? They are not uncommon, by the way and are often bred by weak leaders. I had to coach one such team and I almost became a worrier myself. It took significant injections of resilience to avoid that trap.

What next?

We have met Peter Clarke, visited Ghana and seen Burundi through the eyes of Maggy Barankitse. I hope my description of resilience now gives you an understanding of this ingredient. To round out the chapter, I would like you to now hear from (amongst others) Sir Malcolm Rifkind, a British politician; Julia Immonen, Finnish founder of Sport Against Trafficking; Dr Louise Makin, British CEO of BTG, a pharmaceutical company; Barbara Merry, British CEO of Hardy Underwriting operating in the Lloyds Insurance market.

We will then finish with someone I greatly admire. Willie Walsh, Irish CEO of the International Airlines Group (IAG).

Sir Malcolm Rifkind – the story of the handover of Hong Kong to China

I wanted to pick a politician who has survived the winds of change. Sir Malcolm Rifkind is one of four ministers to serve throughout the whole of both the Margaret Thatcher and John Major Prime Ministerships. That got me wanting to know more.

I spoke to him in 2012. A sightseeing tour through Sir Malcolm's journey illustrates how resilience was a necessary tool to dissolve resistance between different interests. From being in the school debating society to becoming the British Foreign and Commonwealth Secretary, he has had a full and varied political life. Including Secretary of State for Scotland, then Transport, then Defence and being responsible for Britain's relations with the Soviet Union and Eastern Europe, the European Community and sub-Saharan Africa. But the one that attracted my attention was the final negotiation with China over the transfer of Hong Kong in 1997.

As we know, for over 150 years Hong Kong was a colony of the British Crown and before the handover in 1997, was one of Britain's last glimmers of Empire. Britain had won the island and leased the New Territories in 1839 and 1898, after defeating China during the first Opium War. In 1997 the 99 year lease on Kowloon and the New Territories was up and Britain negotiated the Hong Kong handover. China was eager to take back and redeem what it saw as an embarrassment in its history and was backed by international support. Perversely, while Hong Kongers felt an allegiance to China, there was no real appetite to return the world's most capitalist city to a communist country. Concerns about civil liberties and the rights of Hong Kongers after the handover were rife, particularly after the Tiananmen Square Massacre. To try and assuage the local populations fear, Sir Malcolm, with others, had to negotiate (in conjunction with the Hong Kong Governor, Chris Patten and elected Hong Kong politicians) with the Chinese the Basic Law, the premise of which was to assure 'Hong Kong's Capitalist Way of Life' for at least fifty years with a number of laws and measures. No mean feat!

When I discussed the ten ingredients in the book, he said *resilience* stood out for him as the most pivotal through this Hong Kong handover. In our conversation, he told me how much he enjoyed 'making a point' while debating in school. In Sir Malcolm's leadership passages, *'resilience not only provides the wherewithal to argue your point, persuade and see policies enacted, but it helps you survive the very machinery of the game of snakes and ladders that politics resembles – you can be climbing successfully and successively and then .... an unlucky throw of the dice can set you back many moves'.*

This is in stark contrast to the more linear progress in the corporate world, so resilience is essential to keep your bearing and temperament when you reverberate on your pathway around your public posts. And to think a lot of his resilience lies in holding a good dialogue which as we now know has its inception in his school debating society – mental toughness is essential.

Sir Malcolm is now Chairman of the Intelligence and Security Committee appointed by the Prime Minister, David Cameron, in 2010.

Three women in a boat.

That's a play on the title of the 1898 book, *Three men in a boat*, in case you hadn't made the connection. I thought that might be an appropriate title given I am about to present three stories of resilience from three tough women! *I chose them because you may not have heard of them but that is the point – they are ordinary people who have achieved extra ordinary things.*

- *Julia Immonen* who made a maiden voyage of resilience across the Atlantic in 2011 with an all female crew to campaign against human trafficking
- *Louise Makin*, a scientist turned the CEO of BTG (an international specialist healthcare company) whose other passion is sailing 'Journey Maker' in the Three Peaks Yacht race and
- *Barbara Merry*, CEO of Hardy Underwriting who, amongst other sectors, provides maritime insurance and is one of the few senior women in the Lloyd's Insurance market.

The 'water' connection was flowing .

Julia .....

On 7 December 2011, Julia set off from the Canary Islands to row the Atlantic. 45 days, 15 hours and 26 minutes later she arrived 2,613 miles away in Barbados. Julia was the nucleus of a five-woman crew for Row for Freedom. This, in partnership with charities ECPAT UK and The A21 Campaign where she is *Sport For Freedom* Director. Sport For Freedom aims to raise awareness and £1 million to combat human trafficking. This five – women crew achieved two world records; the first female five to row any ocean and the fastest crossing of the Atlantic ocean by an all-female team.

You may think resilience was all about resisting the physical demands of rowing the ocean. It was certainly a significant draw on this ingredient, especially with the loss of their water-maker after day 15, which meant relying on rations from a hand pump...amongst an endless list of technical problems.

But Julia had to summon up resilience well before leaving dry land. Her idea formed around herself and her best friend rowing together. It was a blow when she had to pull out – instead of quitting it inspired Julia to put together a bigger, five-woman crew and campaign. The task of getting to the start-line with sponsorship always loomed at large until the very day they left! Resilience and dogged determination not only kept the dream alive, but drew the other four crew members to her cause and saw enough money raised to literally launch themselves into the Atlantic on that bold December morning.

Louise .....

Louise Makin rows the real life boat race and calls herself 'the journey maker' (namesake to the yacht she crews). She has two passions, leading BTG as a CEO and leading the race when sailing. As a CEO, *It is so much more than doing a race – it is about paying attention to the journey you once set off on.'* Compare this attitude to people who set off on a journey looking only to the destination, then wonder why they never arrive because they are not concentrating on where they are on their trajectory and either tread water or, worse, neglect course corrections.

From a PhD study of lithium, I call her a rocket scientist, I wondered how did she take on a CEOship? *'I liked the challenge. By the time I joined BTG, the company's disparate interests had lurched into a £35m loss in 2004-5.'* *'It really was a bunch of scientists trying to run a business without enough cash savvy',* says one analyst and *'She had to take drastic action.'* Louise says, 'We are in an exciting position. We are building one of Europe's leading life-sciences companies.' Then she adds: 'Shire has made the journey we aspire to.' Shire, the pharmaceuticals company that started above a Hampshire shop over two decades ago, has a market value of more than £11 billion at the time of writing, while BTG is worth over £1 billion. That shows the sort of race that Louise likes to journey.

Running a P&L through crisis shaped her strongly as a leader. The second enabler was her father who always said, 'just do the best you can'. The third influence was her international rowing experience, putting herself 'out there' and managing it. She clearly knows her way around both big business and sailing, leading journeys through troubled waters.

'I used to be very driven and single minded before. Now I am more drawn, I know a solution will come because I am open minded, not just single minded and ready to persist despite all odds. My business is the same. Only one in ten drugs that enter trials gets to market,' she points

out. *'This is a business where things won't always work, things will fail and we have got to stay tenacious. Resilience and belief are life drugs!'*

Louise says, gender has never been an issue in her career. 'I don't think of myself as a woman in business. I think of myself as an individual.' And quite an individual. Bringing an operational focus and commercial strategy to bear and acquiring two companies in two years, Protherics and Biocompatibles, on her own 'Journey Maker', this CEO, sailor, scientist and mother of two is a champion for resilience.

Barbara....

Barbara Merry, CEO of Hardy Underwriting, is one of five children born in East Anglia of parents who had not had formal education themselves. 'I loved school and was taught to read and write before I went to school by my sister.' Writing, as it turned out, was instrumental in Barbara securing her position within the Corporation of Lloyds of London, the world's specialist insurance market.

In 1985, she went for an interview with Lloyds which needed to change its regulatory regime and she was hired because she had writing skills which would be useful to draft new banking rules! But she soon encountered a male boss whose prejudice against her was so damaging that she decided to leave. But before she had actually done so, out of the blue a headhunter recruited her for Hardy Underwriting, where she scaled the ladder to become the CEO. While Barbara took the job at Hardy enthusiastically, she was terrified of the prospect as she had no idea of what being the CEO of a listed company entailed. 'I did not know what I did not know and I did not know who to ask.'

Confronted with a number of tests – financial, personal and operational – Barbara's entire leadership story is about learning from each crisis that was presented to her and converting that into a success. Sometimes these crises happened in such quick succession, there were no margins for reflection or consolidation. The power of resilience and of staying anchored in one's belief of what is right for the company, was the only thing that carried her through successfully.

Hardy Underwriting, founded by Peter Hardy in 1978, has been subjected to bids. Those from competitor Beazley were first rebuffed and then superseded by US insurance giant CNA, who has secured agreement. Resilience was needed both to defend the company's independence and then, in the face of exceptional claims from the significant natural disasters in 2011, to secure the best outcome for its future prospects.

And now to round out our diverse quintet, here's the grand finale.

Willie Walsh – plane good resilience

The book was born in a long haul British Airways (BA) flight a few years ago. I still have the first draft scribbles on ruled sheets that I borrowed from the cabin crew. Like with HSBC, I have a long standing affinity with BA where it feels over the last fifteen years, I have grown with them and they have grown with me. It felt only natural I would want to meet with the man at the helm of BA.

I met Willie Walsh in his open-plan offices a mile from London Heathrow's Terminal 5. Now chief executive of International Airlines Group (IAG), he was then CEO of British Airways. Let us have some insight into Willie's DNA, before I discuss the famous Heathrow Terminal Five turnaround as a core example of resilience. There is an immediate likeability about him that disguises a steely, determined centre. From the geographically themed office plan to the 'man of the world' himself, you know where you are with him – in every sense.

So what is the story behind the success of this Irish glazier's son-turned-pilot-turned CEO? He says, *'I didn't plan any of it. My story is about being in the right place at the right time'.* Interesting.

In his teens, an advert appeared in an Irish newspaper for Aer Lingus's pilot training scheme. He didn't apply. Then a letter came through: 'Because of a postal strike, we may not have received your application. Please come for a series of aptitude tests.' Willie, nudged by his part-time career guidance teacher, went for it. *'I got many questions wrong in the first interview, but made it to the second interview and beyond. I didn't tell anyone until I got the offer. From a chance advert to a chance application, I came to Kidlington (near Oxford) at 17 and learned to fly. I experienced the fragility of the airline industry as it went through another downturn and I often wondered whether I'd have a real job at the end of it.*

'Then at a pilot's union meeting, I made some foolish comments. Someone said 'if you think you can do it better, help yourself'. So I did. I got elected and became the union representative.

'So, three lots of two year terms of flying and trade union work gave me exposure to the management side. Eventually, I was invited to join the management side of the business (Flight Operations and People Management) which opened up my options. Around this time (1992) I also did a Masters in Management at Trinity College, which was specifically tailored to the Allied Irish Bank.

'Mentorship is an incredible thing. Larry Stanley, CEO of Aer Lingus, took it upon himself to mentor me and exposed me to the non-technical side of things. At the time, the CEO of Chartered Airlines, Futura, resigned at a short notice and Larry asked me to take over, overnight!

'I was then the COO of Air Lingus and involved in their business survival plan. Again, I didn't go looking for it [the CEO position], but it came to me. The interview with the board was a character-building experience. Their first question to me was 'Are you mad to join, because Air Lingus could really go down. You could become a national hate figure – known as the guy who took it down. If you succeed, everyone else will take credit. If you fail, you will be responsible.' Those words shook Willie. He claims he never kept a diary, but for the first few months at Air Lingus he did, detailing who he saw, what he felt, the emotions he and others experienced. Against that stress, the resilience training as a pilot stood him in good stead.

Post 9/11, the world predicted the airline industry would go into a slump. He admits he was lazy when it came to academic learning but active when it came to challenges. *'There is something around 'excitement and making the impossible happen which gives me huge emotional rewards of self worth and fulfillment and lets me tell my friends and family, 'I'll prove them wrong. We will show them'.*

'I loved it when the odds are all stacked against me. When someone in the government asked who I was and upon learning I was a pilot, said 'oh, pilots are definitely messed-up people', I thrived on that misperception! So on 18 October 2001 – Act I, Scene I, if you will – I was presenting the survival plan to the board while without much notice or warning. Act I, Scene II found me putting myself forward as a candidate for CEO! The Board didn't come to an unanimous decision and in fact most voted against my candidacy. An interview with a psychologist, late evening and a couple of more sessions confirmed the position.'

Most of us have at some point or other been spurred on by an *'us against the world'* situation, but when Willie shares such moments, his

enthusiasm and mental toughness are so vibrant you wish you could bottle them.

That evening, on his first day as chief executive, he stood in front of his management team and read out his psychological report verbatim to them. 'This is who I am, folks and what I bring is not growth, but cost cutting.' Honesty doesn't get more bare-boned than this. But that disclosure won him trust and respect and people could believe in his potential beyond the message.

Willie offers us a valuable lesson in reality vs. theory. On paper, aerodynamic analysis tells us bumblebees cannot fly. Yet closer inspection reveals that an incredibly powerful muscle structure enables their wings to provide the lift. Likewise, human ingenuity, energy and willpower tip the balance between what looks like a non-starter on paper to becoming a real possibility in life.

Willie says: *'The value of learning is compounded from one's mistakes compared to one's successes. The value of resilience and courage is likewise – doubled in a crises scenario than a growth scenario. Allow the stretch. Allow the discomfort. The measure of success is nil if you haven't failed and tested the limit.'* Quite simply, you will never know. You only need pause to think, therefore, to how anathema it is to the human spirit not to go that extra mile.

Talking about failures, we broached the epic story of the much-awaited-but-disastrous Terminal 5 opening at London Heathrow. Willie didn't even pause to think: *'It was a disaster, I was angry. I just went home that day.'* The biggest lesson, according to him, was the one he learnt about the environment in which people perform. **He attributes the root cause to a terrible compromise on not familiarising people enough in a new environment where there was unpredictability and variance, for which you had to be instinctive and ready. It was a human failure more than a mechanical failure.** The following day Willie faced the media and the BBC asked a killer question 'Whose fault is it?' Willie's said one word – 'Mine'. There was a storming silence after. Sky followed next 'Will you resign?' His response was quick but measured. 'No, I won't. I will fix it first.'

What followed this is most telling. As the disaster unfolded and the enormity of it became apparent, Willie, in his office, decided he would go and face the situation first hand at T5. On the drive to the terminal, his head of communications asked him what he was going to say. Willie had no idea. **His instinct was simply to be present. His instinct would** deliver. **And so it transpired that once he got there, there was an immediate 'transplant' of his honesty and integrity from within to the outer, listening world. No premeditation, no contrived PR and therefore, no loss of credibility. This was straight from the heart and soul. And it is a prime example of how, if we have the courage to let our gut speak, sincerity and responsibility can win out against seemingly impossible odds.**

Brave ownership released the rest of the team to find the solution. **As a leader, his sole focus, selflessly so, was to admit the failure, grab the missile and disarm it. The next step was equally important. He addressed his team to convey, 'I have disarmed the missile and taken sole ownership for the problem. But finding the solution is a collective responsibility. If I am going down, I am taking everyone down with me'. That energy and spirit has its own infectious and courageous pull.**

Leadership in crises is about being honest and facing it, but also about being positive in the worst of disasters. Another story of fear and resilience was the crash landing, short of the runway, of a flight from Beijing in January 2007. No matter how prepared you are, the impact of receiving news like this is physical. However, *'You cannot let the situation control you; you have to take control. Media is immediate and in 24 hours will find its story and if you don't author the story, it will invent one. There is no prep time. No rehearsal. You go 'live' minutes after a crash. You learn resilience as you live it.'*

Yes, Willie. I have learnt that hard lesson in my own life. As he left my office in Covent Garden, which he humbly came down to for our second meeting, I remembered Helen Keller's quote. She was deaf–blind from childhood but learned to speak, read Braille and acquired a comprehensive education: 'A happy life consists not in the absence, but in the mastery of hardships.'

I kept standing at the reception for minutes after he had left. His words didn't leave me. **'The measure of success is nil if you haven't failed and tested the limit.'**

The power of failure

I believe that being a great leader really begins with your first encounter with misfortune. In 1984, the Center for Creative Leadership conducted a study on the 'key events' that contribute to a leader's development. The study found that the greatest opportunity for leaders to learn, grow and further their development came less from successes and more from hardships, failures and career setbacks. Great leaders are people who look at challenges as opportunities to grow, to change and to learn from their mistakes rather than seeing themselves as victims of circumstances and feeling they are not in control of their own success.

Look at the following words of encouragement below. Can you spot the core theme?

- *'People are always blaming their circumstances for what they are. I don't believe in circumstances. The people who get on in the world are the people who get up and look for the circumstances they want and if they can't find them, make them.'* George Bernard Shaw
- *'I have not failed. I've just found 10,000 ways that won't work.'* Thomas Edison
- *'Failure is only the opportunity to begin again more intelligently.'* Henry Ford
- *'Failure is an event, never a person.'* William D. Brown
- *'Never confuse a single defeat with final defeat.'* F. Scott Fitzgerald
- *'You always pass failure on your way to success.'* Mickey Rooney
- *'If you voluntarily quit in the face of adversity, you'll wonder about it for the rest of your life'.* Bill Clinton

The common thread among all these famous people and their wise words is the same. You can't have success without failure. Never give up and never stop trying. There is power in failure, you just have to give yourself a chance. Keep trying, keep failing and soon you'll start succeeding.

I think we know we all have it, but do we truly realise how potent it can be?

The opportunity to learn from our mistakes or failings is what allows us to grow and change as human beings. Take for example the following story. A candidate to replace the retiring chairman of a very successful company was being interviewed by the incumbent himself. The candidate, upon being introduced to the chairman, quickly said, *'I would like to know what the keys to your success have been'*. The older man looked at him for a moment and replied, *'Young man, I can sum it up in two words: good decisions'*. To which the young man replied, *'But how does one come to know which are the good decisions?'* *'One word, young man: experience,'* replied the chairman. *'But how does one get experience?'* asked the interviewee. *'Two words'*, replied the retiring chairman. *'Bad decisions.'*

That reminds me of someone who always encouraged me to make life decisions without 'spoon feeding' an answer. The very epitome of resilience in fact – my mother. She learnt from her mother, my grandmother, the one quality, I now treasure – an ability to make decisions in a crises. The choices she gave me were always calibrated to empower me in making a decision. I found this really made a difference when it came to the more serious cross roads moments in my life. Like a life raft, she is my back-up drive of resilience. Like her mother, who reared a family of eight children through the war, stitched every item of clothing and manufactured every morsel of food for them with her own hands with a 'can do' smile, Ma tells me to this day: *'Make decisions. In that some will be wrong but take a risk and learn from the process, rather than avoiding risk and staying safe.'*

I believe there is a strong link between decisions, risks, mistakes and resilience. I call it character building, DNA making.

How resilient are you feeling now?

Your code for Ingredient Nine: Resilience

Pause. Ask yourself what do you remember from this chapter; list the key takeaways and ideas that had an impact on you – something inspiring, something relevant or something you would like to try.

Now, make a note of the following: the term 'things' below can refer to behaviour actions, conversations, skills or even an attitude

1. List three things you would like to START doing to strengthen your RESILIENCE...

2. List three things you would like to STOP doing to strengthen your RESILIENCE...

3. List three things you would like to CONTINUE doing to strengthen your RESILIENCE...

On an ascending scale of 1 to 10, how robust is this ingredient in your DNA?

Ingredient Ten

LUCK

—'I make things happen'—

---

*Luck itself is a blend of the nine ingredients –
self, focus, emotion, instinct, fear, creativity,
expression , dark side and resilience. Luck is a
choice, not just chance. Make it, rather than
just hope for it.*

CH_{10}

You have seen, touched and sensed the nine ingredients...............

What about Luck?

Stop. You may well be thinking that luck is luck. Pure chance. Beyond anyone's control and something we can't fully explain or understand.

Well – yes, no and yes.

The first and last 'yes' go together. I do not profess to have the answer to these mind mysteries.

I totally refute the 'no'.

There are flukes, coincidences and what can sometimes seem to be divine intervention. The word luck covers a panoply of phenomena. Synchronicity, Luck, Choice, Chance and Coincidence play a larger part in our lives than we realise to describe experiences such as lucky timing, a chance opportunity or being in the right place at the right time. Are we really saying we can have no hand in this? I do not believe so.

If it helps, perhaps think of it as good fortune; and what makes it good? Well you can and you do!

So in a way you could say that the luck I am talking about can be described as how we perceive or label the outcome rather than the input – be it the catalyst or cause of you finding yourself in a state of readiness to strike. In other words, it is more than describing how you feel, it is understanding what you do to be ready to strike when opportunity knocks which can provide part of the explanation of our fascination with being lucky.

So when people ask time and again, what do I need to do to be lucky? What is this (seemingly magic) ingredient? This is what I hear:

- Do I need to try harder?
- Do I need to be at that right place at that right time?
- Do I need more talent, or ambition to be more successful?
- Do I need more visibility?
- Do I need more sponsorship?
- Do I need to pray more or wear a lucky charm? (yes, some have even asked that!)

How often have we all heard something like this? Well, let me expound my simple view on luck.

Having studied other people's luck quotient and my own lucky breaks, I've come up with a mantra which after years of practice, works. Here it is.

To be lucky, is to just 'plug and play'. Plug into your strong belief. Then play it right out there in the universe. You may ask what does playing out in the universe actually mean? Well, going back to the start of the book – even to the cover – the golden key for luck is to unlock the door of self-belief for opportunities to follow. Once you walk through that door, everything else – the universe – is out there for you. So once you believe in yourself, 'play it out to world'. In other words, if you don't put anything out there, nothing can come back, be it connections, opportunities or luck. To attract luck from the universe and bring it to yourself, you simply need to put yourself out there.

Putting yourself out there – what does that mean?
Luck is about Confidence (plug) and Connectivity (play)

The simplest principle is often the most powerful and the most overlooked. **Plugging into your confidence** is essential and those who create their own good luck have high degrees of assertiveness and self-esteem. They keep to their dream, persevere and 'keep at it' to create the conditions that ultimately help them win or be lucky. Also, they are good at visualising their goal – to be 'able to picture the outcome' is a positive affirmation, as if it were a dream that has already come true. It not only helps you work out the steps to make that outcome happen, but boosts your will and skill to realise that dream. Neuroscience proves that affirmations reinforce luck.

Affirmations are ways of planting the seeds of success in our subconscious, helping us to think positively and to be more prepared for success. 'Whatever the mind of man can conceive and believe, it can achieve'. W. Clement Stone

After plugging into your confidence, **playing out your trust in others** and seeing other people as sources of real opportunity is key. Without confidence there is no way to give yourself to the opportunity.

So, my 'aha' moment struck when I realised, luck doesn't always have an exclusive causal relationship with effort. Hard grit (experience alone) may not necessarily bring big luck. Instead luck does have a strong cause and effect link with instinct and networks. Others around you, if they are the right others can help you attract luck

An example. Repeated studies show that inherited wealth accounts for 10% to 20% of today's multimillionaires. Contrary to what many parents tell their children, pure hard work alone is neither necessary nor sufficient for success. Some people enjoy spectacular success by being smart, well networked, creative and focused.

Definition of luck

Before we delve any further, let me clarify that when we talk about luck the meaning is centred around our actions that generate those conditions in which luck can occur. This chapter is about positioning and preparing ourselves to capitalise on a lucky window when it opens up. There are, of course, those events that I mentioned in the beginning, what we term purely lucky happenings – chance timings, a favourable sequence of developments, but again the point is how do we expose ourselves to these possibilities and be ready to benefit from them.

One of my lucky encounters in life, which you may say happened by a random turn of events, was meeting Malcolm Ransome. Back in 2008, the Daily Telegraph newspaper invited me to give a talk on surfing the recession at the Telegraph Business Club. I was travelling abroad at the time and was struggling to make the commitment. Even leading up to the final appearance it was hit-and-miss, mainly down to me being away in India and eventually mis-hearing the dates when contacted on my mobile whilst crossing the notoriously busy streets in Delhi!

Somehow, right at the very last minute, weighing the odds in favour, I decided to go. The talk went off well – nothing amazing or otherwise. However, right at the end, a series of people came up to thank me for the refreshing advice. It was humbling, but right at the back of this group, there was this gentleman, very softly spoken, who came up and said to me he how much he had enjoyed my presentation. I thanked him for his comments. That was it. Months later, I received a phone call in my office. I couldn't remember the name so it was hard to make the connection to the call.

Anyway, Malcolm re introduced himself and we decided to meet up for a coffee. The more we talked, then and subsequently, the more I realised the synergy between my work and his network. This was despite him having no leadership background or consultancy experience. He was a retired philanthropist. He kept saying: 'I don't really know if any of what I am saying will make sense as I have no experience of your world of work but I've a hunch that ....' He acted on instinct and played out the opportunities to me and I plugged into them. Our overlapping orbits in business and leadership issues came together in an almost uncanny way with the concepts and projects I was working on at the time. The more we tapped into this harmony, the stronger the network became, the more I realised this was the sincerest form of advocacy between us – that based on respect, trust and instinct. It is a successful story of plug and play.

Now, here you see a great plug-play pattern that proved a lucky opening. I realised I could learn a lot from Malcolm. As someone from outside the direct consulting world, he offered a fresh pair of eyes and ears through which my leadership consultancy could refresh, reinvent and innovate. He is a great mentor.

The connection though was a sliding door, moment if you have seen the film. Because, if I had not acted on my last minute hunch to go to the Telegraph talk, you wouldn't be reading this story.

Let me relate an example through not one, but two chance confluences. This I how I met Sir George Martin.

(Act 1)

I have a shared interest with most of you. The music of the Beatles. Malcolm, it happened is absorbed by the behind the scenes aspect of their recordings – how it was inspired, written and produced. A BBC documentary on Sir George Martin, the 86 year old producer of the Beatles, was therefore a must see. Relating this and the conviction that Sir George was a natural for the book, the question was how on Earth does one contact him? Enter the second piece of luck.

(Act 2)

Long before the BBC programme was made, when I started CorporateDNA, within months my old accountant did a runner and I was left with a desperate hunt for a replacement numbers man. A *very* chance encounter brought me into contact with Marcus Baker, a down to earth British bloke. You might say my loyal right hand man, managing our assets yes, but for the six years I have known him, he himself is an asset in my books. Marcus once saw a poster of the Beatles in my office. A simple question followed from him – Oh, you like the Beatles? (yes) Well I know someone who is a close acquaintance and did Sir George's accounts. (Well, you mean I could meet him?) I am happy to ask. The contact was passed to Malcolm. Act 1 and Act 2 came together. We met Sir George. The rest, if I may coin the phrase, is history.

So, this is a real example of how a three-way-plug-and-play resulted in a lucky outcome.

The point here is if Malcolm hadn't seen the BBC programme his thought wouldn't have happened when it did and if I hadn't put up the poster, Marcus would have never known my interest in the Beatles and mentioned his contact. Sir George would never have been in this book playing out to you on the very cover 'you can do anything if you really want to'.

So luck, as you see, follows a plug-play-plug-play-plug-play cycle, agree? (feel free to add some music to that). I am smiling writing this.

The universe of luck

You remember I opened this book with a Big Bang moment on the page one of the opening chapter. It only makes sense I close with the universe.

What is the universe? Scientists continue to ascertain its true composition is, in its broadest sense – pure energy – atoms, protons, electrons, human DNAs, you and I. We are all made up of energy – stardust in fact!

In that sense, we all have a small orbit of energy within which we exist or cycle. I call that small orbit our own personal universe. When my orbit of energy comes into contact with your orbit, or your universe, more energy gets created. Hence, knowing what is happening outside your own universe is very important to ensure your awareness of other orbits and when and how to connect to benefit your energy quotient.

What I realised is this. Each individual, has an orbit or space around him/ her which has its own trajectory, pace and energy. Our orbits are made of events, episodes, experiences and encounters. These are as you will agree, an eclectic mixture of planned, unplanned and often 'pure chance' events. Sometimes, what you might call pure chance is actually synapses connecting between two individuals, which brings about a good change or a good outcome. It happens when their orbits touch or overlap, there is a mutual affinity, but one had to be cognisant of the orbits touching.

In other words, life has summed up to me the magic confluence of **social affirmation, reciprocity, listening and preparedness.** Each is outlined below supported by a personal example.

1. **Social affiliation**

   Human beings are born dependent. In order for any new opportunity or idea to survive and thrive, it depends on others for fruition. Synergy is key. Trust in others leads to a dynamic network of connections, which, in turn, provides exponential resources and touch points – the sum being greater than the parts – more than we can ever individually have on a one to one basis. Luck, in our terms, only exists and thrives in human connectivity. Interdependence is greater than independence, just as much as Cooperation is greater than Competition. For social affiliation to work, intimacy needs to replace detachment (or mistrust), otherwise there can be no opening up to others and no room for dialogue or for the genuine exchange of ideas and opinions.

I sincerely believe in the investment in others. Without this ethos organisations are in permanent stalemate. When people withhold information thinking this insulates them and gives them power, they compromise their luck quotient. Whereas mutual investment in each other, in our ideas, integrity and innovation, engenders limitless potential to our creativity and capability – stimulating growth and reinvestment.

Example:

In the case of Vittorio Colao, Group CEO of Vodafone, I knew I wanted him for the book and his office agreed in principle, but over an 18 month period, 99% of the energy and effort went into trying to arrange diaries to meet and discuss the book and with the best of mutual will it didn't work. Then earlier this year, what in fact turned around my luck was a chance bumping into him in a lift and mentioning the book. Being prepared to leverage that 60 seconds elevator window (1% energy and effort), converted that chance encounter into a lucky break. The result you have read in the Chapter on Expression. Do you see the 99–1 point?

Lesson: Social Affiliation is the strength that allows us to use the hidden opportunity in any moment to join with others to create something stronger, more mutually creative than any individual effort. Some call this skill networking or partnerships. I call it social affiliation.

2. **Reciprocity**

Wikipedia defines Reciprocity in social psychology as responding to a positive action with another positive action, rewarding actions in kind. As a social construct, reciprocity means that in response to friendly actions, people are frequently much nicer and much more cooperative than predicted by the self-interest model. In the course of our lives we form many give-and-take relationships, building a healthy interdependence with family, community and culture.

First Example:

You can say, I am privileged to meet thousands of people – delegates, coachees, clients – across cultures, through our Leadership programmes. Inspired people never forget their gratitude and this in turn creates gratifying spin-offs of time and investment via exponential pay back of individual contacts across a worldwide network of countries. It has to emanate from a natural build of sincere reciprocity. Nothing is contrived for it is only the sincerity that will feed back into the personal returns that benefit everyone.

Second example:

When I started CorporateDNA, I was keen to contribute to philanthropy, but not just a token donation here or there, something meaningful with continuity and measurable outcomes. I met with lots of charities, most were frustrating and steeped in bureaucracy. Eventually I chose Action Aid, the only UK international development charity. As we came to know each other a good example of reciprocity developed where I became an ambassador for Action Aid while they helped to develop our Corporate Social Responsibility (CSR) blueprint. Five years on, we have built on this and taken it to a new level where we run a development programme to develop their internal leaders. In effect, we help them instil a corporate mindset in a not-for-profit context, while they help us instil a goodwill mind-set in a corporate context. A meaningful two way reciprocity. Others tell me, this is a rare synergistic partnership. That's luck too.

Lesson: So luck is more an attitude supported by a connectivity to others. We can win. Once, twice – many times not because we are lucky but because we make winning a mind-set, a habit. This attitude is best defined as a pre-disposition to winning. Luck can be cultivated, best in reciprocal relationship with relevant others.

3. **Listening**

Listening is the third important skill. Most people love to talk. If you listen, really hard and pay attention to the small details, you will pick up something, just something, that opens the door to luck. These little stimuli can make big luck...our ability to *recall* can open up amazing connections.

Example:

In 2008 I had just moved to a new house and changed energy suppliers. Faced with a miserable array of issues with the new electricity bill, I logged a complain to the energy provider in no uncertain terms. The call, let us say, was heated. Anyway that afternoon I received a call from the supplier and a soft spoken bright voice said 'Is that Rhea, I am Rose from EDF Energy...' Before she could go any further. I, not having recovered from the morning's shambolic customer call, burst out on the phone repeating the string of meter and bill issues we have had. Rose listened patiently and then after minutes as I paused for breath, she said, 'Rhea I am really sorry to hear about your issues with your bill. But I am calling from the Learning and Development team to enquire about your services. An ex colleague of mine recommend your services for a potential leadership programme we are about to design. Would you be interested?' I was embarrassed as hell. I apologised and listened with great attention, trying to make up for a compromised first impression. As Rose told me about the opportunity she also covered the wider business background and better still offered to get their customer services lead to give me a call to resolve the other personal billing issue. I was touched. Anyway again, this is where two acts converged to bring me luck. We won the work with the company and I later heard the procurement team was impressed with my ability to understand and recall their customer context to such great detail. Apparently the read across and play back of the key issues about the company through the two conversations when I presented back made them feel we knew them intimately. Hmmm, the thing I had done well was to listen really hard even to technical matters of little interest. Today this energy company – EDF Energy – is a valuable client for over four years.

Lesson: Active listening is vital. Often it is more important than talking. Listening helps you inquire and acquire information without doing the talking. This information gives you the cues to make connections, join the dots and attract opportunities.

4. **Preparedness**

Preparedness is about being ready. It can be about being prepared for any opportunities should they arise or any contingencies should they occur. Athletes do that well. Like in martial arts, it is akin to being ready with a response to threat should the threat occur even before the threat emerges. A state of readiness develops through putting yourself in new situations, meeting new people, even when you haven't done your full homework

Example:

Here's a compelling story about preparedness. In 2005, I was in Dublin, as a guest speaker for an international conference while still with a large corporate employer. My topic was talent management. After a delayed flight, I rushed to check in to the hotel to see a large dinner underway of circa 150 people being held by the sponsors including all the speakers and guests. Most seats were taken and half way down the room, as my eyes scanned for a spare chair, I spotted two.

As I took my seat and tucked in to a much needed glass of wine, another lady, also late, hurried to the chair next to me, 'Excuse me is this free?' She was a senior HR person from Reuters in London. Over the next days we spent a lot of time connecting and sharing our career stories and unfulfilled dreams. I told her while I am due for a directorship next year, maybe someday I will run a consultancy of my own. If I do, it will be like this...like that. She encouraged me to go head. Anyway we exchanged cards but after an year or so we lost touch.

Fast forward three years. One evening I was walking towards Waterloo tube station. I got a call. The lady who I met those three years ago remembered me and was in urgent need for a team building intervention for someone fairly senior in a global bank, because their current supplier had pulled out. It was the same person. This is Sanchita, who is now in HSBC and she recalled everything I had said the years before about my dream consultancy and had a hunch I would have started one. I, of course, had! She gave me a day's notice to make myself available. I changed my diary and met the client, who was fussy. But I was prepared to strike.

Today HSBC is a valued prestigious client and Stuart Gulliver a valuable contributor to my work and the book. So, although you may see this as luck, this is a story about one phone call.... being ready ... and delivering mutually beneficial results.

Lesson: A lucky network is a wide network of relationships that may at first have little to do with any business objective, but somehow later come into great relevance and play. Be prepared to strike because the lucky opening is often a fleeting window doesn't last forever.

Here's the paradox, though. I have seen in life, some great people that after getting lucky forget the crucial lucky relationships that helped get them there in the first place. By definition, the top for them becomes less of a journey and more of an arrival point. Power, strength and confidence are expectations we have of successful leader's, but vulnerability and humility humanises leaders, creating a gravitational pull of luck that far outlasts power.

As you progress through the company part of your message is how you would take the company forward, by example of course, not exhortation. In a position of leadership, momentum marries responsibility. As you rise *through* the company, so you now rise *with* the company, still developing yourself, but in different ways as you broaden your focus to lift others with you. It all comes back to gravity – remember our orbits! Your leadership influence works much better when others naturally gravitate to your objectives and goals rather than being pushed or coerced.

A personal example of (young) Spine and (mature) Shoulders:

Remember the spine and shoulders excerpt from the opening chapter?

There is a saying in my business. A combination of broad shoulders that embrace breadth and vision sitting atop a growing spine that forms the building blocks of experience is a great combination. Let me share with you how two separate parts of my life joined together in this way for me.

Sometimes seemingly disconnected events, decades apart, connect to bring luck. Let me take you back to a secret still well kept. I was just finishing university in Delhi and I was bored. A curious turn of fate meant that with my British passport, after university, I couldn't work for an Indian company without a work permit. My mother's friend, a head-hunter, offered me an internship with a British company, Shades of India founded by a British couple. I was initially reluctant about the scope of the job, partly from being unsure of what I wanted to do in life, but I trudged along to meet the founder and to give it a go.

From the word go, a rather tall British gentleman greeted me in pure flawless Hindi and here was a new adventure about to start. Who was this man David Housego? The story intrigued me. David's first trip to India might easily have been his last when, as a student, his overland hitch to Bengal via Pakistan turned into a tour of the sub-continent's nursing homes thanks to a ferocious bout of dysentery. As unromantic as it was painful, the three-month odyssey was the start of Housego's life-long love affair with the country.

The decision to move permanently to India was made for him in 1988 when the Financial Times sent him to Delhi as their Asia correspondent. After stints in Paris and Iran, they thought they'd slip easily into ex-pat life.

However, the family fell sick within weeks of their arrival with Dengue fever. David recounts a catalogue of horror stories including years later, their youngest son, Kim, was kidnapped while on a family holiday, trekking in Kashmir, but 'leaving never occurred to us.' If anything, the experience seems to have confirmed their commitment to the country. India became home and Shades of India was the entrepreneurial result. A hazy plan to use India's untapped traditional textile skills on upmarket products became a reality when the law regarding foreign ownership of Indian-based textile companies changed in their favour.

I became intrigued by the story and thought to myself that even though I know nothing about textile or design, this could be an interesting experience. Undeterred by the lack of a detailed job description David and I agreed I would shadow him in his work and assist him in his customer and supplier meetings, watching and learning how a CEO makes decisions, negotiates, leads and drives commitments.

Although barely three years old, Shades of India's home textiles was already gracing the world's most exclusive department stores: Bergdorff Goodman and Takash-imaya in New York; Porthault in Paris; and Liberty and Joseph Maison and Conran in London. I was enmeshed in learning about their end to end value chain from design, production, marketing and finance. From appliquéd and exquisitely embroidered bed-linen, tablecloths and curtains to mosquito nets – the lot!

Today I realise how invaluable that nine-month experience was, more so than any MBA. An amateurish internship, which randomly came about, in turn set me up for getting inside the mind of a CEO, how a leader thinks act and decides in running a business, how the spine connects with the shoulders. Something that would prove invaluable in starting my own business, little did I know then I would be a CEO someday running a global leadership consultancy. Nine months of induction gave me the preparedness, I needed to build a strong spine and shoulders for something that at the time I was completely oblivious to and which, years later, would fit in perfectly with my business dream.

I learnt never to turn down a chance opportunity however random it seems at the time, for every experience adds a piece to our learning jigsaw. All experiences are building blocks and they all connect like vertebrae in the spine, connecting the elements from my different experiences gave me a lucky start, as some would describe it. I think you can see though that, albeit reluctantly, I ventured out to explore this unknown world and it was this that has repaid me many times over. So yes, this type of event, we call luck, is for us to seize – the choice is ours. You do not have to be lucky or unlucky in this sense, just willing to plug and play.

Putting yourself out there – luck is about winning

Using my plug and play formula, **luck is about winning. Winning is a habit, an attitude and a consequence.** Using the combination of the nine companion ingredients, try the plug and play format below:

'Plug into' your (belief, focus and instinct) and 'Play up' your (creativity, resilience and expression) and 'Play down' your (fear, dark side and negative emotions)

To win – or, to be lucky – let us take each in turn.

Plug into your:

1. **Self-belief:** Knowing what you want and believing in yourself.
2. **Focus:** Go after what you want. You can't deliberate, get distracted or simply wait for things to happen. If you want something, you have to go out and keep at it till you get it.
3. **Instinct:** You have to listen to the small hunches, read the shifts in energy, pick up on cues between people and interactions.

Play up your:

4. **Creativity:** Explore all angles. Dream up new ones. There are so many different concepts and approaches that exist in your imagination that are just waiting to be released and take you places.
5. **Resilience:** Stay dedicated and determined. It is not always easy to put yourself out there and there will be times when you will face rejection. Every failure has a hidden lesson to set you up for success next time. Don't give up on yourself. Make it a point to learn from your setbacks and mistakes.
6. **Expression:** Find a way of expressing your belief (intent or desire) to expand your reach and depth through a bigger network and a bigger universe for meaningful connections to happen.

Play down:

7. **(Negative) Emotion:** take control of the 'bad' emotions as much you do of the 'good'. Remember, you have the upper hand.

8. **Dark Side:** you know your tipping points, so stay aware, avoid inhabiting these zones and use the knowledge of them to your advantage.

9. **Fear (of failure or rejection):** Just as we invite fear in, we can therefore also show it the door. This never needs to compromise you (especially if you fear rejection) when you are putting yourself out there because ultimately you have the choice, to coin Groucho Marx's dictum 'I wouldn't want to belong to any club that would have me as a member'. The choice is yours.

One thing, especially while writing this book, I have always believed in is the power of suggestion; that the universe 'suggests' many choices, clues and opportunities to us in very subtle ways and if you can read the clues and act on them, you will maximise your probability of attracting good outcomes. In other words, one must make oneself the creator of the conditions that increase the chances to win.

Expanding your universe is a pre-determinant for luck. **Learning how to attract constructive attention to your goal is not a selfish act.** The key phrase to remember is 'can someone else benefit from knowing about my idea or goal? Who do I know who knows somebody who would be interested?' The more you participate in life, the more luck will leap your way. The more active you are, the more opportunities you will have and find yourself in the right place and right time.

Luck can be controversial, though. 'He didn't really deserve it but just got lucky'. Who doesn't want to be lucky? Luck is emotionally laden. How often have you heard these phrases and sayings?

Tough Luck	Good Luck	Blind Luck	Beginner's Luck	Bad Luck
Out of Luck	Plain Luck	Lady Luck	Worse Luck	Pure Luck
Lucky Dog				

One thing is proven. Everybody wants to be lucky, but no one wants to rely purely on luck. If you did, you would lose focus or negate the power of the nine other ingredients by just waiting for luck to intervene. So look at how you can bring more luck into your life by being ready for it.

Let us take an example. An inspiring someone recently dropped into my book universe and we spoke a lot about luck; Alan.

Sir Alan Collins

Alan blends the ten ingredients through several eclectic strands in his DNA. What if I told you: the ex British High Commissioner to Singapore and Ambassador to the Philippines, Head of the 2012 Olympic Business Legacy. The Director General for Trade and Investment, USA and the Consul-General New York. On several City Boards. Sir Alan Collins KCVO CMG.

STOP before you even think of the word 'lucky' or 'privileged'. An only-child from white-collar working class parents. A family where work ethic was at the centre of things. The subliminal message from those parents was 'you must do well, you must be upwardly mobile, you must make us proud of you'.

State Schools followed by London School of Economics and a Civil Service career, mainly in the British Diplomatic Service, driven by these imperatives, which represent the ambition to succeed. Or equally by the fear of failure, or rather the fear of being caught out as an imposter. Thinking that one day you will be rumbled and returned to more humble origins. How can you really be an Ambassador? How can you have been knighted by Her Majesty The Queen?

For someone with such strong credentials, Alan remains humble without ever forgetting his roots. This causes us to ask what drives a person in their career? Fear of failure? Or ambition to do well? Or are they the same thing?

We talked about luck. Sometimes something comes along that gives a different perspective on all this.

'Something that transcends the fear of failure. The luck to be in the right place at the right time. High Commissioner to Singapore. Singapore chosen as the place where the venue for the 2012 Olympics will be decided. The chance to achieve as part of a team where the prize is huge for Britain. The chance to see how a successful Olympics bid can be put together in order to come from behind and win. A bid with an air of 'disruptive creativity', the sort of bid where thirty children from the East End of London are brought onto the delegation to illustrate its twin themes of Inspiration and Legacy. Themes that will win the Games for London and determine its nature going forward. The chance to see how Lord Sebastian Coe can lead, bring enormous charisma and strength of leadership and Sir Keith Mills can bring supreme business acumen. The opportunity to work alongside this project and make a contribution to it'

The outcome is success. The vital word in the Jacques Rogge envelope is 'London'. The race is on to stage the greatest and most sustainable Olympics in history, to transform the East End of London to the advantage of all those children. The chance to inspire a young generation. The chance to leave a lasting legacy for the whole of the UK. Business outcomes will form a part of that legacy. The luck is to be the person put in charge of that, working for successive British governments. Or, do we make our own luck? Do we put ourselves in the right place at the right time sometimes? Stop and think about it.

As a successful Olympics unfolded in front of our eyes in London. As we begin to see the Legacy that is the Olympic Park and work towards the business Legacy that means jobs and growth can we lay the ghosts of the fear of failure? Yes, it is in the DNA from those ambitious parents and from the right combination of attitude and focus. Worth thinking about. Overcoming the fear. Riding the luck.

It is easy to prove that actions and consequences follow our thought patterns. If you take any substantial event in your life and try and remember the thoughts that preceded the event, you will see a strong connection. Do you know why? Our attitude determines most of our actions and on that note, our preparedness determines most of our luck.

Are you ready?

Since luck involves taking risk let us next take Dr. Mark Mobius – one of the best known risk asset investors. The 70+-year-old Executive Chairman of Templeton Emerging Markets Group is a global investor and emerging markets fund manager and is considered to be one of the leaders in an industry he has been involved in for over 40 years.

The pied piper of emerging markets

Given his international experience and leadership in emerging and frontier markets investing, this seems an apt moniker for Dr. Mobius who was born to German and Puerto-Rican parents in New York in 1936. With a B.A. and M.S. in Communications from Boston University and a PhD in economics from MIT in 1964. He also studied at the University of Wisconsin, University of New Mexico and Kyoto University in Japan. Okay, so that's solid grounding. At 41, Dr. Mobius joined Templeton in 1987 as president of the Templeton Emerging Markets Fund, a closed end investment company, bringing his knowledge of international markets together with Sir John Templeton's disciplined, long-term value approach to investing in global markets. The first emerging market equity fund available to US investors. Today, he is the Executive Chairman of Templeton Emerging Markets Group, managing over 50 closed-end and open-end funds worldwide, supported by a team of over 50 investment professionals, located in 18 offices around the globe.

Did you hear some great credentials there? What is greater than that is how Dr. Mobius drew on his luck and experience from the road, as a self-declared nomad, to produce successful tips. Indeed, his views on luck, exposure through travel and street smart initiatives in driving opportunity have refreshing parallels to leadership of my plug and play principle.

I believe in getting out and kicking the tires. I'm on the road 250 days a year, visiting companies in almost every corner of the globe. After chalking up over 30 million miles of flight time, I'm proud to have achieved the status of a full-time nomad. I would rather see with my own eyes what's happening in a company or country. Lies can be as revealing as truth, if you know what the clues are. You have to observe and listen to the signals. This is one advantage of getting to know the people who run the show by actually viewing a factory or plant in action. You won't get the same type of information by just scanning through cold, hard data or numbers.

My personal theory is that countries that make it easy for travellers to enter tend to be friendly to foreign investment. Whenever I visit a new country, my radar kicks in the moment I hop off the plane and pass through customs. It intensifies as we drive into town, check into the hotel, talk to the cab drivers, walk around the neighbourhood and chat with the service staff in shops.

He continues, with absolute conviction, that: there is no simple secret, no single blueprint, no rigid roadmap that will guarantee you, me or anyone long-term success as a global investor. However, there are good, solid lessons to be learned from observing the methods of research and analysis employed by long-term investors in these turbulent markets.

I really sensed this in my conversation with Dr. Mobius. I felt his wisdom from the investment world had many applications in the leadership world so here's an interplay over ten areas of our common thinking, of our common thinking between Dr. Mobius and myself.

1. **Mark Mobius: Keep an eye on value.** Is a share selling for below its book value?

   Rhea: I would say, in my world, to win, or to be lucky, leaders today need to first monitor the intrinsic value within their own selves (self worth) rather than seeking external validation of how much they are worth. Ask yourself, is your visible confidence level below your inner self esteem? What value, even a price tag, would a leader attach to their self worth? Would you value yourself more if you looked for and discovered those undervalued assets and hidden strengths?

2. **Mark Mobius: Don't follow the herd.** Many of the most successful investors are contrarian investors. Buy when others are selling and sell when others are buying.

   Rhea: I believe great leaders differentiate themselves.. Set yourself apart. From the Self – ingredient we can see what, at first glance, seems contrarian –opening opportunities where no one else sees any. I always think of Sir Martin Sorrell who bought a wire basket manufacturing company, Wire and Plastic Products and grew it from a two person one room office into a mega billion dollar business called WPP, the world's largest advertising company. He did that by fundamentally changing the way advertising industry was viewed, run and rewarded. An inspirational, yet contrarian, investor.

3. **Mark Mobius: Be patient.** Rome was not built in a day and companies take time to grow to their full potential.

   Rhea: This is so true in today's era of instant gratification, ambition and drive that can tip over to the 'dark side' of impatience. There is a difference between speed and haste we often don't appreciate. As in the business world, so in our personal development, a constant dash for 'here and right now' is normally counterproductive. Blend and blend again your ingredients, building up your personal seasoning to realise your full potential. Invest in both time and energy.

4. **Mark Mobius: Examine your own situation and your appetite for risk.** You should not go into equities if you are the type of person who is nervous every time you read a stock market report.

   Rhea: I agree Mark; everyone must understand their Fear threshold. Or, more to the point, understand and unmask fear itself, as we have spoken about. For taking fear at face value will prevent you doing a lot of exciting and rewarding activities – investment being a good example. If you think 'investment = fear' then you are in a 'no-go' situation. If you think 'investment = risk assessment' you can use the creative tension in fear to objectively analyse low to high-risk investments and match these to your own risk profile. Correct me if I'm wrong Mark, but I believe Sir John Templeton said: 'The time to buy is when the most people are the most fearful.'

[Mark Mobius: yes Rhea, that is very true].

5. **Mark Mobius: Diversify your portfolio.** You must never put all your eggs in one basket unless you have a lot of time to watch that basket – and most of us don't.

   Rhea:, Yes, diversify and open up as many connections, alliances and networks as you can. Diversity of plug and play, gives you the stability as to weather whatever the world throws at you, individuals who prevail crises after crises through investing in a portfolio of choices, interests and networks. I say again, one must make oneself the creator of the conditions that increase the chances to win.

6. **Mark Mobius:** Don't listen to your friends or neighbours when it comes to making investment decisions. Your own situation is different from everyone else's so you should be making the decisions.

   Rhea: I couldn't agree more. Listen to your instincts. Your situation is unique. Others may share their instincts. Listen to that, but don't count it as the only advice.

7. **Mark Mobius:** Don't believe everything you read in newspapers, because things tend to be manipulated and/or exaggerated. Don't be swayed by headlines – instead, look at what is going on behind the scenes.

   Rhea: Ah yes, transparency – leaders need to be savvy and read the tea leaves. I have seen too many examples where people with real potential have compromised their luck by being gullible and, naïve. Most people certainly take 'headlines' at face value and rarely check. 'what is going behind the scenes' or 'what' is invisible in print, but simmering between the lines'. My instinct and expression ingredients comes to mind.

8. **Mark Mobius:** Go into emerging markets because that is where the growth is. Look at countries where populations are relatively young. Countries with young populations are going to be the most productive in future years.

Rhea: Emerging' leaders – rising stars, high potentials – young visionaries are on the rise. The world needs 'more of them' and expects 'more from them'. In today's world, with the growing demands of the future, leadership is not just a choice, it's a necessity

This is something I readily identify with, especially in the younger generation (we met in the chapter on Emotion) that populate/make up the rising stars programmes that I run.

Somewhere towards the end of this book, I wanted to test the luck concept not just with entrepreneurs, diplomats and successful investors but with some everyday, ordinary folk out in the street, people like you and me. I had this urge to pick a small new universe, like a village out of nowhere or somewhere I have never been and ask if and how does luck play out in their lives?

Making your own luck

On that note I set off. In the first few days of 2012, you could say I made my own luck by escaping to Loch Tay to finish off the book in the context of welcoming the New Year. Loch Tay lies in the north of Scotland between the picturesque villages of Kenmore, Killin and Aberfeldy and I pitched up in Big Tony's wood lodge in the first of this trio. The sun was shining which itself for January in the UK is lucky. The snow peaks were glistening and reflecting in the blue waters of the loch. Business looked promising for the coming year. Friends and family were around me. I felt this was a different cycle of my life compared to a few years ago. I felt lucky and on that train of thought, I found myself trapped in an inner restlessness of wanting to crack the luck code. While wandering in the small market village of Aberfeldy, with a population of circa 2000 people only, I wondered whether the residents here, untouched by the big-city-factor, had ever experienced good luck amongst themselves where a chance force has granted them a gift or a power. Could this be my sample universe to see whether this luck thing is real or imagined?

Having just finished refining the chapter on creativity, I decided to indulge in that very creative spirit by randomly picking people from the small length of the high street and asking them the luck question. So I asked the butcher, the baker, the winemaker (who kindly stood in for the candlestick maker that day!), the post office owner, the gift shop owner and the girl in the whisky distillery – do you think you are lucky? They were all taken aback for a second but then the responses followed rapidly – 'yes', 'no', 'never', 'sometimes' or 'occasionally'. These were people with ordinary lives, making an ordinary living and going about their daily routine in the village – how did they perceive their justification of luck?

Stories from Bob, John, Belinda and Rose, from a village

Bob from the wine delicatessen said, 'I'm lucky, I got this job... I used to work in the supermarket around the corner and the owners of the wine shop noticed me – maybe because I have a big smile and it showed positivity'.

John from the gift shop said, 'I'm never lucky. I have been playing the Lottery for almost 20 years and I have only won a tenner!'. When I asked him 'what's the exact thought that goes through your mind when you put your numbers in?', he said 'I doubt I'll win but I know I've got to be in it to win it.'

Belinda, who owns the gift shop with her husband, said, 'I'm lucky because I haven't had any serious failures. I'm just open to what throws life throws at me and seeing how I can turn every adversity into an opportunity'. She showed me her last few days accounts. She had taken £513 two days previous, £67 the day before and £31 that day before I bought my little item and said 'I can look at £513 and think I'm not lucky today, or I can think 'I did £513 two days ago and I will do it tomorrow again'.

Rose from the Dewar's distillery said, 'I'm lucky – absolutely! Four years ago, a Russian friend of mine gave me a pair of red shoes and said red shoes indicate luck. I was sceptical but the shoes were nice so I wore them and within a week, out of the blue and after decades, I met two long-lost friends of mine, one in a supermarket and one on the Internet'.

Across the range of answers, there were two common threads: first, I could almost guess in the first few seconds what someone's answer would be based on their body language; and second, people who thought they were lucky had an incredible sense of positivity in their attitude – they were good humoured, energetic and curious.

I found this encouraging for even in this small sample we can already see evidence emerging of the perception of luck and the forces, actions or context that brought about a result that the individual interpreted as luck.

Bob got his job because his employer noticed he smiled, was positive and was therefore engaging customers.

John has the odds of winning the lottery stacked against him. His participation at least affords him the chance of winning, but you sense his doubtful attitude probably minimises his chances. Although this does not stand up technically, after all it is a completely random lottery which nobody can influence, at the very least he should participate positively as not only could this encourage a positive outcome, if indeed this is ever proven to work, but he would also enjoy the anticipation of a win instead of mistakenly thinking he can pre-empt disappointment by assuming the worst. There is maybe a lesson for us all here in other areas of our lives!

Belinda takes the glass half full approach. Her daily takings display the normal randomness in her chosen retail environment, but she remains optimistic that tomorrow will always bring good sales.

Rose has a positive outlook and sees association in the shoes she feels good in and the fortuitous meetings with long-lost friends. It is about believing even without fully understanding.

So it is the positive state of mind, doing the right thing and understanding the context of the activity that brings about the result that is then viewed as lucky or unlucky. Harnessing this awareness and approach in our lives can attract the outcomes that we describe as luck in all its guises.

Now at the same time of my Loch Tay experiment, my mood was largely influenced by various New Year's Eve celebrations or rituals I had been part of. My thoughts turned to how different cultures associate good luck to mark the New Year and what the common denominators are. Whether it is the Japanese who celebrate New Year (Oshogatsu) at midnight on 31 December, when Buddhist temples strike their gongs 108 times, in an effort to expel 108 types of human weakness, or the Chinese who use the colour red to symbolise good luck and happiness and even paint front doors in red to bring in the good omens.

So you can see a wave of luck-generating activities ripples around our planet every twelve months. What is the common ingredient here to all these practices?

Manufacturing luck might seem to be the objective, but perhaps the real value in practising these rituals is the boost of confidence and a position of personal influence that they provide people with. If you believe that doing a specific action or behaviour will bring you a better year, then you probably will have a better year. Belief is the foundation of human psyche. It is very similar to sports psychology: many athletes use rituals such as visualisation or guided imagery to recreate a particularly successful race which helps them re-live the experience of success from the past. This recall and visualisation prepare them both mentally and physically for competition. That preparation in turn maximises their chances of winning – in other words, being lucky.

The luck factor

Anyone who has spent time researching the question or observing human experience to assess what separates 'lucky' people from 'unlucky' people, has discovered that the main difference lies with each person's attitude and outlook.

I have always thought that of magicians and illusionists. Let us see what a onetime professional magician turned professor of psychology has to tell us about how each of us has the opportunity to become luckier through four essential principles – as described in The Luck Factor by Dr. Richard Wiseman, Professor of Public Understanding of Psychology at the University of Hertfordshire. Richard has made luck his business. His first lucky break came when he was six, went into the school library looking for a chess book and was misdirected into the magic section. He never looked back.

I will illustrate each one with a personal example from my own life:

Maximise your chances

This is all about boosting or multiplying your likelihood of being lucky.

My example: There was a period of three years when I used to travel to the Middle East at least twice a month on a long-term assignment for Dubai Holding, the holding company of the Dubai government under the patronage of His Highness Sheikh Mohamed. As happens with frequent travel, you get to know the locals. I would often be picked up a driver whose opening conversation with me was always about the traffic and then the lottery. One day, I asked him about his fascination with the lottery and if lady luck had ever come his way. He said, 'If I sat and wait to get lucky, nothing will happen! Maximising your chances is the only route for winning sweepstakes. For that I have to enter the lottery as often as I can, into as many sweepstakes as I can and sooner or later I'll win'. His advice also applies to all of us.

Entering the field of luck has certainly happened to me. A chance encounter with a long-lost business acquaintance turned my attention to an advert at

HSBC's London headquarters for the HSBC StartUp Star awards in 2008. In a quick conversation, she convinced me to apply, a few months later, CorporateDNA was declared a national semi-finalist. Had I not bumped into my former client, I had probably never known about the awards, but by taking up an opportunity flagged up to me by my contact and acting on it, I had maximised my company's chances of luck.

Listen to your instincts.

My example: well, I have written a whole chapter on this. This is about listening to your inner voice and acting on the cues and clues it gives you to pursue a course of action that may prove fortunate.

Here is a story of an entrepreneur who used instinct to call upon his luck. There is a great treasure of a restaurant on the same street where I live called The Cinnamon Club. A good friend of mine, Vivek Singh, is the executive chef and CEO. Vivek's own story is for me, a good example of how you can make luck through acting on your instinct. Vivek became a chef by a 'pure freak of chance', as he puts it.

He outraged his family by shunning their plans for him and becoming a chef rather than an engineer. At that time, especially in India, for the son of an engineer to declare he wants to make a living through cooking was pretty hard to digest! Anyway, after graduating from catering college, he joined the Oberoi Hotel group as a specialist in Indian cuisine. He first worked at their flight kitchens in Mumbai where 2,000 meals were produced a day for various airlines.

He then moved to the Grand Hotel in Calcutta where he was fast-tracked to become the Indian chef of the Oberoi's flagship Rajvilas in Jaipur, recently voted by Tatler as the most luxurious hotel in the world and at the age of 26 he was cooking for royalty. Vivek had books by Marco Pierre White and Charlie Trotter so when the founder of The Cinnamon Club, Iqbal Wahhab OBE, a British entrepreneur of Bangladeshi origins talked to him about how he thought Indian flavours and western culinary styles could be married to redefine Indian cuisine in London, Vivek was already on the same page.

But here's what Vivek did differently. He turned winning recipes on their head so out went the ever popular tikka masalas and vindaloos which could have guaranteed him success: 'My instinct told me I needed to show the British palate what they didn't even know they wanted.' Not so different from Henry Ford's faster horse versus car analogy. Since first opening its doors in 2001, The Cinnamon Club has been redefining expectations of Indian cooking.

The start wasn't easy. Armed with a novel concept and a bold purpose, Iqbal and Vivek stuck to their gut feel and did not give up their entrepreneurial dreams, even when the Club initially suffered severe financial difficulties. Using the ingredients metaphor for the book, I'd say they poured dollops of self-belief and resilience in their gourmet vision. There were, after all, high stakes: with a £2.5m investment and when they were looking for a venue to house their dream, they had to convince the landlord of the Grade II-listed Old Westminster Library to choose them over 300 other bidders, including premier league names like The Ivy and Conran. Amateurs with a dream who attracted luck by plug and play?

Walking around in his unassuming white chef's coat with his favourite brass mortar and pestle (which he regards as his ten-year-old lucky charm), Vivek's passion continues to redefine expectations every year, every season. His story of luck always reminds me of the perfect blend between listening to one's instinct with courage and passion. Today the Cinnamon Club serves 100,000 customers and turns over £5 million (US$7.5 million) annually and boasts a fan club from politicians and TV celebrities to mere mortal entrepreneurs like me. In fact I have written several pages of this book, tucked in a corner of their library lounge, cooking my ten ingredients while savouring Vivek's edible versions!

Expect to be lucky

Expecting luck means nurturing high hopes and expectations and believing they will come true. It is all about a winning attitude. The luckiest people believe that their future is bright and as a result they try harder and don't give up on their goals.

It happened to me in 2008. I couldn't present to a prestigious UK board in May of that year as I had a non-refundable holiday booked in Europe – it was a 'financial ouch' situation either way! To be honest, I was feeling a bit miserable on the flight but decided to plug into my laptop to take my mind off things and, in so doing, played out an interesting development. An item long lingering on my to-do list was updating my profile on Google and so I decided to finally do it., for despite our growing presence in the US, Europe and Far East, I was aware that CorporateDNA lacked the same in Central Asia. Anyway that was that, just an item ticked of my list, but guess what? Three days later, I received an e-mail from the Government of Malaysia inviting me to speak at their national day in August to an audience of 1,200 on the subject of being an entrepreneur in the UK, with a planned welcome from their Prime Minister. The opportunity, albeit unnerving, brought a clear message. While I closed the door of making the UK board presentation, another door had opened up bringing a bigger opportunity which was more prestigious from a press, profile and visibility perspective. I couldn't stop asking about how they found me but I later learnt they had Googled my profile, the one I had updated on the flight! What if I hadn't done that? Some of you may say that's a happy accident. I'd say that is an example of attracting luck – in other words using my plug and play analogy, it is about putting yourself in a better position to incur good fortune, which then appears as luck.

Look on the bright side

People who see the glass as half-full thrive during difficult times. They see setbacks as temporary and believe that everything turns out for the best. They take spells of bad luck as lessons to be learned and work through knock-backs determined to turn negatives into positives. Below are events in the life history of a man who failed many times but kept fighting back. See if you can guess who it is. He:

- failed in business at age 22
- was defeated for the state legislature at age 23
- failed in business a second at age 25
- coped with the death of his sweetheart at age 26
- suffered a nervous breakdown at age 27
- was defeated for speaker at age 29
- was defeated for congressional nomination at age 34
- was elected to Congress at age 37
- lost renomination for Congress at age 39
- was defeated for the Senate at age 46
- was defeated for the vice-presidency of the U.S. at age 47
- was defeated for the Senate age 49

Then, at age 51, he was elected President of the United States – Abraham Lincoln.

I make my case.

As Einstein said, 'in the middle of difficulty lies opportunity' and Stephen Covey backs up Einstein's view: 'Opposition is a natural part of life. Just as we develop our physical muscles through overcoming opposition – such as lifting weights – we develop our character muscles by overcoming challenges and adversity.'

First, you are given an opportunity. Then, based on that opportunity, you hatch a dream. And when you try to execute that dream, you meet your opposition. It is here on the battleground, facing the opposition, that success is either realised or lost. Remember the reference to the Hero's Journey in the Resilience chapter.

Not accepting 'No'

As one tries to grow, develop and succeed there will be, no doubt, people and circumstances around every corner that either get in the way or strongly to tell you no. They are like handicaps: your pessimistic parents can tell you no, your envious friends or colleagues can tell you no, your lack of self-esteem causes you to say no to yourself, your society or community can say no, addiction tells you no and so on. The people who succeed are those who don't take no for an answer. They shrug off the pessimism, they choose better friends, they put up boundaries with their family and they surround themselves with positive people and beliefs.

How high do you want to aim

Lucky hunches are something that everyone has had, but lucky people tend to rely on them more. Your intuition is the result of subtle clues that your subconscious has put together.

Inspiring leaders harness the power of visualisation to see the future and convince others that working together they can bring that vision to reality. Going back to the power of visual affirmations from earlier in the chapter; look at the following examples who got others to visualise a future by using language to visualise outcomes:

- Mikhail Gorbachev – 'We need Star Peace not Star Wars'.
- JFK – 'Man on the Moon'.
- Gandhi – 'Be the change you want to see'.
- Martin Luther King – 'I have a dream'.
- Steve Jobs – 'A computer for the rest of us'.

They made the impossible happen by plugging into their belief and playing it out to the world to see, sense, hear and feel.

While our own dreams may not be as big as putting a man on the moon or changing the world, they can still be bold. What do you want to do or be? An Olympian? A CEO? A musician? An athlete? A social entrepreneur? Often when I ask my friends or clients what would need to happen for them to get lucky in achieving what they wanted, the answers range from driving career success to 'making my child a star' to a lovely house in the Italian countryside. However for some, luck is nothing more than change of self-perception; for example, 'I would be lucky if people stopped perceiving me as weak'. That's okay too.

My point here is whatever the size of your goal, take the necessary steps to make it happen. If you want that house in Italy, think about finding the house in the first place and how you'll pay for it. Imagine that you are already living in the house and see yourself waking up in it. How do you feel? If career success is what you want, start visualising what your impact would be like at the next level. What decisions and actions would you drive to that next level? What would your team be like?

We are all stardust – why not release the star from the dust?

It is easy to prove that consequences and events follow thought patterns. If you take any substantial event in your life and try and remember the thoughts that preceded the event, you will see a strong connection. Do you know why? As we said before, everything in the world is interconnected and everything is energy. We are stardust! Quantum physics proves this strongly. We live in a universe of waves and each one has a frequency that touches and affects other waves. Thinking a thought attracts a wave of energy and that energy attracts circumstances and opportunities translate that thought into action. By repeating and reinforcing the same thoughts, the subconscious drives our mind to behave and act in ways that attracts the right action.

Repeating thoughts are like magnets attracting similar thoughts which may belong to other people. This universal attraction literally can bring seemingly new people who don't know each other into contact and almost through a partnership of energy and connectivity, lucky actions can unfold.*

No dream is too small and the universe is large enough to accommodate and help realise most dreams, if not all of them.

---

* Adapted from Visualise and Achieve by Remez Sasson.

Shameel Josoob – the CEO of Vodafone, South Africa

Let us take the story of Shameel Josoob to prove this concept.

When 21-year-old Shameel joined Vodacom – the South African division of Vodafone – as an accountant, no one knew that he would become the CEO in eight years, but that's what he did. Hardly anyone knew where he had come from. Shameel's rags to riches story makes the hair on the back of one's neck stand up because it exemplifies how he made his own luck from scratch – not only from nothing but against great hardship and adversity.

He was born to a family of five and his parents divorced when he was ten months old. His mother raised the family single-handed in difficult conditions and on an allowance of less than a few dollars per child. Triggered by necessity and ambition, young Shameel became a trader when most children of his age were being nurtured and educated. By the age of five, he was selling herbs, spices and samosas and by seven, 'I had my own business where I was selling anything I could lay my hands on – packets of chips, kites, marbles, earrings and popsicles in the school playground'. At eight, the family was living in an Indian township where he would buy and sell in the trading community as he could not by law then venture into 'white' areas. Seeing his growing success, other kids wanted to join his 'business' trade and soon the young entrepreneur-by-default Shameel had a trading team. 'I divided the playground into different distributors and networks and sold through these agents rather than risk looking "uncool" by selling items myself. I gave them a margin and they gave me profits.' Quite a triumph for a ten-year-old.

I asked him about the lessons he learnt in the first decade of his life.

'Firstly, you are never too young to start a business: the child's mind is young, fresh and thinks without boundaries. The dreams are big and there is no voice of criticism holding you back. Secondly, for a business having a great team and a great location is everything. People need to be able to see, hear and experience you. Thirdly, you may be young, inexperienced and with gullibility always a weakness, especially at that tender age, but you have to keep your eyes and ears open so a tray of chips doesn't disappear while you are talking to a customer. Finally and the biggest lesson of all is that things don't happen by themselves. You have to make things happen. If I am given an opportunity that's fairly small sized, with initiative and drive, I can soon make it large – or even extra-large. But I have got to believe in my instincts and affirm the positive that it can happen. I can do it.'

In those words, were sewn the biggest inspiration for Luck.

Shameel's self-belief was driven by fear of failure – he simply couldn't risk not changing his fate – 'I had to change my luck' – and soon enough an astrologer read his palm and said 'the lines of this eight-year-old boy shows he can achieve anything he turns his mind to'. Now whether we believe in cosmic predictions or not, the fact is that this encounter fuelled his self-belief and channelled his energy to take action kick-started his journey of luck. I would say we all have fortune tellers around us. They come in the form of mentors, coaches, family, or even strangers – listening to them and taking action is the foundation for our luck factor.

For Shameel, the location lesson from his difficult trading days at school came in handy when, after a series of promotions, he was sitting just a few doors away from the CEO's office. 'That visibility and proximity may have been a coincidence but I saw it as an opportunity I had to seize. I would often through courage of conviction and credibility built to date, push back my inner voice of being young to boldly push open the big man's door and talk through my ideas, including how to do deals differently, how to maximise profits and create customer loyalty. I was the Head of Procurement for Vodafone Equipment Company. By 23, there came a crossroads moment where the MD said to me, 'You need to pull your socks up. I want you to lead this division/department in two years'. I said 'My socks are already up'. I don't think he quite knew how old I was. The key message here from Shameel is about self-belief and in his words, 'putting hooks out there to help others know you are ready'. This echoed perfectly the current Group CEO of Vodafone, Vittorio Colao's words to me: 'People are always readier than they think they are. It is just about believing and showing it.'

Shameel became the CEO of Vodacom at the age of 29. It was a $5.2 billion business with a 53.5% market share. Still on the right side of 40, Shameel has recently moved to become CEO of Vodafone Spain – a completely different market, different target and an entirely different culture. His words to me in London were invigorating. Looking back at the last decade I will reinforce my lessons from the playground. In business, to be lucky whether as an entrepreneur or a leader in a corporate, there comes a point where you have to value energy, passion and drive over skills and qualifications. For that common sense is the biggest degree you can attain. No different from what Dadu had said to me and I offer my definition of common sense as – 'doing what makes sense but doing your very best under the circumstances'.

I walked away, agreeing to say in touch with Shameel, who shares my prosper-in-adversity principle. He seemed to echo a mantra that luck is also about being able to articulate 'this is what I need to do and why and this is what it will mean for you and why'. If this simple mantra can be delivered clearly, the universal connections we talked about will conspire in many ways to bring luck to you.

Luck and career success

I am constantly amazed at how many of my CEO clients, feel not having gone to top league private schools has held them back. Really? It doesn't work that way. Education is only the starting point of a career. While sometimes the best chances come disguised. You will very likely have heard of that pithy and pertinent saying – attributed in its time to many sportspeople, but apparently first spoken by the golfer Gary Player, 'the more I practice, the luckier I get.' This remark marvellously and wittily dramatizes the link between expertise and hard work and luck. Well, what Gary Player said is nothing new. After all, Seneca the Roman dramatist, philosopher and politician said 'luck is when preparation meets opportunity'.

Andrew Haigh – Head of Entrepreneur's group in Coutts

In the last two years, I have worked closely with Andrew Haigh, who leads the Entrepreneurs Group. This is one of the largest business segments at Coutts Private Bank and has strategic responsibility for supporting 20,000 entrepreneur clients in the UK. I met Andrew at a House of Lords event in 2010 and for someone of his caliber, I straightaway sensed an authenticity where a sense of natural ease and balance sat alongside his great track record and credibility.

Andrew, who began his career as an investment banker in London and then New York, has an unconventional pedigree: he is a linguist by training with a joint honours degree in French and Russian as well as a diploma in Art History. I learned that Andrew, while based in Beijing and Shanghai, had helped the Chinese government set up the first domestic private bank in China. No mean feat! I asked him if he had been lucky. After a reflective pause Andrew said:

'I believe I have been fortunate in that three cultures have shaped my DNA: UK, US and China. The UK, being my home, gave me my heart – my relationships sentiments and identity. But I was a fairly introverted and quietly capable young manager. So a bold move to the US gave me an appetite and a permission to show energy, drive and enthusiasm and as an unassuming young person, that was a key development. China taught me flexibility, followership and humility. It taught me to blend my drive and energy with a mature patience and groundedness'.

For Andrew, it is clear that while he was lucky to be exposed to three very different cultures, it was then about preparation and practice, taking Seneca's inspiration and making the most of that opportunity in realising his potential. I asked him to define in his own words the entrepreneur of today. 'Today's entrepreneur has to be global in a new way, not just a British or Indian person who can adapt and work in different cultures. For tomorrow's entrepreneur to be lucky, one needs to have a truly global identity which is almost a nationality without boundaries. It's like in your passport it would say 'global' as the country of origin.' I endorsed his view that 'life is all about doing something you never thought you would do'. For that to be truly believable, exposure to multiple realities and practising your strengths in them is key. That way, when a real opportunity does strike, you are ready to seize it the best you can.

Your 'luck' quotient

So, if I asked you now, do you consider yourself lucky – try reading the statements below as in an informal luck check:

It often happens that I:

- am surprised by favours and turn of events
- benefit from unexpected support
- meet someone new who opens a door for me
- get help from people whom I know nothing about
- seem to be at the right place at the right time without even thinking about it
- see one, or multiple connections leading to another
- believe 'that was lucky'

Take a moment to reflect on how you have scored yourself. Were you able to tick them all? Can you think lucky? Think about those successful occasions. How did they arise? What had you done consciously, or subconsciously to bring them about? Is this and what you have read in this chapter, leading you to reconsider (if only gently)? If you find you are still on this first rung of the ladder, take a few examples from this ingredient and see how you could, say, raise your profile, extend your interest in others or expand your network and you will find incremental steps towards the top rung easier than you think.

As Dale Carnegie said in *How to Win Friends & Influence People*: 'You can make more friends in two months by becoming interested in other people than you can in two years by trying to get other people interested in you.' Have the humility to be interested in more people and watch more circumstantial luck come your way.

Be willing to learn, approach life optimistically and find the openness and humanness to realise that humility and vulnerability are the strongest magnets of wonderfully unforeseeable and lucky situations.

My luck quotient as an entrepreneur:

I believe that the primary determinant for success is not luck in the first instance; it is the quality of the entrepreneur to be ready and curious to attract luck. For all practical purposes, we entrepreneurs make our luck by being ready to deal with events as they unfold and convert them into opportunities. What we cannot do, however, is to manufacture those 'once in a lifetime' moments that allow the opportunity to create something extraordinary. These moments require a congruence of events that are outside of the control of the entrepreneur and the maximising of the nine ingredients that are inside of the control of the entrepreneur. We simply have to be ready to seize them!

Adding more luck to your leadership DNA

Right time, right place, right people? Well, those who *create* their own good luck do, not credit their success just to a random roll of the dice, they are acutely aware of the origins of their good luck. Moreover, having seen it work before, they know how to repeat it.

Can we succeed without a minimum of luck? The answer is obviously yes! However, there is no doubt that if you did add some luck to your hard work you can not only survive and succeed, you can be genuinely successful or fulfilled.

Here are some deeper connections I have found when people claim luck because of being at the right place, at the right time with the right people:

When someone says **'I was lucky because the timing was right'**, I say that person was ready and prepared when luck struck. Many people are not even aware of the fact that luck is around that they can really go for it. It is the 'right' time.

When someone says **'I was lucky because the environment is right'** or 'I was at the right place', I say they took initiative in creating an environment which was open to luck. This could be them finding the right places to be, or opening those doors they felt through their instinct and foresight could lead to luck. Also as Woody Allen once said, 'Success is showing up when the other guy doesn't!'

Finally, when someone says **'I was lucky because the people around me are right'** or 'I was around the right people', I say without even consciously connecting it to luck, they have built the right network of people – that could be in the form of a team, an alliance, a circle or forum you belong to – it doesn't matter. What matters is by surrounding yourself with those crucial people, you have created a partnership which has unlocked your luck factor.

In all three scenarios, the common factor lies in being prepared and keeping the ground ready for luck to strike – through people, environments and timing.

On top of this, some research shows that people who believe that they are lucky are indeed luckier than those who are more pessimistic! So there is a psychological dimension to the good fortune drive: think you are lucky and it will help you!

From streets of China

Let me leave you with this thought. In China, the names given to streets in certain cities can often be very grand sounding. For example, you find yourself walking down the Street of Golden Profits, The Street of Five Happiness, The Street of Ten Thousand Happiness, The Street of Ninefold Brightness, or even The Street of One hundred Grandsons. The rationale I am told is a combination of make-believe ritual with desired aspirations.

If you lay yourself open to the acceptance of the leadership DNA and metaphorically stroll down these avenues of aspiration with positive self-belief, in the expectation to be lucky and maximise your chances, then I genuinely believe you will get lucky. As mentioned in the introduction, if your preparation of the nine ingredients is sincere and authentic, luck will flow – undoubtedly.

So remember that preparedness is a core element.

- **Prepare yourself to 'luck in' when an opportunity presents itself, but don't rely on luck.** It is what we do and how we position ourselves that can generate luck rather than the other around.

- **Lucky people believe in luck not randomness, they believe in taking charge.** Put yourself in this frame of mind and you can be a lucky person as we perceive others to be. They never quit and are ready to find the miracle in a mess when messes happen as they invariably do. They build networks because they know luck comes mostly through other people – simply by being in a bigger 'luck pool' you exponentially increase your exposure to luck. Lucky people become so by investing positive emotions in their dreams – and guess what? They attract luck.

- **Lucky people have a super power – they remain humble and vulnerable**. Amazing leaders don't necessarily out-smart everyone else; they combine their self-belief with instinct, emotion and creativity while using their focus and resilience to keep that winning attitude alive in the face of big events, whether they are shocks or unexpected opportunities.

In hard cold facts, I would say I have been unlucky more than I have been lucky. But the lessons from my unlucky episodes have exponentially enhanced my chances of luck. I call this 'failing upwards, failing only to move up further!

The concept and reality of what we call luck can be subjective as we have seen and however we view it or understand it at the very least we should move the odds in our favour through making our own luck.

Remember 'luck is when preparation meets opportunity' and 'the more I practise, the luckier I get' as our Roman and South African friends, Seneca and Gary Player mentioned above. Writers and rock stars, chefs and athletes, philosophers and giants of industry, engineers and inventors, poets, politicians, scientists and music legends... have learnt to preserve their belief while absorbing a lot of the opinions and the attitudes of those around them. So yes, you can't be thin-skinned and you have got to allow a bit of controversy. So there is a psychological dimension to the good luck: think you are lucky and you will be lucky!

Luck starts and ends with self belief. With that note, we circle right back to where we started with the first ingredient – the self.

> "A musician must make music, an artist must paint, a poet must write if he is to be ultimately at peace with himself. What one can be, one must be."
>
> Abraham Maslow.

Leadership: It's in your DNA. 'You can do anything if you really want to.

Your code for Ingredient Ten: Luck

Pause. Ask yourself what do you remember from this chapter; list the key takeaways and ideas that had an impact on you – something inspiring, something relevant or something you would like to try.

Now, make a note of the following: the term 'things' below can refer to behaviour actions, conversations, skills or even an attitude

1. List three things you would like to START doing to strengthen your LUCK ...

2. List three things you would like to STOP doing to strengthen your LUCK ...

3. List three things you would like to CONTINUE doing to strengthen your LUCK ...

On an ascending scale of 1 to 10, how robust is this ingredient in your DNA?